D1498304

FIRE AT
Peshtigo
Robert W. Wells

ASBURY PARK PUBLIC LIBRARY
ASBURY PARK, NEW JERSEY

PRENTICE-HALL, INC., Englewood Cliffs, N.J.

FIRE AT PESHTIGO
by Robert W. Wells

© 1968 by Robert W. Wells

Copyright under International and Pan American
Copyright Conventions

All rights reserved. No part of this book may be
reproduced in any form or by any means, except for
the inclusion of brief quotations in a review, without permission in writing from the publisher.

Library of Congress Catalog Card Number: 68-24229

Printed in the United States of America • T

Prentice-Hall International, Inc., London
Prentice-Hall of Australia, Pty., Sydney
Prentice-Hall of Canada, Ltd., Toronto
Prentice-Hall of India Private Ltd., New Delhi
Prentice-Hall of Japan, Inc., Tokyo

Foreword

Nearly a century after, everyone knows that Mrs. O'Leary's cow did or did not kick over a lantern causing Chicago to burn down on October 8, 1871. Few Americans, however, have even a passing acquaintance with a far more disastrous fire that took place that same day in the great pine forests a few hundred miles to the north.

The Peshtigo fire killed five times as many people as that in Chicago. It was the worst tragedy of its kind ever recorded in North America.

This is the account of that conflagration. I have tried to describe its causes and effects, as well as the backgrounds of the lumberjacks, homesteaders, and others who lived on what was then a remote and colorful frontier. But mostly I have attempted to tell what happened to a few thousand people suddenly confronted with the prospect of painful death, and the wise and foolish and sometimes courageous ways they met that challenge.

ROBERT W. WELLS

21569

Acknowledgments

It has been nearly a century since the Peshtigo fire. The passage of time has removed virtually all those who could have told firsthand of their experiences. The history of the disaster has had to be compiled largely from written sources and from the accounts handed down by the survivors to their descendants.

Fortunately, a number of those who lived through the fire wrote of their experiences shortly afterward when the memory was still fresh. Some of these accounts are in a booklet, "The Great Fires in Wisconsin," published by a Green Bay newspaperman, Franklin Tilton, to raise funds to help the victims. Father Pernin wrote his own story to help get money to rebuild one of his two churches that were burned that night. This account, published originally in French, was translated into English and reprinted in the Wisconsin *Magazine of History* of 1918–19.

The Reverend E. J. Goodspeed included accounts of the Peshtigo and Michigan fires in a book he published in 1871 called *History of the Great Fires in Chicago and the West*. Mr. Goodspeed seems to have hurried into print with a mixed bag of stories which have the merit of being fresh but not that of always being reliable. These, where used, have been treated with skepticism, and some of his best tales have been omitted with regret—notably one about a French woman who fled with her son and mad mother through the woods, dodging wolves and other dire perils. The reason this thrilling story is left out is that I don't believe a word of it.

Among other old accounts which were helpful were Xavier Martin's story of "The Belgians of Northeast Wisconsin," published by the Wisconsin *Magazine of History* in 1893; an *Illustrated Historic Atlas of Wisconsin*, printed not long after the fire, which included biographical sketches of some of the survivors; *An Illustrated History of the State of Wisconsin from Its First Exploration Down to 1875* by Charles R. Tuttle; *Through the Flames and Beyond or Chicago As It Was and Is* by Frank Luzerne and John G. Wells, who managed to get that unwieldy title into print by 1872; *Martin's History of Door County*, printed in Sturgeon Bay in 1881; *A History of the Great Minnesota Forest Fires* by Elton T. Brown, in 1894; the *Wisconsin Legislative Manual* of 1872; H. R. Holand's *History of Door County* of 1917, and the one with the most eye-catching title of all, "Report of the Disastrous Effects of the Destruction of Forest Trees Now Going on So Rapidly in Wisconsin," submitted by Increase A. Lapham and two fellow commissioners to the Wisconsin state legislature in 1867.

Among numerous newspapers consulted—mainly the issues of 1871—the most helpful information was found in the *Marinette and Peshtigo Eagle*, the *Milwaukee Journal*, *Peshtigo Times*, *Green Bay Advocate*, *New York Tribune*, *Fond du Lac Daily*, *Green Bay Press-Gazette*, *Milwaukee Sentinel*, and *Shawano Journal*.

The manuscript, periodical, and particularly the newspaper files of the State Historical Society of Wisconsin were used extensively in my research. The United States Forest Service made available reports of modern scientific studies which help explain the nature of such fires as those which occurred in Wisconsin and Michigan in 1871.

Descendants of those who lived through the fire were

helpful in providing anecdotes they had been told by their parents or grandparents. There were too many of these to list, but Mrs. O. R. Dooley of Kohler, Wisconsin, and Mrs. Elmer England of Peshtigo must be mentioned.

A number of Wisconsin residents located books and materials long out of print that had been stored in their basements or attics. I am grateful to them all. A special word of thanks is also due the librarian at Delafield, Wisconsin, Mrs. Hortense Langer, whose assistance in tracking down material is a credit to her profession.

Besides the publications mentioned, the following were among those used in researching the history of the fire and the background of northern Wisconsin:

Stewart Holbrook's *Burning an Empire* (Macmillan, 1943) and *Holy Old Mackinaw* (Macmillan, 1938); John Emmett Nelligan's *The Life of a Lumberman,* as told to Charles M. Sheridan (Madison, 1929); *Wisconsin in Three Centuries* by Reuben Gold Thwaites (Century History Co., 1906); *Famous Fires* by Hugh Clevely (John Day, 1957); *Empire in Pine* by Robert F. Fries (Wisconsin State Historical Society, 1951); *Logs on the Menominee,* privately printed by Fred C. Burke; *Recollections of a Long Life* by Isaac Stephenson (Chicago, 1915); *Great Forest Fires in America* by John D. Guthrie (United States Government Printing Office); *Forest Fire Control and Use* by Kenneth P. Davis (McGraw-Hill, 1959); *Farming the Cutover, Cutover Problems,* and *The Wisconsin Pineries* by James I. Clark (Wisconsin State Historical Society, 1956); *Pine Logs and Politics* by Richard Nelson Current (Wisconsin State Historical Society, 1945); *The Wisconsin Pine Lands of Cornell University* by Paul Wallace Gates (Cornell University Press, 1943), and Vol. 1, *History of the Fox River Valley, Lake Winnebago and the Green Bay Region,* William A. Titus, editor (S. J. Clark, 1930).

To Edith

CONTENTS

•

Foreword

Acknowledgments

Fire at Peshtigo

Index

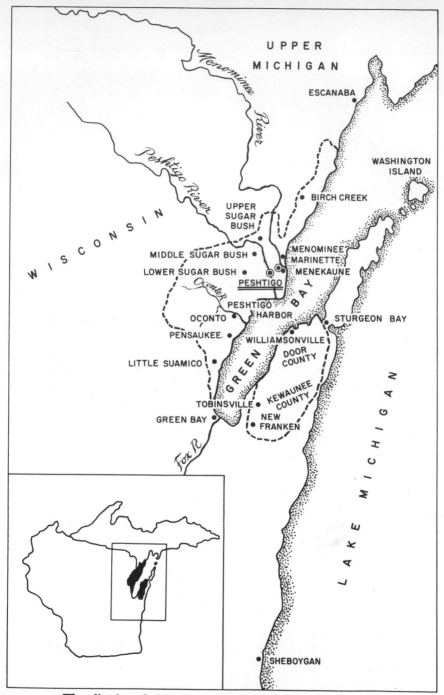

The district of the fire in Wisconsin and Upper Michigan, 1871. Broken lines indicate the approximate area devastated—some 1,280,000 acres. The insert map outlines Wisconsin and Upper Michigan and shows the estimated burned-over portions of the two states.

ONE

•

In northern Wisconsin autumn is the year's most beautiful season. Sumac forms splashes of scarlet on the hillsides. Maples and quaking aspen are transformed to pastel yellow. The oaks, retaining most of their leaves, join reluctantly in the autumnal carnival, their symmetrical outlines changing gradually from green to the color of blood against the sky. When the great pine forests abounded they formed a vast ocean of green that ignored the coming of fall. But in clearings where bushes and deciduous seedlings sprouted, the frosts of late September brushed the woods with color.

A bearded woodsman, stalking with his ax through the timber, might allow himself the luxury of standing for a moment, filling his lungs with the crisp air, and thinking: "Goddamn! I'm glad I ain't shut up in town." Then, perhaps, he would spray a yellow stream of tobacco juice on the foliage to prove his masculinity, scratch himself where the bunkhouse lice had bitten, and walk on under the tall trees that except for brief moments like this represented so many board feet of lumber, so many dollars to be earned, so many pints of cheap whiskey, so many nights with the whores and their loud perfume.

This was what the north country was like in the days when a squirrel leaping from tree to tree could make its way from Upper Michigan across Wisconsin to Minnesota without once touching the ground. In those vanished times, as now, nature gave a final flourish of artistry before blasting the land with chilling winds and swirling snow.

In the fall of 1871, there was no such beauty. The red on distant hillsides was created by flames rather than the glow of frosted oaks. Smoke stung the eyes. In the little towns and on the lonely frontier farms with their stump-filled clearings, there were the dull ache of worry and the nagging of fear.

During that autumn some north woods residents, indulging in the frontier habit of description by overstatement, claimed the air was so dry that "if a man'd touch a match to it, it'd burn." Women walked onto their back porches, looked at the dull clouds of smoke against the horizon, and wiped their hands nervously on their aprons. In the night, children woke up whimpering in the dark lofts. The men looked at the familiar forests as at an enemy and glared up at the sky. "Why the hell don't it rain?" they asked each other when they met on the splintered board sidewalks of lumber towns like Peshtigo. "You think it'll ever rain again?"

The swamps had dried up. A man could drive his mare across places that were ordinarily under water, and she wouldn't sink an inch. It hadn't rained since July 8, except for a hopeful sprinkle on September 5 that disappeared into the parched ground and left the countryside as dry as before. The Indians walked onto what had been bogs to pick cranberries that were scarce and wizened because of the drought. In the marshes where the Menominees were accustomed to gathering wild rice, there was not water enough to float a canoe. The Indians said it had never before been so dry in the fall within the memory of their old men. They blamed the whites. Things had not been like this before the whites came with their axes and sawmills.

Housewives in Peshtigo and in the nearby Upper,

Middle, and Lower Sugar Bush settlements had finished canning the blackberries they and the children had gathered. As they put the jars away in the root cellars, some of the women wondered if their families would still be there that winter to eat the pies made from the berries, for there was the smell of danger in the drifting smoke from the woods. "The swamps and marshes were peat prepared for burning," one resident wrote. "The forests of pine were tinder, ready and anxious for suicide by fire. All nature was so dry and miserable that it cried out for death."

But there seemed to be nothing to do but follow familiar routines and hope for the best. In Marinette, six miles north of Peshtigo, efforts were begun to organize a series of revival meetings. It was felt that a few sermons about hellfire might be particularly appropriate that fall, especially if the lumberjacks and railroad crews could be induced to listen. Respectable citizens felt that the men who would spend the winter in logging camps in the woods could use all the admonishment along these lines that was available.

As it was, the saloons were busy. The sporting houses on the edge of town were finding business brisk. The shanty boys—the lumberjacks' name for themselves—were getting ready for winter in the woods when celibacy would be enforced by a sixteen-hour work day and the rule against going to town except on Saturday night and Sunday. There were sixty lumber camps each winter in the vicinity of Peshtigo. They provided plenty of weekend customers for the fourteen saloons. Whiskey was plentiful. Enough Germans had migrated to the area to make beer a popular drink among some of the customers at the saloons, who had their choice of ample supplies from Henry Rahr's East River Brewery in Green Bay and its rival, the Union Brewery.

One local lumberjack, a six-footer who weighed more than two hundred pounds, was the acknowledged champion of the Saturday night sprees in Peshtigo. A traveling salesman once made the mistake of walking into a saloon where the champ was drinking and bragged that he could lick any man in town. The lumberjack ignored the stranger at first. Then he got tired of watching the drummer walk back and forth, his thumbs in the armholes of his vest, boasting of his exploits. He strolled over and issued his challenge to the upstart by the accepted method—kicking the fellow across the room with one calked boot, size thirteen.

"So you're the best man?" the champ said. "Here's your chance to prove it."

The kick sobered up the salesman, who took a quick look at the lumberjack and slunk away. Someone bought the champion a drink and things settled down to normal again.

"A little less howling nights in certain quarters would be acceptable to families adjacent who wish to rest undisturbed," the *Marinette Eagle* primly suggested.

The *Eagle* had recently opened a Peshtigo branch office, and no wonder. The community was booming, and it was ripe for a weekly newspaper of its own. Its population fluctuated considerably, depending on whether trees were being cut in the woods, but it was estimated to have climbed to close to 2,000 more or less permanent residents, including 350 heads of families who had houses built on both sides of the Peshtigo River, which divided the village in half.

Businesses were moving in at an encouraging rate. Kelsey and Vierke's new drugstore had opened on Oconto Avenue and was advertising "pure imported wines and liquors for medicinal purposes." Down the street was F. J. Bartels' dry goods and grocery store, where a man could buy patent medicines and Yankee notions. Bartels, a German immigrant with a bushy moustache, had come to Peshtigo during the Civil War, left to serve as a captain in a Wisconsin regiment, then returned to open the general store. The Peshtigo Hardware Store, run by the Williams brothers, had Japanned ware along with less exotic items.

It was a three-hour boat ride from Marinette to Peshtigo Harbor aboard what was advertised as the "staunch little

4

steamer, *Union*," captained by Thomas Hawley. It made trips three times a week between Green Bay and Marinette, touching at Pensaukee, Oconto, and Menominee, as well as Peshtigo Harbor.

Adolph Kuchenberg had decided to run a daily stage from Peshtigo to Menominee, which was just across the Wisconsin-Michigan border from Marinette. He was preparing for passengers who soon would be coming in on the Chicago and North Western Railroad that would connect Peshtigo with its principal market in Chicago. Kuchenberg advertised that he had equipped himself with good teams.

Winter was the best time for logging, because pathways could be iced so the logs could be hauled on huge sleds to the river, but cutting had continued during the summer. Along the banks of such rivers as the Peshtigo, Oconto, and Menominee there were huge ramparts of pine logs. It had been planned to float them down the rivers before cold weather, but low water left by the drought prevented that. Several million board feet of potential lumber were included that fall in such collections, with no likelihood of making profits until the melting snows filled the rivers next spring.

There were so many trees that no one worried much about waste. The lumbermen were in what seemed a limitless sea of pine, put there by nature for their benefit. Wherever the men with axes went, great brush piles of what they called "slashings" arose and were left to rot or burn. To the farmers in places such as the three Sugar Bush settlements, trees were simply in the way. Before fields could be plowed or pastures seeded, the pines had to be cleared. To the railroad workers, the forest was also an obstacle. So the farmers felled trees and dragged them by horses or oxen to be left at the edges of their clearing; railway crews chopped down the pines on their right-of-way and snaked them off to the side so that ties and rails could be laid.

Where wood was the primary resource, communities had been created which were unusually vulnerable to fire. The

5

houses were of boards or logs, their roofs of wooden shingles. The closest thing to improved roads connecting the villages were the type called "corduroy," with split logs and brush covering marshy sections. Bridges were constructed of planks supported by timbers. Sidewalks were made of boards.

The sawmills had no easy way to dispose of their waste products, so sawdust simply rose in great piles near the wooden sheds which housed the snarling saws. Various uses were found for it—even the mattresses used in many homes were stuffed with sawdust, and the streets of the woods towns were paved with it to reduce the dust of summer and the mire of spring. But still the sawdust piles rose higher. It was a nuisance. Some of it was hauled out from shore and dumped into the Green Bay, an arm of Lake Michigan, which is bounded on the west by the main part of Wisconsin and on the east by the peninsula which includes Door and Kewaunee counties.

It was a countryside in transition from the backwoods era to what was expected to be a glorious, industrialized future. Iron had been discovered in the upper peninsula of Michigan. It seemed that all that was needed to make a lot of people wealthy was better transportation. The Sturgeon Bay Canal Company had finished surveying a route across the Kewaunee-Door County peninsula to give ships a more direct way to get from the bay to the main part of the lake. Peshtigo Harbor, six miles down river from Peshtigo, hoped to compete with Marinette as the principal port where ore would be transferred from the railroad to lake ships.

By 1871, a great tide of immigration had been flowing for twenty years from Europe and the eastern United States into what was then called the Northwest. In its twenty-third year as a state, Wisconsin had a million inhabitants of the nation's thirty-nine million, most of them living in the lower third of the state.

Luther B. Noyes, who had been a captain in the Civil War, a Monroe County (Wisconsin) judge and publisher of a

6

Sheboygan newspaper, had arrived in Peshtigo Harbor in the early summer of that year. With him the 41-year-old lawyer–turned–journalist brought a Washington hand press and a plan to start a newspaper in the northeastern Wisconsin lumber country. He rented rooms in Marinette and on June 24 published the first issue of the *Eagle*, distributing it to a few hundred subscribers. Soon he added the Peshtigo column and recorded the happenings of a community that had reason to look with confidence toward the future.

"Plenty of chills and fever, headaches and whisky," a typical item said. "Very scarce on the market: Locals (news items) and green apples." Frost had killed the cucumbers and "played smash with vegetation generally," the *Eagle* noted on September 5. School began. A Peshtigo woman became the mother of her twenty-third child. Her name wasn't mentioned. There was no need, since everyone knew her anyway.

William B. Ogden, a Chicago millionaire who owned the Peshtigo Company, and General Moses M. Strong made a tour of the extensive cranberry marshes owned by the company with a view to cultivating them on a large scale. The firm planned to raise one thousand acres of cranberries, employing five hundred persons at the task.

It should not be supposed, despite the howling heard nights in certain quarters, that Peshtigo was devoid of some of the finer amenities. J. F. Jaques, local agent for pianos, organs, and melodeons, had a good supply of such instruments and guaranteed to sell them cheaper than they could be shipped north from Chicago. Such luxuries as oranges, lemons, and "ice cream in its season" were available at George Robinson's meat market. Harter and Horvath, a Marinette store dealing in clothing, laces and embroidery, had opened a Peshtigo branch.

There was one physician in town. The citizens also had available a variety of miracle drugs, such as Dr. Walker's Vinegar Bitters, positively guaranteed to cure biliousness, rheumatism, scrofulous disorders, chronic constipation, and

7

nervous weakness. Perry Davis' Pain Killer was equally versatile. Twenty drops in a little water was an instant remedy for colic, cramps, spasms, heartburn, dysentery, flux, and wind in the bowels.

As September wore on, Noyes was so impressed with Peshtigo's future that he changed the name of his paper to the *Marinette and Peshtigo Eagle*. He continued to tell his readers many of the things they already knew, which is one of the functions of a weekly editor. "The logs are beginning to play out," he wrote. "It will not be long before the mills will all be shut down and the boys off to the woods."

In the log houses and the clapboard homes of more prosperous residents, preparations were being made for the long winter ahead. Fat, black stove pipes were cleaned of soot and put back into place in kitchens and parlors. Great stacks of split wood began to appear near the back doors of the houses, ready to counter the winter cold. Potatoes were dug in the gardens or bought in the stores for seventy-five cents a bushel. Hogs and cattle were butchered. Green winter squash shared basement corners with pie pumpkins. Apples were stored or converted to cider, some of which would be allowed to turn to vinegar.

At Menekaune, adjoining Marinette, a committee collected money for a family man whose arm and leg had been sawed off in a mill accident. Enough money was raised to build him a house. The mill owner contributed a building lot.

People around Peshtigo kept an anxious eye on the weather and the distant smoke from peat and brush fires, but mostly they behaved as though everything were normal. The Congregational Church was given a new coat of white paint. Its minister, the Reverend Edwin R. Beach, got his name in the paper for raising the largest tomato in town. It weighed one pound, ten ounces.

The railroad contractors had sunk pilings into the river at Peshtigo for a bridge to be built when the tracks were laid from Oconto to Peshtigo. Peshtigo was impatiently awaiting its link by rail to the south. The Chicago and North Western had reached Green Bay eleven years before, and it was considered high time the line was extended to tap the forest resources. Much of the best timber along the rivers had already been cut. Once the railroad arrived, the logs could be loaded on freight trains instead of depending solely on spring floods to carry them to the mills.

Four itinerant Italian musicians arrived in town, bearing a violin, a clarinet, and two string instruments described as harps. The men who had come by heaven-knows-what-route from Italy to northern Wisconsin were made welcome.

By mid-September, the Peshtigo Company mill had cut 5,690,384 board feet of lumber that year with its two great circular saws. About the time this impressive total was reached, fire broke out in the sawdust. Everybody grabbed a pail and no damage was done.

With the frost and the dry weather, there was a blessing worth noting in the *Eagle*—the flies were disappearing. Ducks were plentiful in the Peshtigo marshes, despite the low water, and made fine eating. At Nick Cavoit's sawmill located along Trout Creek, a workman forgot that the steam boiler had been drained and built a fire under it. The boiler was nearly melted before Nick realized what was happening. It would cost him eight hundred dollars to repair, Cavoit told his friends, and it would be cheaper to get a new one. Nick's remarks to the workman were not recorded.

One of the railway laborers clearing the unfinished right-of-way north of Peshtigo became ill. Several friends improvised a stretcher and hauled him to the village, where they tried to find him lodging. No one wanted to take him in. As he was being carried down Oconto Road, idlers strolled over to inquire what was the matter. Discovering he had not been the victim of some interesting mishap, they drifted away again, advising the weary stretcher-bearers to take him to see Doc Kelsey. This seemed like sound advice. They took their burden to the office of J. F. Kelsey, physician, surgeon and

9

partner in a drugstore. He needed only a brief examination to make his diagnosis.

"This fellow's got smallpox, boys."

"The pox! And here we been carrying him around."

"Exposed half the town doing it, no doubt."

"What'll we do with the poor bastard, Doc?"

"Get him out of town, and the sooner the better."

And so, cursing their luck but unwilling to abandon a friend, the railroad workers headed back toward Camp Four on the railway line, where the sick man could live or die as chance willed. As they walked unhappily away from Peshtigo, the smell of burning wood filled their nostrils.

10

TWO

●

When large-scale lumbering began in Maine, timber lands sold for twelve cents an acre, but by the time loggers began to move west to Wisconsin and Michigan, inflation had set in—the government had raised the price to a dollar and a quarter.

Isaac Stephenson who became a leading timber baron, arrived in Wisconsin in 1845. The number of immigrants from New England was still small in the Wisconsin north country then, so in conjunction with Daniel Wells, the Canadian-born Stephenson bought up land and timber rights without much competition. Within ten years, however, the migration from the Eastern woods had become a flood. Only nine years before "Ike" Stephenson's arrival, lumber to build the Wisconsin territorial capitol had had to be brought all the way from Pennsylvania. There had been plenty of trees but no sawmills nearby to convert them into boards. When Stephenson got to Green Bay, he found two sawmills there. Another was located near Marinette and there were a few others scattered around the area, including one at Peshtigo. By 1871, the vast forests of white pine were being cut at a great rate, although the peak of Wisconsin lumbering was still twenty years in the future. Some of the pines were one hundred twenty feet tall, three feet across and three hundred years old—so huge that the lumber from three trees was sufficient for a good-sized house, even though cutting methods wasted one-fourth of each tree.

Some of the Eastern lumbermen became prominent citizens of their adopted state. Stephenson was one example, as was Cadwallader C. Washburn, who led Wisconsin troops in the Civil War, then went on to become governor. But most of the lumberjacks brought west from Maine were more interested in eating hearty and saving their wages for sprees in the saloons and fancy houses of the wooden towns springing to life around the Wisconsin and Michigan sawmills. The board sidewalks of such logging towns were chipped and scarred by the lumberjacks' calked boots. The muddy streets were flanked by small log or board dwellings and frame business places, a large percentage of them saloons and gambling houses. Livestock were allowed to roam at large.

There were three men to every woman, and the respectable women generally avoided the rough-talking lads in mackinaws who came roaring into town on Saturday night. This social vacuum was soon filled in part by those women who took a professional interest in the lumberjacks, but in the early days of such towns as Peshtigo the shortage of girls was a serious problem. Some men married Indian girls. Others forgot their loneliness with a bottle. Many of them competed for the attentions of the few unmarried white girls who were there.

In Peshtigo, one such girl was considered the town belle. She had eyes for only one of the lumberjacks—a man who had somehow acquired a store coat, the kind worn in the city. It had immediately made him the cultural superior of his rivals in mackinaws, and they considered this an unfair advantage. One Saturday night, while a dance was in progress, several of them kidnapped the coat. They did something to it which the chronicler of this story described as "unprintable." From then on, the dude wore a mackinaw, and the Peshtigo belle no longer found reason to single him out.

In Michigan, the first principal center of the lumber industry was Saginaw, said to have been built on forty feet of sawdust. As lumbering climbed toward its peak, there were 112 sawmills along the Saginaw River, mostly in Saginaw and Bay City, enough to cut a billion board feet of lumber in a single season. Lumberjacks came from as far away as Green Bay, Wisconsin, to blow their pay in Saginaw. Trains pulled into the Père Marquette depot from the West with every pane of glass kicked out, and from each train poured men in red shirts and sashes. Their mating howls frightened virtuous women and brought an anticipatory gleam to the eyes of the girls on Water Street. As many as 5,000 loggers might converge on the city for a single weekend—an invasion that one student of such matters described as "possibly the greatest mob of bottle-men and door-kickers-in that ever walked." The click of their steel calks on the board sidewalks was like the sound of a sudden cloudburst.

There were said to be 80 houses of prostitution in Bay City at the height of the lumber boom. Saginaw, being twice as large, doubtless hewed to the standard and had perhaps twice as many. In the 200,000 square miles of forest in Michigan, Wisconsin, and neighboring Minnesota, these brawling cities were only two of many that grew up with the dual purpose of sawing lumber and providing places to relieve a lumberjack of his earnings.

The time came where there were 112,000 men working in the lumber industry of these three states. The number was not yet that high in 1871, but it was growing rapidly and the communities that depended on timber for their existence were growing, too. The Yankees from Maine were quickly followed by Germans, Irish and, a little later, Scandinavians. French-Canadians drifted back-and-forth across the border. Indians hired out to help cut the trees. There was considerable rivalry between Indian and white loggers. Sometimes it broke out

13

into the minor battles, with calked boots as weapons, that were the loggers' third favorite sport, behind drinking and wenching.

The lumberjacks spoke a language of their own. Prunes, for example, were called "logging berries" and tea was "swamp water" or "belly wash." A man of low intelligence was a "dead head," the term used for a sunken log. In the 1870's, the disillusioned son of a Wisconsin minister gave his impressions of life in one lumber camp:

"We roll into our soft, downy couch of lousy blankets and lay and listen to the mocking bird, with music by the entire band and snoring in seven different languages, mostly imported—professional snores from Germany and Norway, warranted never to miss a note—while the beautiful odor of wet socks and foot rags is heard from the near distance, and finally fall to sleep to slow music, only to be awakened in a few minutes by the melodious voice of the cook, singing, 'Roll our your dead bodies! Daylight in the swamp!'

"Then we get up and go to our beautiful and sumptuous repast of fricasseed pork and beans on the half shell with a basin of reduced ice water flavored with copperas and called by the low and uneducated 'tea.' Such is life in the woods. But for me, give me six months, twice a year for two years, in [the state prison at] Waupun, or some other place of enjoyment."

When the timber gave out around Saginaw, it was the turn of Muskegon, Michigan, to be the center of lumbering. Loggers claimed they could smell Muskegon whiskey fifty miles up river at Big Rapids and the perfume worn by the girls at Muskegon's Sawdust Flats even farther. Among the proprietors of the bordellos in the six blocks known as "the Dust" was Big Delia. She weighed 225, was six feet two inches tall, and once hit a logger so hard she broke his jaw—he had refused to remove his calked boots, which offended Delia's sense of decorum. She chewed Hiawatha brand tobacco and would have made a fine lumber camp boss.

In the shanties of lumber camps around Green Bay and

14

Oconto, Marinette, and Peshtigo, the logging crews spoke with respect of Muskegon, a town where there had been the biggest celebration of the Fourth of July ever held in a red-light district. The girls got official permission from the city fathers to show their patriotism. They built an open pavilion, 90 feet wide and 120 feet long, and decorated it with bunting, cedar boughs, and a large American flag. Big Delia, chairman of the entertainment committee, hired a band from Milwaukee to play for the dance. Somehow a misunderstanding arose and two bands arrived on the ferry from across the lake. A lesser woman than Delia might have been upset, but she simply ordered, "Fill 'em up with beer and let 'em snort handsome." As it turned out, it was lucky that there was a spare band. One set of musicians passed out from too much Muskegon hospitality, but the other was ready to take over.

The ladies' auxiliary from Sawdust Flats were confident of the members' ability to entertain lumberjacks, but for this special occasion they called for reinforcements. Eighty or ninety volunteers from the Milwaukee and Chicago chapters of the sisterhood responded. As the celebration wore on, a difference of opinion arose between a local brunette known as "Black Jap" and a young woman called "John L." Jap was waltzing with a young logger when, for reasons not entirely clear, her rival slugged her in the jaw. Jap returned the blow and the fight was on. It lasted perhaps a half hour, and when it was over, both participants had considerably less hair and clothing. While it delayed the dance, most loggers found it a particularly enjoyable part of the party, and the Milwaukee musicians who slept through the melee were sorry afterward that they'd missed it.

Muskegon had to be mentioned along with Saginaw and Bay City when the loggers argued about the best place to spend a weekend in Michigan. The names of Seney, Roscommon, Ludington and Grand Rapids were apt to come up, too. As for Wisconsin, it had not yet decided to call itself America's Vacationland, but it had an adequate supply of the

15

entertainment most likely to appeal to red-shirted vacationers. Hurley, which managed to retain some of its old habits when they had passed into history elsewhere, was one such community. Ashland was notorious for an establishment outside of town operated by Price Wade. Hayward, Wausau, Rhinelander, and Barron had no shortage of facilities for a thirsty lumberjack, while in eastern Wisconsin there were Green Bay, Marinette and Oshkosh. Milwaukee, then a wide-open town, was a little too far from the pineries to go to for a weekend.

After the disastrous events of 1871, some people tried to find the reason that Peshtigo had been singled out for destruction while other communities in the vicinity escaped relatively unscathed. Some suggested that it had been punished by God for its wickedness. There is no evidence, however, to indicate that Peshtigo was outstandingly sinful. Virtually every lumber town in those days set aside a district where the lumberjacks could be accommodated in their search for a woman, a drink, and a chance to relax after a six-day week in the woods. Some communities pursued the lumberjacks' trade so enthusiastically that they won a reputation against hard competition. It was said, for example, that the three toughest places in the universe were Hayward, Hurley, and Hell.

Peshtigo was not in their league, although one man who lived there before the fire has described it as a "tough burg." Henry Drees told of brawls frequently breaking out in the saloons, and he personally blamed French-Canadians and half breeds for starting most of them. When the men got drunk enough, Drees recalled, the fights would start. Tables, chairs, bottles, cuspidors, and anything else moveable would start flying through the air. The drinking situation was compounded by a company rule against saloons at the harbor. This required those who worked there to take the six-mile train ride to Peshtigo.

It is hard to determine such things after so many years,

but it seems likely that Peshtigo, in fact, was a little less full of lumber camp hell-raisers than many of the other small communities. Unlike most towns in the timber country, it was the trading center for a prosperous farming district—the Upper, Lower and Middle Sugar Bush—and the rural families were mostly hardworking and respectable. Many of the mill workers in Peshtigo were also family men, whose wives would have kept them in line. Still, there was sin there, no doubt. The preachers sometimes warned against it, as was their duty. After the great fire that took its name from Peshtigo, there was one Green Bay newspaper which compared the community to Sodom, adding: "It seemed as if the wickedness of the place had mocked God until his fiery thunderbolts were loosed for its destruction. And he who had been boldest in sin was first to call on his maker for succor." To counteract such slander, other contemporary observers claimed after the fire that Peshtigo had been a thriving little paradise, where everyone worked hard, went to bed early, and paid strict attention to his duty. It seems likely that the truth lies somewhere between Eden and Sodom.

THREE

●

When he was nineteen years old, John E. Nelligan, who had been born in New Brunswick and learned the lumbering trade there and in Maine, arrived in Oconto. It was the spring of 1871. Jotting down his reminiscences many years later, he remembered his first impressions of the lumberjacks he saw there:

"They were strong and wild in both body and spirit, with the careless masculine beauty of men who live free lives in the open air. They seemed the finest specimens of manhood I had ever seen. They were magnificent. Even in their annual periods of dissipation, when they flung away the wages of a winter's work in a wild orgy lasting only a week or so, they were magnificent. Drunk or sober, they would fight at the drop of a hat and fight to the bitter end. They had their code, and it was a chivalrous code. Rough in dress and speech and manners, gaining their livelihood by the hardest kind of manual labor, living, loving and laughing crudely, still they were gentlemen."

This was the reminiscence of an old man, looking back at his youth and a time lost. Still, no doubt there was considerable truth in Nelligan's evaluation of the lumberjacks as an unusual breed of men. When he called them the "hardy forerunners of our present-day civilization," he was telling no more than the truth.

There is the temptation to look on the era of lumbering in Wisconsin and neighboring states as a disgraceful example of waste of natural resources. The loggers have been pictured as crude despoilers of a wilderness, who left a legacy of ruined land fit only for crops of tourists. But in 1871, when Nelligan arrived in "the small country town" of Green Bay and took the Hart Steamboat Company's flat-bottomed boat to Oconto, nearly everyone agreed that clearing the land of trees was both socially desirable and profitable. Farmers wanted open land for their crops. It was not realized until too late that much of northern Wisconsin country was fit for raising nothing but trees and that their removal would change the water table, permit erosion, and cause other problems that future residents would blame on those lumbermen then riding high.

One of the first sawmills in the forests north of Green Bay was constructed by Judge John P. Arndt at Pensaukee in 1825—the Indians had given him permission on condition that he pay them fifteen dollars a year and supply six boards to the tribe annually for making coffins. In 1836, David Jones built a small sawmill in Peshtigo, and a few years later he laid out the streets and offered lots for sale. Settlement was slow, however, and though Oconto County was the largest in the state, with an area of five thousand square miles, in 1852 the population of the entire county was only 415. The first wagon road from Green Bay to Marinette wasn't built until 1856. Prior to that, settlers had used Indian trails. After the Civil War, however, the lumber trade boomed, and settlers and lumberjacks began arriving by the thousands. By 1870, Oconto County had fourteen thousand residents, about half of them in its three principal towns—Oconto, Peshtigo, and Marinette. In twenty years, in fact, the Wisconsin population

19

had tripled, but most of the state remained predominately rural.

When he got there in the spring of 1871, John Nelligan estimated the city of Oconto's population at four thousand, about double that of Peshtigo a few miles to the north. His description of Oconto would do for most of the other small lumbering communities: "Plank sidewalks, punctured and chipped by the calked boots of rivermen, lined the muddy streets. Behind the sidewalks stood the mercantile establishments of the booming little city, most of them saloons."

One saloon was operated by the Klause brothers, who held dances in an upstairs room on Sunday nights. A gang of particularly rowdy lumberjacks developed the habit of dropping in on such dances and starting trouble. The Klause boys got tired of cleaning up the debris after such visits, so they hired an armed bouncer. The roughnecks showed up as usual, led by a Canadian named Denny White. When things got out-of-hand, the bouncer drew his revolver and fired at White. But he was nervous, his arm shook. The bullet killed a young bystander named Joseph Rule. The bouncer was willing to apologize for his error, but nonetheless was hauled off to jail. Rule's friends discussed the matter over their whiskey and decided to teach the bouncer not to be so careless with his aim. Using a small log as a battering ram, they smashed open the flimsy door of the jail and dragged the prisoner from his cell. By the time the crowd reached the middle of a bridge, the victim had given up hope of escaping, but he requested time to say his prayers. The mob was in a hurry to get back to the saloon—having wasted too much good drinking time as it was—so they declined. They dragged their prisoner across the bridge and hung him from a tree in a field where the Oconto courthouse was later built. Afterward, cooler heads regretted the lynching, but others pointed out that anyone who aimed at one man and shot another wasn't safe to have around.

Lynchings were not common, but they did occur. Another example of that type of logging-town justice took

20

place in Marinette, where two brothers named McDonald were jailed after killing a half-breed in a fight. Ordinarily, killing an Indian was not considered very illegal, even if the Indian were half-white. But for some reason the death of this half-breed and the unpopularity of the McDonalds aroused the mob instincts of about five hundred Marinette citizens, many of them drunk. They smashed into the jail and grabbed the brothers. As the McDonalds were dragged face down through the streets by ropes fastened around their necks, some of the mob leaders jumped on the backs of the helpless men and rode them. By the time the tree chosen for the hanging was reached, the brothers were dead. Just to make sure it was official, however, the lynchers hanged them anyway.

Drunken brawls in saloons and on the sawdust streets did not usually result in fatalities. Mostly they caused nothing worse than a bad case of "loggers smallpox," easily distinguished by the marks made on a loser's chest when his opponent jumped on him with calked boots. But if a participant in a fight died, no one worried very much, perhaps because the lumberjacks were accustomed to seeing men die. In the woods death was commonplace. A dead branch or "widow maker" might fall, a tree might crash down in the wrong place, a log in the river might twist and send the man riding it to a quick end. When such an accident happened, it was customary to bury the victim on the spot, hanging up his boots on the nearest tree as a memorial.

When the shanty boys swapped tales, the talk was most likely to be of some actual character of the camps, such as the Canadian who always wore a stiff boiled shirt or a white cardboard dickey over his mackinaw when he went to town to celebrate the arrival of Saturday night. After a few drinks, he would stand in the center of the street and bellow: "I am T. C. Cunnion, the man-eater from Peterborough, Ontario." The cry was meant as a challenge, but as T. C. measured roughly three feet across the shoulders, the consensus was that it was better to let him howl. To help build his public image, Cunnion often stopped in a butcher shop and demanded a piece of cow's liver. Then he would head down the street, chewing on the bloody morsel and letting forth his cry. According to the tales told around the fire, it was the unusual combination of raw liver and a woman that laid the mighty man-eater low. Emerging from a butcher shop, his face covered with cow's blood, Cunnion had opened his mouth to announce his name and origin when he nearly collided with the woman, who was on her way to buy some meat. She was, quite naturally, startled. She gave a piercing scream and swung her umbrella at the bloody apparition. The umbrella caught Cunnion full across the face and sent him sprawling. He slunk away to the woods, his bellow permanently stilled by the disgrace of having been bested by a woman.

This was the kind of story, based on fact and doubtless embellished as the years went on, that the shanty boys favored. Their humor was robust. On one occasion, for example, John Nelligan was on a train that stopped at Seney, conceded to be among the toughest towns in Michigan. He estimated that there were five hundred drunks on the main street that day and two of them, deciding to have some fun, boarded the train with drawn revolvers and started threatening the passengers. The male passengers could see it was all in jest, but some of the women and children "almost died from fright." The railroad officials, unable to see the humor in a pair of drunks brandishing revolvers aboard their train, had the fun-loving pair arrested. "The court gave them five years in Jackson prison to think their joke over and analyze its weak points," Nelligan said.

Life in the north woods was far less fun and games, of course, than long hours of hard work. The timber crew bosses were judged on their ability to improve production. By 1871, oxen were beginning to give way to horses in the camps. The change came after someone figured out a method of icing the trails, making it possible for a team of horses to drag an astonishing quantity of logs down the trail to the nearest river.

22

A lumber camp's routine began at 4 A.M. when the chore boy crawled out of his bunk and lit the fires, then shook the teamsters awake. They headed for the barns, being careful not to disturb the other sleepers. By the time the teamsters had finished their morning chores, the cook had the day's first meal nearly ready. It was time to arouse the lumberjacks. They would roll out of bed, put on the heavy socks that had been perfuming the air from the drying racks, and wash for breakfast—wash their hands and possibly their faces, that is, for no one took a bath in a lumber camp unless he was willing to be considered eccentric. A breakfast horn called a "gaberal" was sounded, and the men began the stowing away of great mounds of flapjacks and baked beans. There was plenty of food, but no talk—it was traditional to maintain silence during the serious business of eating. Any man who spoke was severely reprimanded by the cook.

Work was from first light until dark, with time out for a big noonday meal. In 1871, the trees were still felled with an ax, no one having yet discovered that a two-man crosscut saw was more efficient. The choppers were the aristocrats of the crew. To qualify as one, a man had to be able to chop down a tall pine in a high wind, making it fall so accurately that it would drive a stake into the ground. Once down, the trees were swarmed over by barkers, who trimmed off the branches and stripped the bark from the log so it could be snaked out of the woods to a logging road. The tree itself was sawed into logs small enough to fit on a sled. Meanwhile, other lumberjacks had been preparing the road. A specialist might drive back and forth on it all night with a huge watering device made from a barrel, icing the twin ruts down which the sleds could travel. In the spring, lumberjacks assigned to drive the logs down the river attached spikes to their boots, filing them down so the points were sharp enough to dig into a slippery log or, if a fight developed, into the chest of a fallen foe.

Visitors were scarce in the lumber camps, but now and then a hunter or a hobo would show up. The rule was that the stranger was welcome and could eat his fill, but he had to leave the next day. If he smoked cigarettes, however, he was seldom allowed to linger. The lumberjacks considered a cigarette-smoker effeminate. "Take them pimp-sticks out of here," someone would growl, and the offender would have to be on his way before anyone decided to boot him out. Actually, the shanty boys were tobacco chewers in the early days. Later, after Scandinavians became plentiful, many of them switched to snuff, which the Norsemen called snoose.

Catholic nuns came in pairs to the wilderness to seek donations for orphanages, and most of the lumberjacks gave generously, which Nelligan considered only fair. "It was through the humanitarian efforts of these women, they were well aware, that their illegitimate offspring—the unintended results of their wild revels—were reared in decency and given a chance in the world," he pointed out.

Most loggers were said to be honest men who seldom stole anything but whiskey. If the shanty boys were trustworthy in money matters, however, those who preyed on them were not. The lumbering regions of the north country attracted the unscrupulous parasites who are always found where law enforcement is casual. Nelligan was an old lumberman who looked back with nostalgia on his days in the woods, but he admitted that having money there was an invitation to thievery and sometimes violence. A lumberjack who passed out in a town saloon seldom awoke with his pockets unpicked. At the few drinking places run by honest men, it was the custom to leave all but the money needed for the night's spree with the owner, who returned it when the logger had sobered up. But in many saloons, the most profitable part of the business was the take from dead-drunk lumberjacks.

In the pivotal year of 1871, then, it was a different sort of world in the Wisconsin north country than either the residents or the tourists see now. The lumberjacks, facing a disaster none of them could yet imagine, were men accustomed to a

24

rough, sometimes dangerous life. As Stewart H. Holbrook wrote, the men who "at intervals emerged from the dark, savage woods for the purpose of calling on soft ladies and drinking hard liquor" were pioneers who chopped down the forests so houses could be built. They were different from the farmers and the town-dwelling clerks, a tougher race. The lumber they produced was required by the nation pushing west beyond the Mississippi to settle the treeless plains. They took in stride the days when the thermometer stood "two feet below zero" and the log jams which might be broken only at the cost of a young man's life.

There was one danger, however, that even the toughest lumberjack feared. When fire swept out of control through the seemingly endless forests, all his courage, brawn, and skill were puny weapons. And in the Wisconsin north country in the fall of 1871, the air was thick with smoke and foreboding.

FOUR

•

In that dangerously dry fall weather, the residents of such communities as Peshtigo found some comfort in numbers. But on the remote farms, scattered in clearings near the eighty-mile length of the Green Bay, each family faced the peril of fire alone. The most isolated settlers were on the Kewaunee-Door County peninsula. Most of them were Belgians and Bohemians, with a scattering of French, Irish, Danes, and other immigrants. The men were mostly heads of families and resembled the roistering lumberjacks only in being hardworking and self-sufficient. Any one not of that sort would not have come there, or if he had come, would not have stayed. The small woods fires that had been burning for several weeks on the eastern as well as the western side of the bay held a special threat to these pioneers, some of whom had only recently escaped the grinding poverty that had been their introduction to the new world. Now their hard-won prosperity was being threatened.

Wisconsin is shaped something like a man's right hand held with the palm facing him, the fingers touching each other, the thumb at a slight angle from the hand. The arm of Lake

26

Michigan that is called the Green Bay is represented by the space between thumb and forefinger. The thumb itself represents the peninsula occupied mainly by Kewaunee and Door Counties. Green Bay, the city, is where the thumb joins the rest of the hand.

The county occupying the upper half of the peninsula is named from the Porte des Morts—"door of death"—the passage between the peninsula and Washington Island to the north. That water passage got its name from a legend about a flotilla of Chippewa canoes on a raiding expedition against the Pottawatomies. A sudden squall came up as the warriors were off the tip of the peninsula. Many of them drowned. Their bodies, it is said, washed up on shore for days.

Door County became a separate entity in 1851, when it was separated from Brown County, but in 1871, communications were still primitive in many parts of the county.

Kewaunee County split off from Door in 1852. Its settlement was helped by a rumor that rich gold deposits had been found near the village of Kewaunee. Such wealthy speculators as John Jacob Astor and Chief Justice Salmon P. Chase bought land there. Chase paid nearly forty thousand dollars for eighty acres that proved to be worth only a few hundred dollars when the story of gold was proved a myth. The village had hoped to rival Chicago, but had given up such dreams by 1871, when its population was a modest 1,050.

There was no railroad in Door County. Its public transportation consisted of an occasional stage coach and the small steamers operated by the Goodrich Transportation Company which stopped at a few backwoods hamlets in Kewaunee and the county to the north.

The first wave of European immigrants to the peninsula arrived in the early 1850's. Perhaps "wave" is not the word for an influx that came so quietly and unspectacularly. The newcomers were mostly peasants in the European social scale—pioneers, to give them their due as Americans. They came singly or in small family groups and vanished into the

27

woods, carrying only what could be borne on a man's back—an ax, a gun, a few cooking utensils. They had no money to spend in Green Bay and the other settlements at the edge of the wilderness, and they didn't linger long enough to make much of an impression on the townsfolk.

In the woods, each man chose the land that seemed best to him and began to clear it. The first trees that were felled were used to build primitive log cabins. The women worked beside their husbands. The children—and there were soon lots of children in this difficult land—helped as soon as they were old enough.

The first cash crop on such farms was not grain but shingles. To make them, a pine log was sawed into chunks. These were then split into pieces with an instrument called a frow. Such work was generally done in the winter, and the pieces of split pine were laid in a warm place until thawed, then put in a vise and tapered with a draw knife. An expert could shape three thousand shingles a day.

It soon became common to see a roughly dressed fellow walking along the streets of Green Bay with a bundle of handmade shingles for sale. He might not know a word of English, but somehow he had learned how much the shingles were worth, down to the last penny. He would head back to his cabin only after his price was met. After a few such trips, the profits from the shingles would be enough to buy a cow. The shinglemaker then became a farmer, which was what he had intended when he set forth across the Atlantic. With only one cow, however, it was not yet time to lay down the ax. Each tree cut for shingles was one less in the path of the crops he would plant. Meanwhile, the cow would earn her keep by pulling a home-built wagon on the new farmer's next trip to Green Bay. This, of course, enabled him to bring a much larger load of shingles, but it also gave him fresh milk to drink during the two or three days it took to make the trip. On the way home, perhaps the cow's owner could arrange for her to stop at the farm of some settler prosperous enough to own a

28

bull. By the time a calf was born, the cow was no longer needed to haul shingles—enough had been sold by then so the family now owned a team of oxen.

While such painstaking economic progress was going on in the woods, daughters of the immigrant families were finding jobs in town as hired girls. Besides getting room, board, and a small wage, they were able to learn the language. There were other opportunities open to them. Because of the surplus of men, an immigrant's daughter often found someone who was eager to marry her whether she spoke much English or not. Meanwhile, the girls dutifully sent their wages home.

One of the best accounts of what life was like in those days comes from Xavier Martin, who became a prominent politician and real estate dealer in Green Bay. He was a young member of the first group of Belgians who set out for Wisconsin from Antwerp aboard a three-masted sailing ship in 1853. Martin stopped off in Pennsylvania for four years, long enough to learn English, then followed his parents to Wisconsin.

The Belgians had planned to settle near Sheboygan, but soon disillusioned by the ignorance of French there, they headed north to Green Bay where about half the inhabitants were of French ancestry and spoke a civilized tongue. A Belgian priest, Father Daems, was in charge of a church at Bay Settlement, a small community northeast of Green Bay. He persuaded his countrymen to settle a few miles from him, where they could buy government land for $1.25 an acre. The site, which became known as the First Belgian Settlement, was located in Green Bay township near a little community now called Champion. Martin described what it had been like for the original settlers:

"The little party was ten miles away from any house, in a virgin forest consisting of a thick growth of pine, maple, cedar, basswood—many of the trees being five and even six feet in diameter and some over a hundred fifty feet high —without roads of any kind, not even a trail, with no neighbors, no horses, no cattle; nothing but the occasional visit of a wolf, a deer or a bear coming around their little huts and, on more than one occasion, taking the pork they had brought with them."

Until they could build hewed-log houses covered with cedar bark, the Belgians slept in the open air. Despite the hardships, however, the settlers wrote enthusiastic letters to friends and relatives in Belgium describing the cheap land and rich soil. The nine original families soon became the forerunners of thousands of their countrymen who sold everything they owned and emigrated to Wisconsin. They established several settlements with names like La Sucrerie, La Riviere Rouge, La Riviere des Loups, Rosiere, Brussels, Thiry Daems. In 1855, hardship overtook many of the families. Times were hard. Many homes went without bread for weeks at a time and had to depend on fish, wild onions, and roots. Then cholera broke out. Some families lost five members in a single week. The bodies turned black soon after death and were buried hastily in the woods. When relatives and old friends heard what was happening, the tide of immigration stopped. It resumed after a few years, but on a much smaller scale.

When Xavier Martin arrived in 1857, there were fifteen thousand Belgians in the region, and according to Martin not one could speak English. They came by the dozens to ask him to teach them. "They were emerging from their first years of hardship, full of hope and courage," Martin wrote. "What they desired the most, they said to me, were schools and school-teachers, churches and priests, and the full enjoyment of their political rights, which up to this time they had not exercised."

The Belgians complained that the German, Irish, and Scandinavian settlements nearby ignored them, giving them no help in building roads or schools. Drawing upon his experience among the Philadelphians, Martin explained that there was nothing that attracted the attention of American officialdom quicker than votes. So in the 1858 election, 230

Belgian men marched two abreast from the First Belgian Settlement to the polling place near a windmill at Bay Settlement, ten miles away. They all voted for the same candidates and from then on, Martin said, were looked upon by their neighbors as honest, industrious, and intelligent people.

The roads, hacked out of the woods by hand, had been so narrow and full of stumps, stones, and water holes that it had been difficult for the settlers to haul their crops to market. Now that the Belgians had demonstrated their voting capacities, the county politicians suddenly realized that the settlements deserved a full share of road and drainage funds, not to mention schools and other facilities. A post office was established at the First Settlement, whose name was changed to Robinsonville, and Martin became the first postmaster.

On August 15, 1858, there occurred what Martin described as an "alleged miracle, which made quite a noise at the time." A young woman, Adele Brice, had been to Mass at the Bay Settlement. Walking home, she was in the vicinity of Robinsonville when, by her account, she saw a vision of the Virgin Mary standing between two trees. The vision addressed her, speaking in French, telling her to build a chapel on that sacred spot. According to Martin, the church authorities were skeptical and declared the apparition was a "myth and an imposition." When Adele refused to cease talking about it, she was refused Communion. But many of the settlers sided with Mme. Brice, and they flocked to the site to stare thoughtfully at the two trees. Services were held, although at first no priest would attend. Finally, the bishop permitted a small chapel to be built. This was soon followed by a boarding school, a larger chapel, a church, and a convent. Pilgrims came from miles around and some of them claimed to have been cured of their ailments.

By 1860, many of the immigrant farmers had become relatively prosperous. Old country feasts were revived. The boys held tournaments called "carrousels." Riding full speed

31

on a fast horse, a youth would try to catch a ring suspended at the edge of the track to win a prize. Dancing would last far into the night in the log schoolhouse. Brass and string bands were organized. Best of all, Phillip Hannon put up a brewery, so the Belgians no longer had to drink the product of the German brewmasters in Green Bay and Manitowoc.

The outbreak of the Civil War brought changes to the settlements of Belgians and other immigrants. They had voted, therefore they were Americans and obligated to march off to war. The women went to work driving the teams, harvesting, or plowing. When the veterans returned, life changed. In the phrase of those times, the soldiers had "seen the elephant." They had new ambitions. Some of them built sawmills so the logs and trees were no longer a nuisance but could be turned into cash. Planing, shingle, and grist mills were constructed in a number of the peninsula settlements and in neighboring Brown County. One new mill was built near Brussels by a family named Williamson. Around it soon grew a thriving little settlement which they named Williamsonville.

Now that their trees could be converted into lumber, shingles, and railroad ties, the immigrant settlers had money to buy threshing machines, reapers, and other farming implements. They enlarged their farms. They acquired more and better livestock. Some even began to live in board houses instead of cabins. By 1871, after more than fifteen years of hard work, the Belgians and other settlers were beginning to prosper on the farms they had carved out of the Wisconsin wilderness. Immigrants who had walked into the forest with little more than their axes were now able to ride to town behind their own horses and to entertain friends in board houses nestled in the shadow of large barns. The log cabins remained, however, as outbuildings or as part of the more elaborate homes. It would have been wasteful to tear them down. Of all the sins known to the Belgians and Bohemians, the Danes, and the French, waste was the worst.

So the rural residents of Door, Kewaunee, and Brown counties had special reasons that fall of 1871 to regard the threat of fire with heavy hearts. It is one thing to be a clerk in Peshtigo or Marinette or Green Bay and to look out at the glow of distant flame and know that all you are risking by staying in the vicinity is your life. It is quite another to be a patriarch, with memories still fresh of what it was like to dream of owning a single cow, and to look at the comfortable home you've wrested from the wilderness, thinking: "If the wind shifts, we may have to run for it. But if we run, what will happen to all we've built?"

Not many of the families in the isolated clearings on the peninsula could bring themselves to abandon their homes as the smoke grew thicker and the danger more obvious. They clung to the philosophy that had sustained them: If a man works hard, saves his money and fathers numerous children, he is fulfilling his destiny and will prosper.

FIVE

•

The drought of 1871 both helped and hindered the building of the railroad between Green Bay and Marinette by way of Peshtigo. The winter of 1870–71 had far less than the customary four feet of snow expected in that region. As the year wore on with the drought continuing, the swampy areas along the right-of-way dried up. This made it easier to build there but made it hard to get water for the construction crews. In some places the men dug ten feet below what had been a swamp to find the first signs of moisture. Some of the workmen laid down their axes and shovels and refused to continue until they were supplied with enough water for drinking and for making coffee—bathing was not an issue. Wagons were dispatched from Peshtigo with barrels of water from the river and the men went back to work.

"The railroad embankments in the sand were like hot ash heaps into which the feet would sink at every step," a visitor reported. "The swamps, which had been considered the greatest obstacle to the cheap construction of the road, proved the best working ground."

William Ogden was one of those who had encouraged the

34

railroad to push north. He was in a position to do so, since he was a former president of the Chicago, St. Paul & Fond du Lac, one of the railroads absorbed into the North Western system. The railway was entitled to 3,840 acres of government land for each mile it built between Fond du Lac and the Michigan line, which helps explain why Ogden and the other railroad magnates were anxious to finish the job. By late September, three railroad camps had been established between Peshtigo and Marinette. Although the line had not yet been completed south of Peshtigo, there was preliminary work to be done to the north of it—chopping, mostly, and hauling felled trees to one side to make way for the rails.

Every forest dweller, including the railway workers, was conscious of the danger of fire. Although scattered fires were burning in the woods, no one as yet was too concerned about them. Such smolderings in the humus that had accumulated for centuries were regarded as normal for that time of year. As soon as a good, soaking rain came, the danger would be over.

But the rains did not come. In the backwoods communities, residents sometimes groped through smoke thick enough to obscure the sun. "I wish to heaven the fires would take everything and be done with it," one man told another that fall in Peshtigo, "and let us see the sun once more." It was the kind of foolish remark that would have been forgotten had it not begun to seem likely that the wish might be fulfilled. Yet when danger persists long enough men learn to ignore it, or pretend to, and hope that if no one looks the peril full in the face it will be discouraged and slink away.

So living continued. Railroad officials arrived at Peshtigo to inspect the site where workmen had begun to sink pilings in the river for a railroad bridge. The Odd Fellows lodge prepared for an anniversary social. The Good Templars Lodge, not to be outdone, began rehearsals of *Ten Nights in a Barroom*. In the Upper Sugar Bush, Philip Weinhart bragged that he had raised eleven hundred bushels of potatoes. In the

35

village saloons, red dog and stud poker helped to while away the time.

The smoke in the air and the danger of the woods fires spreading were not allowed to interfere with production at the Peshtigo Company. The town, as it existed in 1871, was a tribute to the enterprise of that company and to its president, William Ogden. Ogden, who had been Chicago's first mayor, was an operator on a large scale. His company had made the harbor into one of the best on Lake Michigan. The mill there had ninety-seven saws, with a daily capacity of 150,000 board feet of lumber. It operated by steam. Around it were a company store, houses for workers with families, a boarding house for two hundred unmarried mill hands, two schools. In the village, many of the houses were also company-owned, along with the woodenware factory, lumber mill, a sash, door and blind factory, a machine shop, a grist mill, a large store, and a boarding house. The woodenware factory was said by residents of Peshtigo to be the largest of its kind. Over two hundred men and boys handled its saws and lathes, which were capable of turning out each day 45,000 shingles, 170 tubs, 250 fish kits, 5,000 broom handles, 50 boxes of wooden clothespins, 96 barrel heads, and almost 1,500 pails for various uses. The company employed eight hundred men in all, including those in its logging camps.

Still, Peshtigo was not entirely a company town. Many of the business establishments were privately owned, including two wagon shops, two livery stables, and such minor industrial enterprises as Cavoit's sawmill and David Lister's foundry. There were several hotels, including the Peshtigo, the Jacobs, the Forest House, and Joseph Gregy's Hotel de France. A telegraph line had been strung along the future right-of-way for the railroad and a telegraph office had been established in one of the grocery stores, where a clerk, W. C. Oakes, operated it.

The village houses were said to be "prettily built and carefully painted," with a number of them having ornamental gardens. The spire of the Congregational Church east of the river was the most conspicuous object on Peshtigo's modest skyline, but the Roman Catholics under Father Pernin were preparing to meet the architectural challenge. In fact, they were not only building a church a little west of the river but had already completed a home for the priest. The Evangelical Lutheran Church had organized a congregation but had no permanent meeting place. The Episcopalian Society met in Good Templars Hall.

The Reverend Edwin R. Beach, the Congregational pastor, held two services on Sunday, morning and evening, besides prayer meetings on Wednesday nights. Father Pernin divided his time between Peshtigo and Marinette, and on alternate Sundays in Peshtigo he held a morning and an afternoon Mass. The Lutherans, with the Reverend Carl Huebner, met on alternate Sundays at 10 A.M. and 3 P.M. in members' homes.

The dominating feature of the landscape was the forest. It began at Peshtigo's edge, so close that the families on the outer fringe of the village were walled in by towering pines. A traveler going east from Peshtigo would soon reach Lake Michigan; traveling south for a day or so, he would emerge into an area of cultivated farmland. But if he headed west or north, there was nothing but trees for hundreds of miles, except for an occasional small lumber town or a clearing where an isolated farm family lived.

By early fall of 1871, small fires were smoldering in the woods in an area one hundred miles long and seventy miles wide. A few of the farmers in the area had fled to Peshtigo. Most of the backwoods settlers stayed where they were, however, hoping things would get no worse. But as a precaution a number of them piled all their valuables — ranging from furniture to stacks of marsh hay — in the middle of their clearings.

Franklin Tilton described in his Green Bay newspaper how the woods fires gnawed at the roots of tall trees "as a cancer eats away the life of a man." Then if a wind came, the big trees would topple over and "their trunks would be wrapped in a winding sheet of fire.

"Again, the fires would reach a clump of cedars or tamaracks," he continued. "The flames would dance around their roots, reaching up forked tongues toward the branches as a beast would leap for his prey, just beyond his reach. Then there would be a momentary hiss as the sap turned to steam, a flash like that of burning powder as the leaves took fire, and in an instant the entire tree would be in flames. Then would the flames leap from tree to tree, borne on the wings of the wind . . . and in a few minutes the beautiful grove would be a blackened, dismal forest of dry poles. . . . The flames would insidiously work their way into the swamps and here develop almost a furnace heat, actually burning from one to three feet into the ground and completely burning out the peat, roots and alluvial soil, leaving nothing but ashes and the subsoil of sand. Thus the fires lived and increased for weeks, until the dwellers in this section began to be terrified for the safety of their homes, their mills and even their lives.

"The whole air was filled with a dense, suffocating smoke, almost obscuring the vision, over a tract of hundreds of square miles. The sun shone down through the smoke with a red, angry glare. The heavens at night would be illuminated on every side with the holocaust of fire."

Tilton stood observing the dismal picture one late September evening in Oconto. Looking to the north in the direction of Peshtigo, he could see nearby buildings outlined against a line of fire that swept along much of the horizon. When he faced south toward Pensaukee, a village of a few hundred persons, he noticed a dull glare through the smoke. He spoke to a traveler who told of miles of burning woods between Oconto and Pensaukee, with the telegraph line burned down and the wooden ties of the newly built railroad destroyed. Pensaukee, the traveler told him, seemed to be doomed.

38

The destruction of the telegraph line meant that Peshtigo, Marinette, Oconto, and the rest of the region north of Green Bay was cut off from rapid communication with the remainder of the state. If help was needed—and Tilton was convinced disaster was ahead—it would have to be summoned on foot or horseback.

There was further evidence of peril within Tilton's view. "A bright light shot across the eastern sky and the whole heavens seemed ablaze in that direction. The fire was sweeping over the low meadows, comprising many hundreds of acres, and halting but for a moment to lick up an occasional stack of hay. Some two or three hundred tons of hay were burned on these marshes.

"We turned away to face a new quarter of danger. In another direction and fearfully near the city was a bright light, with now and then a tongue of flame shooting high above the general glow. Repairing to that quarter, we found the flames advancing into the city, between it and the fair ground, fanned by a fair wind and threatening several buildings.

"An alarm was struck. A sleepless night and judicio is fighting warded off the destroyer. Thus the city was encompassed by fire and no one knew but in a few hours their homes would be reduced to ashes."

South of Oconto and Pensaukee was another small settlement called Little Suamico. It had grown up around two sawmills. On September 21 the fire threatened the town. Led by one of the sawmill owners, A. C. Conn, the workmen fought to save their homes and mills. Two small streams met in the village, so there was water available. Every barrel was filled and hauled by horses or oxen to the edge of the burning timber, ready for use. Ditches were dug around the village— shallow burrows plowed hurriedly to try to keep the fire from creeping from the woods into the town through the humus and dry grass.

Sparks from the burning trees were blown onto the roofs. Conn's mill caught fire several times. But bucket brigades,

39

working desperately, doused the wooden shingles. When the day was over, the houses and both mills had been saved. A corduroy road leading to Conn's mill was destroyed. Two nearby railroad camps were burned, the crews narrowly escaping with their lives. Thousands of railroad ties on the railway line south of Little Suamico were consumed, along with more of the telegraph line. There was now an estimated gap of twenty miles in the line between Green Bay and Marinette, which meant that there was no chance of restoring wire communications before winter.

Fires were also burning on the Kewaunee-Door County peninsula. Messengers came galloping into Green Bay, hoping to hire extra hands to help save valuable sawmills. On the night of September 30, for example, Oscar Gray hurried into the city from his mill in the town of Pittsfield. He had no luck finding men who wanted to return with him to fight the fire—it was Saturday night and the saloons were full of men trying to get the taste of woods smoke out of their mouths. Gray did manage to buy a length of hose before he turned his horse's head toward home again. He arrived in time to join his men in saving the property, but two nearby houses were burned down.

The fires approached within three miles of Green Bay itself that day, burning twelve hundred cords of wood at a charcoal kiln.

On October 2, the stagecoach arrived in Green Bay from the north after a harrowing trip. The smoke had been so thick that the horses could hardly pick their way along the road. The driver said he had encountered delays because of fallen trees which had crashed down after their roots were weakened by fire. He told of a large force of men working hard to try to save McGovern's Hotel at West Pensaukee.

Older's Circus, with eighty horses pulling twenty wagons, headed southeast from Green Bay to Manitowoc and barely escaped being trapped in the burning woods. Some of the wooden bridges were burning while the circus caravan

40

crossed them. Soon after the last of the wagons got across, three of the bridges were destroyed. Fred Scheller took a crew of men out to rebuild them, but was forced to turn back because of the heavy smoke and the danger. Big pines were crashing all around, Scheller reported, and if he hadn't known he was in Wisconsin and the war was over he would have thought the Confederate artillery was firing again as it had at Chancellorsville.

As the first week of October wore on, Green Bay—then the second largest city in the state—was in danger of being isolated by land, although its situation at the foot of the bay made access by water possible for a skipper who could get through the smoke. The plank and corduroy roads which connected the city with nearby communities were mostly burned. The culverts were made of heavy timbers, and these had also been destroyed in many places. The fire seemed to be running along the ground, or even under the ground in the smoldering humus. It got under the bridge timbers and set them afire.

So far, casualties were light. A number of volunteer fire fighters had singed eyebrows and minor burns. Green Bay heard that "a team of horses and an Indian" were burned to death near Oconto on October 2. But most of the damage had been to lumber, hay, an occasional building and, of course, to the great forest itself.

By October 4, the smoke was so thick on the bay that steamers blew their fog horns and navigated by compass in what should have been broad daylight. Woods on both sides of the bay were burning. In Green Bay, the air was filled with flakes of wood ash. The residents had nearly grown accustomed to breathing smoke, but it was making some of them ill. Apprehension was mounting. Tilton, a New Yorker who had migrated to the Wisconsin frontier to become a newspaperman, was as worried as everyone else, but it was his job to write of what was happening:

"By day, flakes of white ashes were continually falling in

41

the streets like snow. Now and then, if the wind blew high, partially burned leaves would fall. A settled gloom fell upon the whole community. [There was] scarce a man or woman but who, before retiring at night, would go out and gaze ruefully upon the red glare in the heavens to the east, west and south of us, estimate the distance of the flames and take note of the direction and force of the wind."

If a bell rang or there was any other unusual sound, everyone stopped whatever he was doing and listened, fearful that it heralded the approach of the fire coming to wipe out the city.

"Thus sped the days—fearful days—but they brought no relief," Tilton said. " 'The sky was brass. The earth was ashes.' "

At Peshtigo, the danger had been obvious since mid-September. By September 24, the village was nearly cut off from Oconto and Green Bay. The fire had also burned through to the river about a mile north of the settlement. The day was a Saturday, but when night fell the saloons were empty. Everyone was either preparing to fight the fire or watching it in mingled awe and fear.

One man who was in Peshtigo that night described it as a grand sight. Unless the danger is immediate and personal, there is a kind of primitive pleasure to be found in watching a fire. This one, it was clear, was awesome. Venerable pines, towering above their offspring, were wrapped in flame. The trunk of a hundred-year-old giant would burn fiercely for a time, the flames shooting higher to catch the top branches, then flashing out along them to form a blazing canopy. When the tree had been sufficiently weakened, it would crash down in a shower of sparks and embers.

Those who were in Peshtigo that night recalled that thousands of birds flew about the village, having fled to this seemingly safe haven from the burning forest. Some would flit about in the darkness for a time, calling out their alarm, then head off above the fiery woods, only to be caught in the rising columns of heated air and fall into the flames.

42

Peshtigo Company workmen spent most of the night protecting the company buildings. Several times sparks caught in sawdust or slab wood at the mill. But the fires were extinguished by buckets of water or by the stream played on the blaze by the hose of the Black Hawk, the company's hand-operated fire engine. That engine was the only such equipment north of Green Bay.

Prayers were said that night for rain. The next morning the wind died down. The danger was apparently past, but the pews of Peshtigo's churches were filled. At the Congregational Church, the minister announced his text and had just begun his sermon when the congregation jumped to its feet and vanished, leaving him gaping before a vacant church. "The steam whistle of the factory blew a wild blast, which told us there was danger from terrestrial fires more immediately pressing than from those infernal," a member of the flock explained later. By the time they arrived at the scene, the fire which had caught in sawdust near the sawmill had been put out, but there was no disposition to go back and listen to the minister's sermon. The wind had risen and was blowing hard from the northwest. The fire was getting close to the river bank opposite the factory. Burning coals filled the air, blown by the wind from the forest. The Black Hawk was wheeled into place again. Every man grabbed a wooden pail and filled it with water. Whenever an ember lit on the shingled roof or the sawdust pile, someone doused it, then hurried off to fill his bucket at the river again.

A gust of hot, blinding smoke swept over the men near the factory. When it had cleared slightly they could see a new danger—a second fire was approaching from the southwest. Women hurried to their homes. With the children helping, they packed their valuables and loaded them on wagons or buried them in the sandy ground. Families who lived in the houses nearest the approaching fire fled to what they hoped were places of greater safety, away from the river.

One man who was at Peshtigo that day wrote a comparison some weeks later between a prairie fire and a forest fire. The latter, he said, was "intenser, hotter, grander" than the prairie fire. "The fire on the prairie before a high wind will rush on and lap up the dead grass and it is done in a breath. In the timber it may move almost as rapidly but the fire goes not out with the advance waves, which sweep over the tops of the trees and catch the light limbs and foliage. Nor is there the same chance to resist the approach of fire in the timber. It is as though you attempted to resist the approach of an avalanche of fire."

Still, resist it they did that September Sunday in Peshtigo. The company's horses were set to hauling water from the river. The hose company and bucket brigades managed to save the buildings. Toward evening, the wind died down. The danger was temporarily ended.

Thick smoke remained until Monday morning, when the wind veered to the south and blew it away. Peshtigo could breathe again. Everyone was exhausted from anxiety, exertion and lack of sleep. Superintendent Ellis made an announcement that demonstrated that this was an unusual situation. The factory would be shut down all day Monday, he declared, and no one need report for work. In 1871, when only the Sabbath was allowed to interfere with free enterprise, this gesture of gratitude to the men who had saved the factory was nearly unprecedented.

The unexpected holiday gave people a chance to recover their spirits. Peshtigo residents felt a weary triumph. They had fought off the danger and saved their town. With much of the nearby timber destroyed, there seemed less chance that another shift in the wind would bring the fire back to threaten them again. The blackened forest, with partially burned pines rising above the general desolation, could be expected to act as a barrier.

The following day, the factory was back in operation and the normal life of Peshtigo resumed. There was still fire in the woods. There was still smoke in the air. But the worst of the

44

danger seemed to be over. The *Marinette and Peshtigo Eagle* claimed in its September 30 issue that "the fires have nearly died out now in this vicinity," but Editor Noyes was apparently misinformed. Other observers reported the woods fires were still burning, although they found no cause for alarm.

The October 7 issue of the *Eagle* was less optimistic.

"Fires are still raging all over the country," it reported. "The raw air of autumn is being well cooked by fire."

Noyes felt he ought to find one ray of optimism in the generally gloomy situation, and he did. "The thick smoke of the past week," he told his readers, "has been tough on mosquitoes." And he found another fire-borne blessing in disguise. "A certain establishment down on the bay shore that has been somewhat obnoxious to the respectable citizens" had burned down.

"We now breathe a little easier," Noyes wrote, "for it seems that the greater part of the combustible matter around the village . . . must be already destroyed. However, Peshtigo is yet very far from being out of danger. Unless we have rain soon, God knows how soon a conflagration may sweep the town."

That fear was equally justified for any of a dozen other communities on both sides of the bay. Knowing the danger, each family tried to decide what it would do if the fire came toward its home. Some had special reasons to worry.

David Maxon, for example. He and his wife were ill with what was diagnosed as a fever. Mrs. Maxon was too sick to get out of bed. He was able to get up and take care of their five children, but he wasn't strong enough to go to his job in the woodenware factory. On the eve of October 7, he stood looking out of the window, hoping that if hell broke loose he would find the strength to save his family.

J. G. Clements, a young Peshtigo man, was a newlywed, having married a Menominee girl on Thursday. His mother-in-law, Mrs. Theodore Trudell, had waited a decent three days before paying them her first visit, and as she started to leave for home she admonished her new son-in-law, "Take care of my girl." Clements put an arm around his wife. Of course he would take care of her; he would, if necessary, die for her. Mrs. Trudell climbed into her buggy to make the dangerous trip back through the smoke-filled woods. As she left, she turned and looked at the young couple. They seemed young and happy, and very vulnerable.

On his farm in the Lower Sugar Bush, C. R. Towsley and his wife talked of what they would do if the fire came closer. Mrs. Towsley sat nursing the youngest of their four children, the Bible open in her lap. She had faith and assured her husband that God had not brought them to this wilderness to abandon them. Towsley kept his doubts to himself. He considered himself a religious man but also a practical one. If the time came when his family had to be saved from being burned, he expected to have to accomplish it himself.

At Peshtigo the night of October 7, a group of fifty immigrants from Scandinavia arrived. Few could speak any English. At best, this frontier land would have seemed strange to them until they had learned a little of the language and settled down into the new life. As it was, it seemed to these newcomers that they had traveled five thousand miles to search out opportunity and had found trouble instead. The air was filled with smoke. The Norwegians and Swedes among the Peshtigo residents told the new immigrants that when the ship had dropped them at the pier in Peshtigo Harbor to board the company train for Peshtigo, it had brought them into what might be a trap ringed by fire.

46

SIX

•

In our time, when it is possible to learn almost instantaneously more than we really wish to about disasters halfway
around the world, it takes some imagination to understand
how Green Bay could have slept through the worst fire in
American history that was right at its doorstep.

The glow from distant fires was noticed the night of
October 8, 1871, but Green Bay residents had grown
accustomed to such sights. The smoke was thick, but no
thicker than on some previous nights. Occasional hot puffs of
wind were felt—"sometimes startlingly hot, as if the breath of
a furnace," one man recalled. But the night passed quietly in
the north country's principal city, with no one there realizing
that fires were destroying one thousand square miles of
countryside to the north and northeast of them.

It was not until the morning of the 9th that Green Bay got
its first hint of what was happening. George W. Watson
arrived back in the city in a horse and buggy with his three
sisters, looking like a man who had seen a small corner of
hell. He reported that New Franken, only twelve miles away,
had been completely destroyed, and the fire had swept on up

the Kewaunee-Door County peninsula. He was a prosperous and fairly prominent citizen of Green Bay, so when he said there was a disastrous fire on the peninsula side of the bay he was believed.

He had left Green Bay on Saturday, the 7th, to drive to Kewaunee, thirty-six miles away. With him was G. A. Lawson, cashier of the National Bank of Commerce. They knew that travel might be difficult, so they hitched a good pair of horses to a buckboard, a stripped-down carriage that was light enough for the two men to lift over fallen trees and other possible obstructions.

New Franken was on the route they took to Kewaunee. It had been settled in 1845 by a party of Bavarians, although in the surrounding area there already were a few French, half-breeds and other settlers. In 1871, Watson's brother-in-law, Willard Lamb, owned most of the property in the little village, including the lumber and shingle mill. Lamb was a pioneer lumberman, having started Green Bay's first shingle factory in 1847, and his New Franken holdings were only one of his lumber interests. He and his wife—Watson's sister—lived in a two-story frame house there. Nearby were a boardinghouse for one hundred of his mill workers, a dozen tenant houses, a company store, as well as some other buildings, including a schoolhouse, a post office, and Anton Burkhart's blacksmith shop.

Watson arrived in New Franken with Lawson for a midday dinner of roast goose at his sister's house. Lamb was not at home, so after the meal Watson decided to take a look at a fire that had been smoldering in the woods for two weeks to see if it threatened his brother-in-law's mill. He and Lawson satisfied themselves that there was nothing to worry about. Men were on day and night guard at the fire. At times it had flared up alarmingly, but on the early afternoon of October 7 it seemed nearly out. The Green Bay men were in no particular hurry, so they lingered in New Franken until 3 P.M. and then climbed into the buckboard and headed toward Kewaunee.

48

Along the way they saw the ruins of several houses and barns. A number of one-room schoolhouses had been burned, along with miles of fences on both sides of the road. At times the fire was so close that Watson had to whip the horses to a gallop past rows of burning trees.

The men spent Saturday night in Kewaunee with a man named Decker, who was worried about a report that Casco had been burned. This hamlet, about fourteen miles from Kewaunee, included a sawmill owned by Decker, so he joined Watson and Lawson when they left at 7 A.M. Sunday to see if his Casco holdings had been wiped out.

When the buckboard got to Casco, Decker was relieved to discover that the report had been false. Casco had been threatened, but the workmen at his mill had fought off the fire. The three men returned to New Franken, arriving there about 2 P.M. They ate lunch, fed and rested their horses, and made ready to go back to Green Bay. But Watson's sister begged him to stay with her. With her husband away, Mrs. Lamb was worried about the fire.

"There was no man around that could take charge except my father, who was completely exhausted by being up nearly all the time, night and day, for nearly two weeks previous," Watson recalled. "She said that if I would stay with them that night, if all was well in the morning she would send a man with their team to take me home. I did not apprehend any more danger that night than at any other time during the past two weeks. But as she was so urgent in her request for me to stop, I finally consented."

Lawson and Decker left for Green Bay in the buckboard. Shortly after 5 P.M. Watson and his father set out to walk around New Franken's outskirts and see if anything more needed to be done to guard against the fire. They decided that it might come at them from any direction except the south, where the countryside had already been pretty well burned over. They stationed a dozen men to watch the woods in the other directions. They appointed another crew to relieve these guards at midnight. Then Watson decided it was time to eat.

49

He was not the sort of man to let very much interfere with satisfying his appetite.

His sister fixed a hearty dinner. The family was about to sit down when one of the watchmen burst into the house shouting that fire was sweeping toward the town from the south and was a mile from Lamb's mill.

Annoyed at having his dinner interrupted, Watson pointed out that there couldn't be any danger from that direction—fire could not burn twice over the same ground. The watchman suggested with some heat that Watson take a look for himself. He did. "The fire was coming at a frightful rate over the same ground that had previously burned over. It seemed as though every tree in the woods was on fire. The wind commenced to rise. The fire spread from tree to tree, in some instances twenty to thirty rods in advance of the fire on the ground. It seemed as though the heavens were on fire."

Watson took time to pull out his pocket watch. It was shortly before 7 P.M. The wind was from the southwest and was quite strong—"blowing a gale," according to his account. The fire soon reached the town. A log barn caught first, then one of the tenant cottages. A huge pile of wood—three thousand cords of it—began to burn. The mill caught next. In a matter of minutes, five more small houses caught fire.

Watson decided that unless the wind shifted they might be able to save Lamb's house, the boarding house, the company store, and one barn. "But as there was no certainty of anything, I hitched up Mr. Lamb's carriage team, took a few things, and then drove out west about a half mile and put them in a farmer's barn, and then went back."

While he was gone, other men had loaded two wagons with valuables and sent them toward Green Bay, but it was obvious that they had no chance to fight a fire like this. On his way back to his sister's house, Watson found that the road he had just driven over was nearly blocked by flames. Three farm houses and two barns were on fire just west of the store and Watson had to make a run for it to keep from being seared.

50

He found Mrs. Lamb and his two other sisters in what he described as "a perfect panic." He told them that if they stayed in New Franken they would be killed; he could see that the village was doomed. He proposed to head south, the direction from which the fire had come. The woods was still burning there, but the worst of the fire had now passed through and around the village, so he felt that their escape was less likely if they went north, west, or east. It was his plan to run across a portion of the burned-over land until they could turn west and make their way to the barn where the horses had been left. "It was a long time before I could induce the ladies to try the woods," Watson said. "They said they would burn up, that the trees would fall on them. But they soon saw that to remain where they were would be sure death, so they consented to follow me."

Watson ran on ahead to pick the least dangerous route. His sisters stumbled through the smoky darkness behind him. When he found the fire was impassable in one place, he doubled back and tried another, shouting directions to the women. "We had got nearly through," he said, "when I discovered that the fire had leaped from the main fire . . . and was running from where it last took fire at the speed of a race horse. I could see that unless we got through the gap, which was only a few rods ahead of us, our time had come. . . . But I succeeded in getting them through safe. In less than three minutes, the gap was closed up. The ladies all fell on their faces, completely exhausted."

There was no time for rest. The heat from the fire forced them to move again. Heading across a plowed field, they came to the Green Bay road near the barn where Watson had left the team. He had made the mistake of unhitching the horses from the carriage. While he was hitching them to it again, the women ran west along the road, heading toward a farm owned by Casper Schauer. By the time Watson and the carriage caught up with them there, the barn where the horses had been was in flames.

Looking back, he could see that all the buildings around Lamb's mill were on fire. There was nothing to be done about it. He rushed his sisters into the carriage and they made their way to Green Bay, arriving about 5 A.M., October 9.

Now that his sisters were safe, he decided to go back to New Franken and see if he could do anything to help. Before he left, however, he ate a hearty breakfast. It helped make up for the meal he had missed the evening before. By the time he arrived at the ruined village, the fire had burned itself out for lack of fuel. There was nothing remaining to show that New Franken had existed. Every building was gone. Within a half-mile radius, fifteen farmhouses had been destroyed. In New Franken, every family was homeless, but somehow not one of the eighty residents had been killed. Watson considered this "almost like a miracle when we consider the extent of the fire and the rapidity with which it came upon the people."

New Franken was at the lower end of the eastern wing of what for convenience has been called the Peshtigo fire. Actually, this conflagration was not a single fire but several. The portion that swept on up the peninsula after burning New Franken had no direct connection with the even more disastrous fires on the west side of the bay, although they all occurred at approximately the same time and from the same cause—a change in the weather that fanned small woods fires into big ones.

There have been suggestions that the fire on the peninsula was started by embers blown across the Green Bay from the mainland. It is true that burning coals fell on the deck of a lumber schooner, the *C. I. Hutchinson*, two miles off shore. The steamer *Atlanta* reported that a fragment of flaming board fell on its deck seven miles out in the bay. But the theory that the fire on the peninsula was touched off by the one on the mainland—or vice versa—is disproved by the direction of the wind and the location of the burned areas.

From New Franken, the peninsula portion of the fire

continued across Kewaunee County and the lower half of Door County, traveling in a northeasterly direction. The Sturgeon Bay, which extends nearly across the peninsula, saved the upper half of Door County. From his own observations and from talking with other eyewitnesses, Watson estimated that the fire traveled at a rate of about eight miles an hour. In some other places, it apparently moved faster than this, but Watson didn't want to seem to exaggerate. Besides, eight miles per hour seemed quite a rate of speed to a man dependent on either a horse or his own legs to save him.

Among those he talked with was a farmer, Michael Hime, who lived about a mile northeast of New Franken. Hime's barn had contained four hundred bushels of wheat, considerable hay, several head of cattle, and a team of horses. The fire must have reached his farm shortly after 7 P.M., but he and his family were already in bed. Hime was not yet asleep. He noticed a bright light shining into his room and got up to peer out of the window. "The woods and the heavens were all on fire," he told Watson. As a good farmer, Hime's first thought was for his livestock. He ran to the barn. Grabbing his two horses by their halters, he led them into an open field—the cows, he assumed, would find their own way out through the barn's open door.

Having taken care of his team, he then roused his wife and three children. He stopped long enough to fill a pail with water to carry with them. With the youngsters still in their nightclothes, the family ran away from the burning forest to the middle of the clearing. Moments after they fled from the house, it caught fire. The family huddled together. The heat was intense. The air was filled with sparks. Now and then, an ember caught one of their garments on fire, but Hime was ready with his pail of water to put out the flames.

"They saved their lives, but lost every dollar of their property," Watson said. "As soon as the barn was nicely on fire, the horses ran in and were burned."

53

Judging from Watson's account, it can be suspected that when it reached the New Franken area the fire was a big one but had not yet attained the awesome power of its later stages. It surprised Watson by coming from a direction where the underbrush and forest debris had already been burned, but otherwise it did not behave in an unusual manner.

By the time the peninsula fire reached its northern limit at the Sturgeon Bay, it provided quite a spectacle for two men from the village of Sturgeon Bay who were in a batteau a little distance off shore. "Great volumes of fire would rise up, fifty feet from the top of the trees, leap over thirty acres of clearing and, in an instant, flame up in the forests beyond," one of the men said.

Along the way, the fire claimed numerous lives—several hundred of them on the peninsula probably, although estimates vary widely. The bodies of forty-four Belgians were found at Rosiere. In Forestville, the total was nearly as high. Williamsonville was the hardest hit of all, but others died in Brussels, Union, Nasawaupee, and other small communities. In addition, an unknown number of isolated farm families were caught in the clearings they had chopped out of the wilderness.

Many of the farmers still spoke little English, and the accounts of what happened on those isolated homesteads are scarce. What happened at the Belgian settlement of Rosiere was reported by a storekeeper named Charles Rubens, who had six children to worry about when the fire came and was too busy trying to save them and himself to pay much attention to the neighbors' situation.

Rubens' first thought was to get into the stone-lined well pit. He threw some bolts of cloth and other items from his store into it, then ordered the children to climb down. It was a frightening thing to do, clinging to the rocks, but they obeyed. Rubens planned to follow them. But he lingered to watch the flames moving toward him through the woods. He had seen forest fires before, but it was plain that this one was much

54

worse. He decided the well was not a likely refuge after all. He told the children to climb out again.

By the time the last one was above ground, the fire was so close and the heat so intense that Rubens' shirt caught fire. He ripped it off and flung it away but not before his face was painfully burned. With the children clustering around him, he hurried to the middle of a field. They threw themselves to the ground, burying their faces in the dirt while the fire raged around them.

They survived. When the danger was past, Rubens found he was temporarily blinded from his burns and the smoke. One of the children took his hand and led him back to the well. Only one fragment of flannel cloth remained unburned at the bottom.

It should not be assumed from this that a well pit was always a trap—although it often was that night of October 8—or that the center of a clearing was always safe, although the Rubens and Hime families had found it so. If Rubens' children had stayed in the well, they would have died. But in Red River township, a farmer and two children who climbed into a similar well survived; his wife, who refused to join him, died. She and three of their children were burned to death in the middle of a clearing.

Some of the reports of incidents on the peninsula managed to find a little grim humor amid the tragedy. One such account deals with "Praying Peter" Bernson, who lived just south of the Sturgeon Bay. After the fire, Bernson spent a lot of time telling anyone who would listen how his pipeline to higher authority had saved him. Two days before, he said, he had fallen on his knees and inquired, "What shall I do?"

A voice seemed to say to him: "Wet down your house, Peter."

So Bernson spent the day throwing buckets of water on his house. But he was still worried. He dropped to his knees again.

"What shall I do with my cows?" he implored.

55

Once again the voice spoke to him: "Let them be in the stable, Peter. If they go out they will be lost in the dark and burned up."

"But what shall I do with my clothes?"

"Put them in a bag, Peter, and keep them in the house."

"It is needless to add," the contemporary account of "Praying Peter" concluded, "that Peter and all that was his were saved to the uttermost."

Like Bernson, every farmer on the peninsula worried about his livestock, especially any horse or cow that had the reputation of being "breachy"—that is, apt to break through a fence and go tearing off into the woods.

The tale was told of an Irish family that lived south of the town of Sturgeon Bay. The wife joined her husband in fighting the fire until it became obvious that it was too much for them to handle. She grabbed up their baby and fled with her husband. Going across a stretch of burning timber, they came to a pine log fence four feet high. Pinning up her long skirts, she put the child on her shoulders and cleared the fence like a hurdler.

"Why, Kate," her husband told her as they fled on through the burning woods, "you jump fences so well, I'm afraid you'll be breachy after this."

When they had reached a safe place, Kate sat down, unbuttoned her dress and put the baby to her breast. Two other small children—strangers, fleeing from the fire—looked on hungrily. When her baby's hunger was satisfied, she motioned to them. There was room for both, she told them.

Another Irishwoman, instead of fleeing, fell to her knees. The day of judgment had come, she told her husband.

"Stand up, you fool, and run," he ordered.

She refused. Instead, she bowed her head to the ground.

The husband studied the tempting target she made, then drew back his leg and gave her what was described as "an affectionate lift with his boot." This got her off her knees and into motion. To make sure she didn't slow down, he kept using the same method of persuasion all the way across the clearing. Bowing to superior authority, the wife kept running until they both were safe.

Another story that came out of the peninsula fire involved a settlement of fifteen families a few miles south of Williamsonville. They were Belgians who had entered the woods three years before, put up log cabins and started to clear the land. They were still living lives of poverty in 1871, although most had sold enough bundles of shingles to buy a pair of oxen and a few tools and utensils. Because their possessions were so few and so hard won, they clung to them grimly when the fire approached. Their clearings were still small—five to ten acres—which made the families especially vulnerable. But each one took time to dig a pit in the ground and bury their clothing, bedding, tools and even sides of bacon. Every one of the cabins was burned down. The farm animals were killed or scattered. Several of the Belgians died and the others narrowly escaped with their lives.

Because for the immigrants thrift was a byword, their neighbors found it appropriate that in spite of the devastation the Belgians had managed to save their bacon.

●

SEVEN

The Williamson brothers were also newcomers to Door County. They had come in the late 1860's to what was said to be the most desolate part of the peninsula, Gardner township. They were not foreign immigrants, but they had the same respect as such settlers for hard work and family ties. They had arrived in the wilderness with more resources than the Europeans and had at once taken possession of 480 acres of timbered land near Brussels and had become shinglemakers. Instead of making the shingles one at a time by hand, however, they began to manufacture them in a mill they erected in the 480-acre tract of pine, hemlock and hard woods next to a swamp. They built a barn, then a boarding house, store, blacksmith shop, family house and a number of shanties for the mill hands. The Little Sturgeon Bay, a safe harbor connected with the Green Bay, was only a few miles north of the community they founded, and they could haul wagon loads of shingles there for shipment on lake boats. They called their settlement Williamsonville. Others sometimes referred to it as Williamson's Mill.

The brothers had brought along their parents, as well as

their wives and children and their sister, nineteen-year-old Maggie. She was said to be the "most beautiful girl and sweetest singer" in the entire region. Miss Williamson was engaged to a young man who was in charge of the mill's steam engine, a job which entitled him to call himself an engineer.

Her cousin, who was also named Maggie, lived with the Williamsons. The single description that has come down to us of Maggie O'Neil—some accounts call her Maggie Neil—indicates only that she had rosy cheeks, but it is known that she was being courted by someone described simply as "her lover elsewhere," who had given her some jewelry to demonstrate his admiration.

In 1871, there were seventy-six persons living in Williamsonville, including fifteen women and sixteen children. The buildings were at one end of a ten-acre clearing. At the other end was a two-acre potato patch with a wooden fence around it. The only road leading away from the community contained considerable debris from the shingle mill.

During September, the threat of the woods fires was recognized—not to the point where it seemed necessary to clear the debris from the road, but prompting the Williamsons and their men to set "back fires" when the wind was favorable. Backfiring is a technique that takes advantage of the fact that hot air rises. When the woods are on fire, there is a constant flow of hot air rising, while cooler air is drawn toward the base of the fire to replace it. Thus, in the immediate vicinity of a fire, the cooler surface air tends to flow toward it. In backfiring, a second fire must be touched off at just the right moment so its flames will be drawn toward the main blaze. It can get out of hand, but if it works properly the small fire advances toward the larger one, burning off the strip of ground between them. Then when the main fire reaches that area, there is no fuel left to feed it.

Backfiring is a risky device in any but expert hands. A shift of wind at the wrong moment can result in the second fire turning on its creators and heading for the buildings it had been designed to protect. But with the glow of forest fires approaching within a half mile of Williamsonville, desperate measures were called for. Back fires were set, the wind did not shift, and a circle of burned-over land was created around the little community. "Then we thought we were safe," Thomas Williamson, one of the brothers, wrote some weeks later. It was assumed here as at New Franken that fire would not burn over the same ground twice. They all were able to sleep soundly again, confident that the danger was past.

Then, on the afternoon of October 8, the wind began to blow from the southwest. Tom and Fred Williamson spotted a small fire in their potato patch. With their father's help, they tried to put it out. It was still smoldering by evening, but it seemed of so little importance that the three men went home to eat.

Thomas went outside after his meal to check on the fire in the potato patch. It had sprung up again. He ordered a teamster, John Conlon, to hitch a pair of mules to a wagon which held a wooden tank filled with nine barrels of water. The mules hauled the tank to the potato patch. Williamson and Conlon threw buckets of water on the blaze and put it out. They they filled two barrels with water and put them in the field in case the fire should start up again in the night.

John and James Williamson joined the men in the potato patch—the other brother, Fred, had arrived earlier. They all took the wagon to a nearby creek and filled the wooden tank again. Then Conlon drove the wagon to the vicinity of the store, unhitched the mules and started leading them toward the barn. "Leave the harness on them," Thomas Williamson told him. There seemed to be no great danger, but the wind was blowing hard from the southwest and he wanted to take no chances. He stationed several workmen around the premises, ordering them to stay awake through the night and watch for fire. Then he took a walk around the clearing. He could see fire in the woods here and there, but not as much as there had been two days before. Satisfied that he had taken all

60

the necessary precautions, he walked over to his parents' house. His sister and Maggie O'Neil were sitting on the stoop talking with a young man named Con McCusker. Williamson joined them.

"In a few minutes," he said, "there came a heavy puff of wind. The trees fell in all directions and I saw the reflections of a big fire south of us. I thought it was a mile and a half off. In less time than it takes to write this, there came another heavy gale and the flames came rolling through the woods up to the back of the barn."

The fire that had already destroyed New Franken had picked up strength as it rolled north over the peninsula. Williamson leaped from the porch and ran to the store where he ordered some of the men to wake up the mill crew. Then he went to the mill, climbed to the roof with a hose, and wet down the shingles. By then the sparks were showering down.

"I wet the end and side of the mill and all around on the ground as far as I could reach with the hose," Williamson said. "The fire seemed to catch as fast as I could put it out. Some of the men came down to the mill. One took the hose. The rest helped man the pumps. I went to the west side of the clearing. The fire caught in some sapwood. I told some of the men to put it out, but they could not."

His brother, John, came running up, greatly alarmed. "He asked me what I thought of the fire. I told him not to get excited. At that time, I did not think our lives were in danger."

The houses in the settlement were linked by a four-foot-high fence of sapwood—green timber too small to be used in the mill. It was designed not so much as a barrier as a source of the winter fuel supply that could be taken a little at a time as it was needed. Thomas could see that the sapwood fence had caught fire and threatened to ignite all the houses. He rounded up as many men as he could and joined them in trying to make a gap in the fence to protect the houses. The fire drove them off. They tried another place, but the flames were being whipped by the wind and they failed again. Some

61

of the men brought buckets of water and threw them on the blazing fence, but it did no good.

Williamson hurried to the mill, which was still safe. He told his brother, John, that their parents' house would soon be on fire. John didn't seem surprised. "If we can save our lives," he said, "I'll be satisfied."

Thomas was generally inclined to think everything would turn out all right, providing everyone behaved sensibly and listened to the orders he gave them. But he saw enough merit in John's pessimism to start back to his parents' house to tell the women what they should do.

When he had left his sister and her cousin on the stoop, the two girls had decided that this was just another of those evenings when the men got all excited about a fire that turned out not to amount to much. They went inside the house and began to get ready for bed. Maggie Williamson's mother was less sanguine. She kept looking anxiously out of the window. Finally she threw open the door to get a better view. She saw great plumes of fire rolling through the tops of the trees.

"Girls!" she shouted. "Come here!"

When they saw the flames leaping from pine to pine, moving rapidly toward the clearing, they burst into tears. Fred Williamson arrived just then.

"Don't cry," he told the girls. "It won't be as bad as you think."

His mother grasped Fred's arm.

"Go and wake up the McAdams family or they'll be burned alive."

Fred ran to the home of Frank McAdams, the settlement's blacksmith. McAdams leaped out of bed when he heard Williamson pounding on the door and pulled on his clothes, shouting to his wife and their three young children to get dressed. By the time the family got outside, their house was on fire. McAdams ran off across the clearing, looking for the most likely place of safety. He told his wife he would come back for her and the youngsters.

62

Two other houses were on fire by now—George Bucklin's and Michael Whalen's. Thomas Williamson came hurrying into the home of his parents to take charge of his mother and the other women and girls who had gathered there.

"Put on men's pantaloons," he ordered.

It was a shocking suggestion to make, but these were desperate circumstances. Thomas was accustomed to obedience from the males around the place. But these were females and in 1871 no decent woman wore trousers. The ladies of the Williamson household did not intend to have the mill hands gawking at them, fire or no fire. The mother and James Williamson's wife did take the precaution of putting on long woolen underwear beneath heavy woolen dresses. But Maggie Williamson and Maggie O'Neil simply ignored Thomas' good advice.

The women and children who had taken refuge in the Williamson house ran outside. The elder Mrs. Williamson glanced back. She had left the kerosene lamps burning. Leaving lamps burning in an empty house was not only wasteful but might be dangerous. For a moment, habit took over and she started back to blow out the lamps. Then she realized that it couldn't matter.

All the women and children gathered at the boardinghouse. Most were in tears. Some were praying. Outside the building, Thomas was still stoutly issuing orders. He sent a teamster to get the mules out of the barn. "And shut the door after them," he shouted as the man hurried off.

McAdams, the blacksmith, rushed back from his scouting trip. He had concluded that the safest place in the clearing was the potato patch. Except for the dried tops of the potato plants, there was nothing in the plowed two acres to burn. He ran into the boardinghouse and grasped the hand of his oldest girl. In his other arm, he took a younger child. His wife followed him outside, carrying their baby. They ran for the potato patch. McAdams was the kind of man who commands respect. And at this moment he seemed to be the only one about who had a definite plan. With hardly any discussion, all the women and many of the men decided to follow after him.

Thomas had nothing better to suggest. The plowed field seemed as likely a refuge as any. But he did not let them leave without one last word of advice. "Take wet blankets," he shouted.

Some of the women turned back, found blankets, dipped them in a barrel of water and then hurried after the others. Many paid no attention to Williamson. His sister, Maggie, was one of them. Thomas grabbed her and handed her the moistened blanket he had been wearing. She took it and ran off after the others. He watched her disappear in the smoke, but he was still optimistic. "I did not think there was any danger in the potato patch."

Williamson went back to his parents' house. His father was there, carrying out furniture. Thomas told him to forget about such things and concentrate on saving himself. "And put on some boots, Pa. You can't get far in those slippers."

Mr. Williamson ran back into the house to find his boots, but found only one. He returned to the yard wearing the boot and a slipper. The houses were all on fire. So was the mill. Everything the family owned was going up in flames. At last even Thomas had to admit that the situation was desperate. He headed back to the boardinghouse. No one was in sight there except one of the workmen, Thomas Cryin, who was standing next to the well pit next to the door.

"Here is a good place to go—down in the well," Cryin told his boss. "I paid no attention to him, as my sister had left a few minutes before and I intended to catch her," Williamson wrote. "I picked up a blanket and started for the potato patch. I tramped through fire. There was fire almost all over the potato patch and the smoke was so thick I could not see more than a rod ahead. . . . I came up to where there were thirty-five persons all huddled together, sitting on the ground. The smoke was so thick I could not tell who they were. Some were crying and some praying."

About ten yards away, several men were "walking back and forth in the fire." Williamson's account becomes considerably less precise at this point. It is not clear whether the men were simply moving about in panic or, with death staring at them from the flames, were still trying to stamp out embers and keep the fire at bay. At any rate, Williamson did not pay much attention to the men. He did not remember later who they were. As for his sister, the lovely Maggie, he had given up any hope of finding her. He was candid about his state of mind: "I was so excited, I thought of no one but myself."

Before the elder Mrs. Williamson had left the boardinghouse with the other women, she had seen her son, John. She asked him what she should do. Thomas no doubt would have had a suggestion to make, but John was too distracted to be much help. He moved his hands in a gesture of despair. "Mother, save yourself. I give up."

Mrs. Williamson could think of nothing to do but follow the blacksmith with the other women and children. Among the youngsters was the little daughter of a man named Desautel. A mill hand remembered turning to look at her just as she stopped short, terrified. Her clothing caught fire. "She burned like a swift candle," the mill hand said.

To get to the potato patch, Mrs. Williamson had to cross the sapwood fence. It was still burning, but she found a place where the green wood had not yet caught fire and she got safely to the plowed ground. The heat was so great there, however, that she climbed back to the other side of the fence again. But this was no better. The boardinghouse was burning, sending forth so much heat that she crossed again into the potato field. She sat down beside Mrs. Nelson Demereau. In a moment, Mrs. Demereau cried out: "Nelson! I am on fire!"

Mrs. Williamson's only reaction was to move away. It is plain that the situation was now so desperate that only the primitive instincts of self-preservation were operating. She then got to her feet and groped through the thick smoke to a

65

tall stump. She leaned against it for support until that, too, caught fire. She moved again, this time to a place where two small stones protruded from the ground. Somehow these rocks comforted her. She wedged her feet between them. Wrapping the wet blanket around her, she stooped down, her chin resting on her knees.

There were shouts and confused voices in the darkness. Someone stumbled against her, giving a loud cry and nearly knocking her over. Parting the blanket, Mrs. Williamson peered out. A woman was stretched out beside her. The woman's body was on fire. Mrs. Williamson never learned which of her friends or relatives it was, but she remembered one thing about the corpse—it was wearing earrings.

The flames from the body were blowing directly toward her. Mrs. Williamson put out her hand, keeping it covered with the blanket, and tried to push the dead woman's head away, but could not. She drew back in horror when she heard the flesh of the burning body crackle. The flames from the dead woman singed Mrs. Williamson's blanket, but it did not catch fire. Her shoes were burning, however. She groped around under the blanket and clawed up handfuls of dirt to cover them. The dirt was so hot it burned her hands.

Meanwhile her son, Thomas, was nearby. He had decided he must run. In the few moments he had been in the potato patch, his self-sufficiency had given way to panic. He later estimated that he ran for five rods—eighty feet or so—when he came to a place where a heap of logs had been burned the previous spring while the men had been clearing more land. The vegetation was gone, there was nothing left to burn. He threw himself face down on the blackened earth. "The smoke was so thick that I thought I could not live. I rolled on my side and back and rooted with my face in the ground for air."

Each time a gust of wind came, it carried great streamers of flame toward him. He thought each such time would be his last. He could hear trees falling. One came crashing down a few yards away. "My feet were burning and my vest caught

66

fire. I could feel the fire burning my back. Twice I put my hand on my back and tried to wring the cloth of my vest to put the fire out. Then I thought I would roll into a big blaze and die quick. Still I lay there. I think I became unconscious."

The thirty-five persons Williamson has seen huddled together were crowded into a small hollow next to a fallen tree. Their refuge was only fifteen feet square. When he wrote his account of his escape, Thomas was able to be precise about the number. The thirty-five were still there the next morning, all of them dead.

"Apparently the men had circled outside to afford slight protection to the women," another man who saw the bodies said. "Some had tried to shelter their heads with clothing. Next to the group and fallen outside lay the blacksmith, holding a fragment of burnt shawl over the face of his little girl. Two feet from him lay his wife with her two little ones nestled beside her.

"Maggie Williamson lay a step from the rest, with a handful of curling black hair which she had torn from her head. Maggie was beautiful as she lay.

". . . Her betrothed, the young engineer of the mill, had stood by her side, fleeing only after she had sunk to the ground and saving himself, half alive, in the well.

"Maggie O'Neil, her rosy-cheeked cousin, could only be recognized by pieces of jewelry in her hands, which had been given her by her lover. . . ."

Sometime before dawn, Thomas Williamson regained consciousness. The smoke had cleared away. He could breathe again. He thought he was the only one in Williamsonville left alive. "I would have given all I ever had for water," he wrote. "I cannot tell you how I suffered for it. I tried to get up, but could not. I lay some time longer and finally got upon my feet. I was so weak I could not stand and lay down again."

He thought he heard someone shouting. He yelled back, or tried to—his throat was dry as ashes and the best he could do was make a croaking sound. He listened for some time,

Then he struggled to his feet and called again. This time someone answered. He hoped it was his father or one of his brothers, but it turned out to be an old man called "Cap" Richmond. It seems likely that Richmond was looking for help rather than offering it. When Thomas asked him to get some water and bring it to him, Richmond left but did not come back. Williamson lay back down on the ground until he began to feel a little better. Then he started in the direction from which he had heard a voice calling. "I staggered like a drunken man. I was so weak, and was almost blind. I could see nothing left to tell where I was, as every building was gone. I hallooed again and was answered by someone about two rods ahead of me."

Con McCusker, who had been sitting with the two girls on the stoop before the fire came, was there. So were Thomas Bush, James Donlon and Williamson's mother. She and the three men were lying on the ground, the remnants of the blankets they had carried through the fire protecting them from the chilly air of the October morning. McCusker had found Mrs. Williamson about 5 A.M., still crouching under her singed blanket, her feet still wedged between the two small stones. He had touched her shoulder, wondering if she was dead. She had looked up at him. He had lifted her to her feet and helped her make her way to the place where Thomas found her.

Williamson noted his mother's survival without emotion. His mind was still on his consuming thirst. He asked for water, and one of the men nodded toward a half-filled pail. Thomas reached eagerly for it. But Bush put up his hand. "I got it out of the well," he said. "Tom Cryin's in the well. A little French girl's in there, too. They're dead." Williamson grabbed the pail and tipped back his head and drank deep. Death was no longer something strange. So many were dead. "I did not care," he said later. "I was suffering so. I drank about a quart. But it did not taste like water."

In the dim light before dawn, Williamson could see

68

bodies lying nearby. They must be relatives, friends or at the very least acquaintances—he had ties of some sort with everyone in Williamsonville. Some of the bodies were as close as six feet away, but he was too full of pain and shock to crawl over to see who they were. His mother asked if he had seen any of the family. He said he had not.

When daylight came, he no longer felt quite so much like a man trapped in a nightmare. Some of his normal feelings returned including concern for what had happened to his missing relatives. He climbed stiffly to his feet and walked around the clearing, now a blackened wasteland. He came to the heap of thirty-five bodies in the potato patch. Maggie Williamson's brother did not know her.

"I did not recognize any of them, as they were so badly burnt," he said. "I got Cyril Jarvis to halloo, as I thought there might be some survivors in the woods. He did so and some one answered. I thought it was John Williamson's voice. I asked if it was John Williamson. The person answered no."

Thomas found John by wandering around the potato patch, stopping now and then to peer down at a body until he found one that he recognized. His brother looked natural, he said.

Thomas bore the confirmation of John's death to their mother. It deepened her despair. There was no time for tears. She was painfully burned, as was her son. It seemed to her that they must leave this place where her husband and children had died. Thomas agreed. There were no horses, mules or oxen left—they had either run off or been burned to death. The mother and son set off on foot, vaguely planning to walk the twelve miles to Sturgeon Bay or find help at a house along the route to the town. Another survivor, Byron J. Merrill, came with them.

The nearest house had been more than three miles away, the home of a family named Murray. They started toward it down what had been the road. Now it was covered with smoldering hulks of trees. Instead of winding through a forest,

69

it was a dimly defined track that was so strange to them that they lost their way several times and went stumbling around through the ruined woods until they found the road again.

Williamson in his dazed condition had not remembered to bring water with them and they were soon suffering from thirst. Surely, they thought, the fire had not gone as far as the Murray homestead and they would find help there. But when they came within sight of the clearing they found there was nothing left of the buildings and nothing to indicate whether the Murrays were alive or dead.

There was an inch or two of muddy water in a swampy area near the side of the road. They fell to their knees and took some of it, Mrs. Williamson drinking eagerly until her son finally pulled her away.

The next home was only a half mile away. Its owner, whose name was Langley, would surely lend them a team to take them to Sturgeon Bay. But when they got there, all the buildings were burned and no one was there. Two of Langley's horses were standing near where the barn had been. It is likely that when the fire approached, Langley had turned them loose. Somehow, they had survived to pick their way past the black snags of charred trees and to stand, heads hanging, waiting for an owner who did not come. Williamson was not in condition to catch the horses if they proved to be skittish, but like the human survivors the animals were numbed. He grasped their halters and led them to where his mother had sunk to the ground, too tired to walk farther. He put her on the back of one of the horses. Merrill, who was also in a state of near-collapse, climbed aboard the other. Thomas walked off down the road, leading the two animals.

The next building on the way to Sturgeon Bay had been a mill. It was gone. A house had stood nearby. Nothing was left of it. But finally they found that the Daily house was still standing. They had left Williamsonville at daylight. Now it was 3:30 in the afternoon. In that time they had covered six miles.

Half a dozen families had taken refuge with the Dailys. There was not much room left for the refugees from Williamsonville, but it would have been unthinkable to turn them away. They were fed and a place was found for them to sleep. The next morning they were taken to Sturgeon Bay.

Mrs. Williamson found it hard to understand why she had survived and her children, except for Thomas and Fred, had died. It did not seem fair that "the providence of God preserved me, an old woman with my days fulfilled, and took my sons and daughters."

After several days of recuperation, Thomas felt well enough to go back to Williamsonville to determine the losses. They were considerable. Of the seventy-six persons who had been in the settlement, only seventeen were alive. Among the fifty-nine who perished, nine were his relatives—among them his father, his brothers, John and James, with their wives and two of their children, and his sister Maggie.

The accounts are vague about the identity of Maggie's prospective bridegroom, but it seems likely he was Byron Merrill, the painfully injured survivor who accompanied Williamson and his mother to Sturgeon Bay. That it was said that Maggie's fiancé had stayed with her until she died and then saved his life in the well indicates that he was Merrill, for Williamson said Merrill was the last to climb down into the well and, in fact, was responsible for saving the lives of all but two of the seven who had chosen that place of refuge. As he ran toward the well pit, Merrill saw that the wooden curbing on top of it was on fire. He tore off the burning boards, then spread his blanket over the top of the well before climbing down into it.

Besides Thomas Cryin, a child belonging to Maxeme Coneya perished in the well. But Coneya survived there, along with Merrill, Joseph Cryin, Cyril Jarvis, and a visitor to the settlement named Louis Leaguee. What Leaguee was doing in Williamsonville is not known. He may have come to see a friend or relative or could have been one of the drummers who traveled about the backwoods in search of orders for everything from saws to yard goods. All that is known is that Leaguee was from Oshkosh and that he suddenly found himself crouching in the shallow well while the most disastrous forest fire in American history raged overhead.

Besides the thirty-five bodies found huddled together in the potato patch, others were found in various places about the clearing and in the nearby woods. One twelve-year-old boy was discovered in a crude outdoor oven built of mud. He literally had roasted to death.

The death tolls at Williamsonville noted in different contemporary reports vary somewhat, but it seems reasonable to accept the total given by Williamson, who had recovered his equanimity if not his optimism by the time he wrote of his experiences a few weeks later. He not only listed the names of most of the fifty-nine persons who died, but was specific about the livestock lost—sixteen horses, six oxen, thirty-eight hogs. Among the dead were fourteen of the settlement's sixteen children and eleven of its fifteen women.

EIGHT

●

While Peshtigo was growing into a flourishing lumber town, the Sugar Bush settlements had become a prosperous enclave of well-to-do farmers. The Lower Sugar Bush extended for about seven miles southwest from Peshtigo toward Oconto and off to the west. It was populated by about one hundred families, mostly German immigrants. The Upper Sugar Bush was centered on the Lake Noquebay Road, which ran northwest from Peshtigo. The Middle Sugar Bush, now called Harmony, lay along a road connecting the upper and lower settlements. The Upper and Lower settlements had perhaps one hundred twenty farms. Their owners were described as "Yankees and Canadians," the latter generally of French ancestry. Most of the homesteads were typical Wisconsin farms, which raised grain and dairy cattle, along with pork, vegetables, eggs, and chickens that could be sold within the village and at nearby lumber camps.

The Peshtigo River lies to the north of this region. It flows east until it reaches a point about eight miles above Peshtigo, when it turns abruptly south and widens out into a considerable stream before it reaches the village. At Peshtigo,

73

it bends to the southeast and continues on a meandering course to the bay. Some contemporary accounts indicate there were no streams in the Sugar Bush settlements. Actually, there were a number of small ones, including Bunday Creek and Trout Creek. In the fall of 1871, however, such streams were dry except for an occasional pool left by the drought.

The settlements had been established long enough so that some of the original owners had sons who had grown to manhood and taken up neighboring farms of their own. The clearings were comparatively large. The threat of fire, the main topic of conversation in the region that fall, seemed like someone else's problem to the families who lived in the Sugar Bushes. They worried about what a forest fire might do to the lumber camps, which provided a good market for their produce, but they felt safe in their clearings. If the woods burned, it would save them having to chop down the trees to clear more fields for plowing.

The maples were mostly gone on both sides of the Peshtigo-Oconto Road in the Lower Bush. Franklin Tilton reported that this cleared space was several miles long and half a mile wide so that "no ordinary fire in the woods could have done more than destroy fences and burn an occasional house." It is clear from other contemporary accounts, however, that the cleared fields still contained plenty of stumps rising several feet above the ground that could feed a fire. And along the perimeters of many of the clearings were great piles of slashings, for the work of expanding the fields was still going on.

One of the several absentee owners in the Lower Sugar Bush was Edward Kittner, who operated a wagon and blacksmith shop in Peshtigo. On the morning of October 8, he and his son drove out to the farm. They found fire burning in the woods along the outskirts of their land. Kittner and the boy joined the hired hands in fighting it, working so steadily that it was 7 P.M. before they felt it was safe to quit and get something to eat. They were near the home of a man named

74

Backman. The Kittners walked through the darkness to ask him for some food. Backman's family was preparing to go to bed. "I wouldn't do it," Kittner told his neighbor. "There's a lot of fire out there in the woods. You'd better be ready to make a run for it."

As he spoke, he walked to the window and looked out toward his own land. The stumps and corn stubble in the clearing were on fire about a thousand feet south of his farm. Kittner rushed out. Backman hitched up a team and went with him to the threatened farm. Kittner sent his son home to the village on foot, keeping his horses with him. As the danger drew closer, Backman hurried over to the homestead of David Heydenberg, shouting a warning. The Heydenbergs started for the village.

Backman drove back and found Kittner's brother now helping fight the fire. The three men concentrated on trying to save the barn. They worked feverishly for perhaps forty-five minutes, soaking the barn with water and shoveling sand on fires from windblown embers. By then the house and corn crib were burning. It became obvious that the barn was doomed, too.

"Let's go over to the preacher's new house," Kittner shouted. "Maybe we can do some good there." Kittner was one of five officers who had signed the constitution of the "German Lutheran Congregation of Peshtigo and Surrounding Territory" when it was organized on September 11, 1870. So he had a special interest in saving the parsonage still being built near what is now called Hartwig's Corner. The congregation had spent $654 on the building and owed $225 to the Peshtigo Company for lumber being used for the home of the Reverend Carl Huebner.

Mr. Huebner, a circuit-riding minister, had been persuaded to start an independent congregation in the village. Not yet settled there on October 8, he was holding services in the public school of Peshtigo. After a 6 P.M. Communion service at the school, the Peshtigo Lutherans were meeting to

75

organize themselves into the Zion Evangelical Lutheran Church of Peshtigo Village and Peshtigo Harbor. By morning, many of those who helped organize Zion Church were dead. Mr. Huebner was presumably among them, for no one ever saw him again.

When Kittner and his companions got to the parsonage in the Lower Sugar Bush, they found the building still untouched by fire. But it was obvious that it was doomed. They decided to try to salvage the windows by removing them from their frames and carrying them away from the building. They had finished prying out two of the windows when the house caught fire. The barn, only fifty feet away, was also burning briskly. They saw they were nearly hemmed in by the fire—the burning house on one side, the barn on another, a heavy log fence blazing in front, the woods aflame to the rear. "There was not much time for consultation," an account of their experience said. "But they laid their plans, took each other by the hand and ran through the fire. They could not see but, as it afterwards proved, they ran about sixty rods into Charles Bartels' field and dropped down near a family burying ground, where they lay until morning."

On another Sugar Bush farm, owned by a family named Nevermann, the husband was not at home when the fire approached. Alone with two small children, Mrs. Nevermann fought down her panic. One youngster was a toddler, the other a baby. Her first impulse was to grab them in her arms and run. But she remembered that she and her husband had agreed that if fire threatened the house she would take two pails of water with her when she fled into a nearby plowed field. It had sounded simple enough. Now it seemed obvious that she could not manage the pails and the children. She stood there in the kitchen of the doomed cabin, forcing herself to remain calm enough to think. The older child could cling to her. But what if he lost his grip on her skirts and fell or wandered off into the smoke? She grasped a length of rope, and knelt down.

76

"Get on my back," she ordered. The toddler obeyed. She put the loop of rope around their bodies and tied it tight. That took care of one child. Perhaps one bucket would be enough, leaving her a hand free for the baby? No. Nevermann had insisted she would need two. Hurrying, for the fire was getting close, she put the baby in a blanket and tied it around him securely. She picked up a filled pail in each hand. She grasped the blanket in her teeth. Then she set off for the plowed field, carrying the baby as she had seen a mother cat carry a kitten.

The house caught fire soon after they left it. As the young mother and her children lay in the open field, embers from the burning forest fell on them, repeatedly setting their clothing afire. Each time, Mrs. Nevermann was able to extinguish the blaze with the water she had brought with her. When the fire passed them by, they were still alive.

Some Sugar Bush parents were less successful than Mrs. Nevermann in keeping their wits about them. Terrance Kelly, who lived in the upper settlement, lost control entirely. Grabbing the oldest of his four children, he ran in one direction while his wife, equally panic-stricken, took the youngest child and headed in another. That left their seven-year-old son and five-year-old daughter to shift for themselves. The children tried to follow their mother. "Wait, Ma," the boy called. "Oh, Ma, wait." But she was out of sight in the smoke and darkness. The children turned in the direction their father had taken, shouting for him. Either he did not hear them or was afraid to stop. It was soon certain that they would never catch him. The world was on fire all around the two young children. The smoke brought tears to their eyes. It was hard to breathe. Flakes of burning wood swirled through the air. The wind pushed at them. In the woods nearby there were the sounds of crashing trees, like cannon fire.

Though the Kelly children had been abandoned by their panic-stricken parents, they did not abandon each other. The boy grasped his sister's hand. As they ran, they picked burning embers from each other's clothing. They headed back for what had been the safe and settled center of their existence. But the house was burning, the flames whipped into long tongues of fire by the wind. The barn was ablaze. Still holding firmly to each other's hand, the children crouched beside the garden fence. As the heat became almost too much to bear, they lay on the ground. Protectively, the boy put his arm around his sister and hugged her close, and they waited out the fire.

On another farm in the Upper Sugar Bush, a settler named Adnah Newton first realized that the woods fires were out of control when he heard a distant roaring that grew rapidly closer and louder. His first thought was for his son, Samuel, who lived with his wife and children on a neighboring farm. Adnah hitched up a team of horses and went galloping down the road to Samuel's house, rousing the family. Then he returned home. The roaring was louder now. Seeing the fire across the fields he had cleared, he decided that the barn might offer more protection than the house—it was a more substantial building. He herded his wife into it, along with their fourteen-year-old granddaughter, Augusta Bartels, and Mrs. Newton's eighty-four-year-old mother, Mrs. Sally McPherson. The wind was so strong that Newton had to hold the door of the barn shut with all his strength. He could see sparks falling all around. He put his hand on the glass of the nearby window. It was hot to his touch. Certain that the barn would soon catch fire, he ordered everyone outside.

Mrs. Newton and Augusta took off across a field. Mrs. McPherson, too old and weary to flee even for her life, lingered near the barn. Newton ran to the house, hoping to save some of his valuables. Then he thought better of it and hurried back to the shed next to the barn to try to rescue his new wagon. As he struggled to drag the wagon outside, the roof of the shed blew off. He gave up the task as hopeless. He looked around for his family. His mother-in-law must have been nearby—her body was found near the barn the next day—but he did not see her in the smoke. The house and barn were blazing now. Newton headed down the road toward the farm of L. H. Hill. He found fourteen persons standing a hundred feet from Hill's house. No one spoke when he approached, but some were moaning. Newton kept on running. Without saying anything, the group followed him. Newton estimated later that he ran about thirty or forty yards until he came to the corner of a fence. He stopped there to look around. Seeing a gap in the woods about fifty feet wide that had not yet began to burn, he struck out for it. The others followed. He stumbled and went sprawling. His followers may have assumed he had fallen into the fire, because they stopped and huddled together, having lost sight of their leader. Newton struggled to his feet again and ran on, alone.

It was hard to breathe. He threw himself to the ground every few yards, trying to get a whiff of air, then climbed to his feet to continue his flight. As portions of his clothing caught fire, he ripped them off and threw them from him. Finally he was dressed only in his trousers and boots. He got through a half-mile patch of woods, then crossed an extensive clearing. As he came to the bed of a dry creek, a young man joined him. They lay down under the slight protection offered by the bank of the stream. They gasped for breath, looking up now and then at the light made from a house and barn which were burning nearby. As he turned away, Newton's naked back was exposed to the heat and to the sparks and embers, but he clung to the dry creek bed.

In the lower settlement, John Hoyt was one of three brothers who ran a farm for their widowed mother. John was the middle son. His younger brother was still in his teens. On the afternoon of October 8, John was in a woods near the farm fighting a fire that was threatening to get out of control. One of his neighbors came over to help. After dark, the two men went back to Hoyt's house, where John got a lantern and walked home with the neighbor. On his way back to his own house, he heard the roaring noise that most survivors remembered as their first warning of what lay ahead. Some

79

compared it to the sound of a great waterfall. Even to the least imaginative of them, it seemed the roar of approaching doom.

It sent Hoyt hurrying into his house to consult with his mother and brothers. The Newton family had chosen the barn as their first refuge. To the Hoyts, it seemed that the house was less likely to catch. They brought the cattle out of their barn and tied them with ropes to the side of the dwelling. Then they filled buckets with water and prepared to do battle. But it was soon plain that this fire was bigger than anything in their experience and that all of the buildings, including the house, were doomed.

The oldest and youngest brother ran off toward a nearby marsh, which still had a few shallow water holes left despite the drought. John was left to take care of his mother. He wrapped her in a soldier's overcoat—a Civil War keepsake that perhaps had belonged to her dead husband—and they set off for the marsh about a hundred yards away. "I'll carry you, Mother," John shouted.

She was no longer young. The accounts of the fire describe her as feeble. But Mrs. Hoyt was determined not to hinder her son. "I can manage, John." They had to cross a field from which the trees had recently been cleared. It was full of stumps. Each was a torch, with flames shooting up from it. The heat was almost more than the Hoyts could bear. The smoke choked them. In the darkness, the mother and son stumbled. "Save yourself," she ordered, as they lay gasping for breath. "I'm an old woman. Leave me here. I can't go any farther. If you don't go on by yourself, you'll die, too." "If you die," Hoyt told her, "then we'll die together." He climbed to his feet and hoisted her onto his back. She clung there, her arms around his neck, while he raced toward the doubtful refuge of the marsh.

Along the road to the nearly dry swamp was a great heap of brush. It was too late now to regret his shortsightedness at having piled the branches there when the field was cleared. The barn and brush pile were burning fiercely. There was an

80

opening between them. Beyond it was more brush that had been thrown down to surface the road into the marsh, and this was burning, too. The only way to safety was through the blazing brush on the road, so he ran through it with his mother, still wrapped in the old army coat, clinging to his back. Once they were safely beyond the flames, Hoyt knelt until his mother got off his shoulders, then threw himself full length on the ground. His mother lay close beside him. When the worst of the fire had passed, she asked John how he felt. "I'm burned bad," he told her. "I doubt if I'll live more than a few days." He did not die, although his burns were so painful that there were moments when he thought death would be welcome. Hoyt had chosen to flee on foot even though burdened with his mother. Charles Lamp, whose farm was also in the lower settlement, was among those who discovered that horses were not necessarily a surer means to safety. He hitched his team to a wagon, put his wife and children aboard, and set off toward Peshtigo ahead of the great wall of flame that roared through the forest behind them. The way led generally through cleared land, but at some places the woods pressed close to the road. At one such point, a tree fell, its roots destroyed by the fire. Some said later that the tree hit one of Lamp's horses. Others said the horse, panic-stricken, ran over the trunk of the fallen tree, winding up astraddle it, lunging desperately, its eyes rolling, the lines connecting the animal to the wagon becoming hopelessly tangled. Lamp leaped from the wagon seat to try to straighten things out. As he struggled with the frightened horse, a great wave of heat and flame burst at them all. His wife screamed. Turning, he saw that she and the children were on fire. Flames were shooting from their clothing and from his wife's long hair. Before he could take the few steps from the front of the wagon to where they were sitting, they were dead. Lamp ran to a shallow brook nearby and threw himself into it. When he was able to return to where he had left the wagon, there was nothing left of it but its ironwork. His wife, children and the horses had been reduced to the anonymity of a few charred bones and a heap of white ashes.

NINE

●

Joseph Lasure, one of a considerable number of Sugar Bush residents who still spoke their ancestral French, was among those who decided to fight instead of run when the great fire drew near his farm. With his wife and all but the two youngest of their five children helping, he tried to save their house and barn. In common with others who lingered to save the homes they had built in the wilderness, the Lasures never had a chance against a conflagration beyond anything they had ever imagined. Lasure himself soon realized that the buildings could not be saved. He gave the order to flee and picked up his three-year-old son. His wife grabbed the baby. There were two other boys, the older thirteen. There was also a nine-year-old daughter, Floy. She was said to have been the smartest student in the nearby district school, able to "read finely in the fifth reader and spell down all the scholars." She and her brothers followed their parents as they ran across the clearing.

But the family had delayed too long. The fire was close behind them. Burdened with the two youngest children, the parents stumbled through the smoke for perhaps a hundred yards. Then Mrs Lasure could go no farther. She fell to the ground, the baby still clutched in her arms. Lasure was so nearly overcome that he could do nothing to help his wife and baby. In fact, he had to put down the three-year-old he was carrying. The eldest son picked up his brother and bravely carried him for a quarter of a mile before he sank down to the woods floor. The other boy had already collapsed, leaving only Floy and her father still on their feet.

The pretty dark-haired girl, who was her father's favorite, "stood it the smartest of all," according to an account written a few days later. She ran on ahead and could have easily outdistanced her father if she had not stopped now and then to encourage him. Lasure could see her ahead of him in the flickering light from the flames. Come on, she told him, waiting for him to catch up. Don't stop, she told him. And so he forced his legs to keep moving, following this child he loved, as she ran ahead of him through a landscape out of a nightmare. His lungs were full of the choking smoke. His throat was raw. His tongue seemed too large for his mouth. His eyes were full of tears from the smoke so that he was nearly blinded. Still he saw her ahead of him and followed.

They were in a clearing now. The grass was as high as his knees. It had turned brown weeks before. It was brittle against his legs, making a rustling sound as he moved through it. It was so dry that a single spark would set it afire. The woods were flaming behind them. Pieces of gray ash swirled through the air. The wind gusted. A shower of sparks passed over their heads and suddenly the field was ablaze around them, the hay catching fire in a dozen places at once. Floy was running through tall grass that was all aflame. For a moment, Lasure thought she would escape. But then her dress caught. For a moment she stood there, this bright and beautiful child, her clothing a torch in the light of the blazing pines.

Later when Lasure had somehow stumbled out of the burning woods to safety and was telling about what had happened, it was not his dead wife and four dead sons he spoke of, but Floy, repeating over and over to anyone who

84

would listen the thought that would haunt him as long as he lived: "Oh, if I could only have saved that girl!"

The same visitor who talked with Lasure and recorded his story designated another as the "pluckiest hero of the fire," although to many it might seem that a child who kept fighting for her life and encouraging her father to fight for his was more deserving of the honor than Lovell Reed, a youth of twenty, who decided that suicide was preferable to death by burning.

Reed had been living with a cousin in the Sugar Bush, helping out with the chores. When the fire approached, he joined his relatives in trying to save their home. As he later told the tale from his hospital bed in Marinette, he had fought the flames until ready to drop from exhaustion, deciding not to run because "number one ain't my cry, when there's trouble ahead." The time came, however, when running was the only thing left to do. He set off alone toward a creek that was about two hundred yards away. The ground felt as if it were burning under the soles of his boots. His clothes caught fire. The flames licked at his face. "I made up my mind I wouldn't be burned to death," he told his visitor. Reaching into his pocket, he pulled out the jack knife that every male carried in those days. He fumbled with it, finally opening the blade, then plunged it into his chest. To his surprise, he was still alive. He drew the knife out and stabbed himself a second time, giving the blade a twist after it penetrated his flesh, trying to find his heart. His anatomical accuracy was wanting. Moving forward, his legs working automatically, he reached the creek bank. He fell forward into the mud and water of the small stream that saved his life.

For most of those fleeing for their lives in the Sugar Bush settlements, no such refuge was available. Charles D. Robinson, in an account written while the fire still smoldered in the forest, described what it was like there:

"Men, women and children, horses, oxen, cows, dogs, swine—everything that had life was seized with panic and ran without method to escape the impending destruction. The smoke was suffocating and blinding. The roar of the tempest deafening. The atmosphere scorching. Children were separated from their parents and trampled upon by the crazed beasts. Husbands and wives were calling wildly for each other and rushing in wild dismay, they knew not where.

"Others, believing that the day of judgment was surely come, fell upon the ground and abandoned themselves to its terrors. Indeed, this apprehension that the last day was at hand pervaded even the strongest and most mature minds. All the conditions of the prophecies seemed to be fulfilled. The hot atmosphere filled with smoke supplied the 'signs in the sun, and in the moon and in the stars.' The sound of the whirlwind was as 'the sea and the waves roaring' and everywhere there were 'men's hearts failing them for fear and for looking after those things which were coming on the earth; for the powers of heaven shall be shaken.' "

Those in the Sugar Bush who believed the Biblical prophecy was being fulfilled would have found agreement among many of the European settlers on the Kewaunee and Door County side of the bay, including those who lived at the first Belgian settlement in what was then called Robinsonville. In that community, however, the residents knew what they must do about the trumpet of Gabriel, which seemed to them to be blaring through the smoke and flames. When the danger approached, even the non-Catholics remembered the talk of miraculous circumstances associated with young Adele Brice's vision of 1859. Frightened families began converging on the site ahead of the fire. Falling on their faces, according to reports from those who talked with some of them later, they "crawled 'round and 'round it with long-continued prayers, in the belief that the world was being consumed." Robinsonville, as it turned out, was in a part of the Wisconsin countryside where the fire did not cause widespread destruction. The devout—and those who had suddenly become devout—went home convinced that their prayers had saved them.

In the Sugar Bush, a few houses and barns escaped and some of the farm district's residents somehow survived. But the toll there was high. In the lower settlement, which was hardest hit, every member of twenty families was killed. Within a few days after the fire, 140 bodies were found and buried in the Lower Sugar Bush, 50 in the middle, and 77 in the upper settlement, according to one contemporary account, for a total of 267. Another later reckoning differed somewhat. It listed 120 burials in the lower settlement, 75 in the middle, and 60 in the upper, for a total of 255. Part of the discrepancy was due to confusion over the vague dividing line between the settlements. But both estimates were conservative. In such a region, after a fire that sometimes completely consumed the bodies of its victims, there were a number of persons who simply disappeared, with no trace of them ever found. For example, searchers tramped back and forth across the blackened farm of Pat Doyle without discovering a sign of him, his wife or their eight children. Not even a charred bone remained. Doyle's friends felt that the least they could do was find his remains and give them burial. But repeated searches of the 180-acre farm in the Upper Bush were fruitless. The Doyles had vanished from the earth.

Livestock as well as humans perished in the farming settlements. On the Austin Phillips' farm the bodies of one hundred horses and cows were found in the corner of a field, having herded together for protection against the peril moving toward them from the woods. Not far away, the corpses of sixteen persons were discovered in a shallow ditch where they had taken refuge.

The suffering did not end with the fire. One mother who survived with her young daughter was unable to find anything to eat in the wasteland the flames had left behind. By the time rescue parties discovered them, the girl was dead from starvation.

One man was found several days after the fire carrying his small son in his arms. As a farmer, the man knew that the potato harvest had not yet been completed. Digging in a field burned bare by the flames, he found a few potatoes for them to eat. Even so, the child was nearly dead from hunger and exhaustion. He revived when the bearded rescuers, with lumberjacks' confidence in the powers of liquor, gave the boy a mixture of wine and brandy to jolt him back to life.

Some tragedies that occurred on the lonely farms can be reconstructed only from circumstantial evidence. No one survived to tell what happened. There was, for example, the John Church family, parents and three grown sons, whose clearing was along the banks of the Little River, a tributary of the Peshtigo. When the fire came the family tried to save their house and barn. The parents and two of the sons perished before they could flee to the nearby stream. The third son, who was twenty-two years old, also died, but how it happened is a matter for conjecture. It is not known whether he was away from home when the flames struck or, less foolhardy than the rest, chose to flee to the river while the others stayed to battle the fire. All that is certain is that when the burying parties reached the Church farm they found the parents and two of the boys on the ground near where the house had stood, their bodies blackened by the flames. Nearby was the body of the twenty-two-year-old, untouched by the fire. The young man's throat had been slashed. The lumberjacks talked things over and could only conclude that the son, having returned and found his home gone and his family dead, killed himself in despair.

Charles Towsley, who had decided ahead of time to trust in his own strength and let his wife do the praying, did not survive to tell what happened when the flames came sweeping down on his farm in the Lower Sugar Bush. There, as at the Church homestead, the evidence was circumstantial. It seems likely that Mrs. Towsley died first. Her body was a little apart from the others. It had not been burned. The verdict of the men who arrived after the fire was that she had died of suffocation. Did Towsley, seeing his wife die and facing the likelihood of fiery death himself, decide that his duty as a father called for him to save his children from needless suffering? It would seem so. He apparently cut their throats and then his own.

William Curtis, a homesteader near Peshtigo, tried to save himself in a well pit. Such refuges occasionally proved safe, but generally the shallow wells were death traps where smoke and heat and lack of air killed those who sought safety in them. It can be assumed that Curtis decided as the fire got worse that there was no use postponing the inevitable. Those who discovered him found he had looped the bucket chain around his neck and hanged himself.

Christ Diedrich, a scaler in a sawmill in the Lower Bush, had gone to Green Bay with a friend and so escaped the fire. He and the friend, John Lemke, hurried back as soon as word reached them of the disaster. They stopped at the home of Diedrich's brother. The brother's body and those of his four children were charred beyond recognition. Nearby was the body of his sister-in-law, still erect, leaning against the remains of a tree as if standing watch over her dead family.

Most of those caught up in the fire were too busy trying to save themselves to do much about helping anyone else. A farmer named Henry Bateman was one of the memorable exceptions. He lived in the Lower Sugar Bush with his wife and their six children. There was no stream in the vicinity. When the fire swept through the woods toward their farm, Bateman hoped that his clearing would be protection enough. This was generally a forlorn hope that night, although in lesser woods fires, a few acres of cleared ground was adequate refuge. Bateman's clearing was larger than that of a neighbor, Henry Bartells, so the eight Bartells children were sent there in the hope that they would find refuge. That gave Bateman a total of fourteen children and his wife to safeguard. In the face of catastrophe, Bateman was able to keep his head. He herded the children into a plowed field, and told them and his wife to lie down. He had forgotten to bring a shovel, but with his bare

89

hands he managed to cover them with the sandy soil, leaving only their faces exposed. Then he threw himself on the ground and did his best to scrape dirt over his body. This desperate means of protection from the fire was successful. Bateman, his wife and the fourteen children all survived.

One of the few farmers in the Sugar Bushes to have a roof over his head after the fire was Abraham Place, an old-timer in the region, a "squaw man" whose Indian in-laws did not forget him when he needed them most.

Formerly from Vermont, Place had come to Wisconsin on foot in 1837 when he was twenty-nine years old. A year later, he settled in the Peshtigo area and soon began trading with the Menominees and buying up land. It was lonely work and Abe felt the need of a wife. He married an Indian girl, and she cooked his meals, kept his cabin swept and provided him with a son or daughter nearly every year. Such an arrangement was socially acceptable around Peshtigo when Place first settled there, but by 1871 the attitude had changed. It was then considered not quite proper for a white man to be married to an Indian, unless he was a logger who used the marriage to get his hands on choice timberland owned by the Menominees and stayed with his bride only until all the pines were cut. Abe Place's neighbors rather looked down on him, even though he was a substantial citizen who owned eight hundred acres of land.

When the danger of fire became apparent that fall, the neighbors saw old Abe and his sons plowing great circles of land around his house, forming a barrier between it and the woods. Some of them wondered uneasily if Place might have had some secret word from his in-laws on dangers lurking in the forest, but most dismissed his precautions as the kind of foolishness to be expected from a man who had not merely lived with a squaw but had married her. When the fire approached, Mrs. Place's relatives came to aid. Each grabbed a blanket, soaked it in water and laid it on the shingle roof of the combination home and trading post. As the heat dried the

90

blankets, Place's sons and the relatives soaked the blankets again and again with water drawn from the well. One of the Indians is said to have kept pumping steadily for nine hours, "showing an endurance possessed by very few white men."

In the accounts written shortly after the disaster, there is a persistent note of grudging respect for the Indians' knowledge of how to survive a forest fire. It is hard to judge how much of this was based on fact and how much on a superstitious feeling that the red men understood their ancestral woods better than the white intruders. It is unlikely that wetting twenty blankets and spreading them on the house roof would have been enough to save the building if the full fury of the fire had reached the Place clearing. It seems probable that Abe was luckier than his neighbors, as well as better prepared. Still it is a fact that his home northwest of Peshtigo was one of the few buildings still standing in the three Sugar Bush settlements the morning of October 9. Many of those neighbors who had scoffed at his activities before the fire tried to reach his clearing the night of October 8. Bodies were found of thirty-five who failed to get there. A hundred refugees gathered at Place's cabin during and after the fire, most of them staying two weeks or more. Any prejudice they may have had against Abe's wife did not keep them away when the woods burned.

Another house to escape destruction in the Sugar Bushes belonged to Reuben Slattery, a logging contractor. He had a capable crew of lumberjacks whom he put to work plowing up an eighteen-foot strip of ground around his home. When the fire he had feared and prepared for actually came, Slattery decided to stay where he was. His wife had given birth to a daughter, Mayme, nine days before and was still bedridden. Her sister, who was staying with her, drew the bedroom curtains. But Mrs. Slattery decided she wasn't going to lie there and not catch a glimpse of the most exciting spectacle of her life. "Pull them curtains back," she ordered. "And prop me up so's I can see out." From her bed, Mrs. Slattery saw a night sky the color of blood. Great clouds of smoke rolled across the clearing. Sparks poured down on the wooden house. But Slattery and the bearded shanty boys who worked for him stood fast, cursing the fire and dousing it with buckets of water. In the morning, the house was erect.

Martin Race also stayed put. He was less fortunate. His neighbors, Mr. and Mrs. George Peck, stopped at the Race farm to urge Martin and his family to flee with them to a wheat field. They planned to scrape holes in the ground and breathe into them, a method they had heard the Indians used when caught in a forest fire. Race told them thanks, but he would abide where he was. His wife was visiting a sick friend nearby. Besides, he said, this was the end of the world and he might just as well stay and die in his own home. Race's younger children, Ida and Charles, obeyed his orders to remain with him. Two other sons, Lorenzo and Harley, decided that if the Lord wanted them, He would have to hunt them down. They fled into the night, leaving Race waiting with some trepidation for the final conflagration. Lorenzo found safety in a small stream a quarter of a mile away. He later located his brother in a hospital, seriously burned but alive. The neighboring Peck family survived in the wheat field. Race and the two children with him were burned to death, and Mrs. Race, trying to reach home to help her family, died on the way.

John Emmett Nelligan, the young man who had arrived in Oconto full of enthusiasm a few months before, was camping in the woods along the Oconto River that October 8. He was in charge of twenty head of oxen, waiting for the other lumberjacks to arrive for their winter's work in the woods. He ran out of groceries that morning and set off on a twelve-mile hike to the nearest source of supplies. He got there about noon and was on his way back to camp with the provisions when his way was blocked by fire. Changing his direction, he headed for a backwoods farm owned by Anson Eldred. When he reached it he found the tenant, an excitable Frenchman,

92

hysterical with fear. According to his own recollection, Nelligan took full charge. He hitched up a team of oxen and with the help of the Frenchman, who "soon forgot his fears and tears under pressure of hard work," hauled barrels of water and managed to fight back the fire, which was eating at stumps and trees in the little clearing around the house. The two men worked all night. By dawn the flames were under control and the buildings saved.

Nelligan was on the periphery of the fire, which did far less damage in the Oconto area than it did a few miles farther north. Oconto itself escaped.

The Frank Lezotte family, including a twelve-year-old girl and her two young brothers, had moved to a farm about four miles from Peshtigo the previous spring. They had spent the summer clearing the land and building a log cabin. By fall, the cabin was completed. The children were asleep in their bunks in the loft when the fire came. Lezotte grabbed the younger boy and ran outside, followed by his wife. Celestine, the daughter, followed them. Then she realized that her other brother was still in the cabin. She hurried back inside, took hold of the sleepy boy's hand and led him out into the clearing. By the time they got there, the parents had disappeared into the smoke. Celestine and her brother ran into the middle of the clearing and flung themselves to the ground. The wind swept great sheets of flame over them, but when the fire slackened they were not much hurt. When morning came, they found their parents and the youngest child close by, still alive but temporarily blinded.

Celestine's hands were burned from beating out sparks and her back was blistered from the heat, but she took full charge. She remembered a potato field she had helped plant during the spring. She would have been willing to eat the potatoes raw, but when she got a supply for herself and the family she found this was not necessary—the fire had roasted them. After the breakfast of roast potatoes, Lezotte took his younger son on his back. Celestine found a charred stick.

93

With her other brother clinging to her and her still-blind parents grasping the stick, she led the way toward Oconto. It was not until 4 P.M. Monday that the family met a wagon driving out from that community to look for survivors and Celestine was able to relinquish her responsibility as head of the house.

In some places in the Sugar Bush settlements, the heat from the fire was so intense that large boulders were cracked. Stumps that had been left when the land was cleared were now gone. In their places were gaping holes, the fire having burned away the stumps, roots and all.

When October 9th dawned, each Sugar Bush survivor took stock of his situation. Those who were able to do so started stirring about, looking for help for themselves or their families and friends. Adnah Newton, still lying in the dry stream bed where he had taken refuge, roused himself. He retraced the route of his flight to look for the little band that had tried to follow him to safety. Thirteen of the fourteen were dead where he had last seen them — once they had lost sight of Newton they apparently had given up hope. Only John Oleson had saved himself by lying face down in a ditch.

Newton also counted the bodies of twenty-three horses, fifteen sheep, two cows, an ox, two calves, and a dog. They were all lying within a hundred yards of where Hill's barn had stood. L. H. Hill, his 75-year-old wife, and all his family were among the dead, along with the L. C. Spear family and Oleson's wife and children. In the vicinity of the Hill farm alone, forty-five bodies were found by the burying parties.

Newton's wife was still alive, though severely burned. Like him, she had taken refuge in a stream bed. Their granddaughter, Augusta, was dead. Some accounts say she was burned to death. Others claim she "threw herself into the creek that ran through Stephen Storey's farm, where she was drowned." Considering the shortage of deep pools in the streams in the Sugar Bush area that fall, the former account seems more likely.

94

Monday's dawn found John Hoyt still lying where he had collapsed after carrying his mother through the burning brush. Mrs. Hoyt was worried about her other two sons. John thought he heard voices nearby. "Who is it?" he shouted. It turned out to be his brothers. The younger boy was seriously burned. The oldest of the three sons was in better condition than John, but once again it was John who took charge. He set out to seek shelter for their mother. There was a fourth son who was married and lived on a nearby farm. John went in search of him. He found him dead, along with his wife and child. Hoyt then traveled all day, looking for a house that was still standing and for some food—his last meal had been one raw turnip eaten at 4 P.M. the day before. When he returned to where his mother and brothers were waiting, he had to tell them he had found no shelter and nothing to eat. It was three days after the fire before John managed to get his mother and brothers away from their burned-out farm. They were taken to an improvised hospital in Marinette, where they all recovered.

Kittner, his brother, and Backman, whose house they had reached on the way back from town, also began to rouse themselves into action after daylight came on October 9. When they called out, they discovered that the owner of the field, Charles Bartels, was nearby. Kittner and his brother were so blinded by the heat and smoke that they could not see to walk, but Bartels was all right. He led them to a small creek. They threw themselves down beside a stagnant pool and drank greedily. The water tasted like lye. After they had washed off the grime, the Kittners could see well enough to start back toward the village. On their way they met two farmers who told them Peshtigo had been directly in the pathway of the fire. No, they told Kittner, they had not seen his wife and children. Kittner forgot his burns and his own close call in his worry over his wife and the young ones. He hurried as fast as he could to the village—that is, to where the village had been when he had started to drive to his farm the day before.

Kittner was one of the lucky ones. His wife had proved to be a resourceful woman, quite capable of getting along without him. When the fire approached, she hitched a team of horses to a wagon. She put her three children aboard it, along with her mother and her sister's three youngsters. Onto the wagon she piled a trunk containing books and papers, $60 of her husband's money and $390 that belonged to the Odd Fellows' lodge. With seven people and the trunk in the wagon, there was no room for Mrs. Kittner, so she followed along behind carrying more books and a piece of silk she had been saving to make into a new Sunday dress. The Kittner home was on the west side of Peshtigo, but Mrs. Kittner decided it would be safer to cross over to the east bank of the river. A lot of other families had the same idea, and Mrs. Kittner ran into a considerable traffic jam. Another wagon swung past hers, tearing off a wheel. The Kittner wagon tipped over. Passengers and trunk were thrown to the ground. Another team, following close behind, smashed into the trunk, crushing it and scattering money and papers to the wind.

Mrs. Kittner decided that not even the most loyal Odd Fellow would expect her to try to retrieve the club treasury under such circumstances. She continued on foot to the river, along with her mother and the six children. They plunged into the water and survived, as Mr. Kittner was delighted to discover when he came hobbling in from his two-mile walk. They were not only alive, Mrs. Kittner informed him proudly, but she had saved the silk for her new Sunday dress.

Lumberjacks from a number of nearby camps set out for the Sugar Bush settlements to help the living and bury the dead. The Kelly farm, where the panic-stricken Terrance Kelly and his wife had left two of their children behind, was one of the first to be reached. Mrs. Kelly and her baby were found alive near the edge of their land. Her husband and the oldest child were discovered a mile away, dead.

With shovels on their shoulders, the lumberjacks moved across the blackened fields toward where the Kelly house had stood. It was gone. So were the barn and outbuildings. There was nothing left of the garden fence but a few charred pieces of wood. Next to where the fence had been were two children, wrapped in each other's arms, their eyes closed, their faces pale as death. The men came closer and one bearded fellow stooped to take a closer look at the Kelly children. Then he stood erect, grinning. "Hey, boys, would you look at this now?" he said, his voice full of wonder. "They ain't dead at all. They're fast asleep."

•

TEN

P. Pernin, as he modestly signed himself, was the French-speaking priest who had come down from Canada to minister to the Roman Catholics at Marinette and Peshtigo. He was a man of considerable energy and determination, as is obvious from the fact that in 1871 he was in the midst of building not one church but two. By fall, the church at Marinette, called Our Lady of Lourdes, and a nearby school were completed and Father Pernin could concentrate on the church he was building in Peshtigo.

The priest was a man of some education and was familiar with such cosmopolitan cities as Montreal. When he arrived in the Wisconsin north country he looked around him with the detached interest and fresh viewpoint of a city dweller. Driving along the roads in his buggy, he found himself moving between endless tracts of tall pines that hid the sky. "Trees, trees, trees everywhere," Father Pernin wrote in describing his first impressions of this northern Wisconsin countryside. "Nothing else but trees as far as you can travel from the bay, either towards the north or west."

In his comings and goings that summer of 1871, he

98

noticed that farmers were taking advantage of the drought to enlarge their clearings by cutting down and burning the trees that stood in their way. Axes and fire were also being used to push the railroad northward. In the woods that autumn Indian and white hunters stalked deer and other game. Fishermen walked through the dry underbrush beside the streams. "At night," Father Pernin noted, "they kindle a large fire wherever they may happen to halt, prepare their suppers, then wrapping themselves in their blankets, sleep peacefully, extended on the earth, knowing that the fire will keep at a distance any wild animals that may happen to range through the vicinity during the night.

"The ensuing morning, they depart without taking the precaution of extinguishing the smouldering embers of the fire that has protected and warmed them. Farmers and others act in a similar manner. In this way the woods, particularly in the fall, are gleaming everywhere with fires lighted by man and which, fed on every side by dry leaves and grasses, spread more or less." Under such circumstances, the priest noted, a brisk wind could easily fan such fires into a blaze which would become "formidable."

Father Pernin's observations were written after the fact. There is no indication that during the summer he was more concerned about the woods fires than was anyone else. By September, of course, every thoughtful resident of the pinery area was worried. Father Pernin had the danger demonstrated to him on September 22. He decided to go hunting for pheasant on a farm in one of the Sugar Bush settlements. The woods were too thick for a man who did not know the landmarks to venture into alone. A twelve-year-old boy, the son of a nearby farmer, agreed to act as his guide. The priest and the child set off happily. The pheasants were plentiful. The hunting was good. Toward evening, Father Pernin was satisfied. He asked the boy to take him back to the farmhouse. The lad set off confidently, but soon stopped and looked around, then started hesitantly in another direction.

"Can't you find the way, my boy?"

"I'm not sure, father."

They walked faster now in the fading light. They went to the right, then to the left, then back to the right again. The woods were hushed, except for a small crackling sound. Rounding a pine, Father Pernin saw that it came from a tiny tongue of fire that ran along the ground, in and out, among the trunks of the trees, leaving the pines untouched but burning up the dry leaves and pine needles on the woods floor.

The wind began to increase. They could scarcely feel it, but the tops of the tall pines were swaying, making dark and mysterious sounds. The boy was thoroughly lost. Father Pernin stopped walking. He began to shout. His voice was lost in the forest around them. He raised his gun and fired several shots in the air. It was some time before there was any response, but then there were distant voices, one of which the boy recognized as that of his father. With a feeling of relief, the priest and his guide hurried toward the men who had come out to look for them.

By this time, the fire which had been darting about through the dry leaves had felt the wind. It had grown into a considerable blaze and now blocked the way between the priest and the farmers. Father Pernin and the boy stopped short, uncertain of what to do. But the other men ripped down trees branches and flailed about, beating out a narrow passageway in the ring of fire so the priest and the boy could run through it without getting scorched.

Another indication of the lurking danger was experienced by Father Pernin early in October as he drove from his Marinette church to the one in Peshtigo. Along the road, he noticed small fires in the woods, now on one side, now on the other, but did not worry much about them. Then he came to a place where the flames were crackling on both sides of the narrow road. The smoke was too thick for him to tell how far the fire extended. He hesitated. Then, deciding to risk it, he whipped his horse forward.

It took five minutes or so before the priest emerged into clear air again. Then he found about a dozen wagons and buggies lined up on the road, their drivers trying to determine if it was safe to continue to Marinette. When Father Pernin's buggy emerged from the smoke, one driver asked him if it was safe for them to go forward. He told them he thought it was, since he had just come through safely, but added: "Loosen your reins and urge on your horse or you may be suffocated." Some drivers took his advice, gave their horses a smart crack with the whip, and hurried along the road through the smoke. Others disregarded the priest's reassurance and went back to Peshtigo.

In retrospect Father Pernin decided such incidents were God's warning to Peshtigo of the ordeal which lay ahead. But at the moment he disregarded the signs of approaching disaster. "I allowed things to take their course," he admitted, "without feeling any great anxiety as to consequences or taking any precautionary steps."

Work proceeded on Peshtigo's new church, with Father Pernin watching the progress with satisfaction. Even before the building was entirely completed, he held services there. During the first week in October, the altar, pews and ornaments were removed to permit the inside of the church to be plastered. Lime and marble dust were stored in front of the building. An announcement was made that there would be no Mass on Sunday, October 8.

Father Pernin decided to hold services at Cedar River, in the upper Michigan peninsula about twelve miles north of Marinette, and sent word to Catholics there to expect him. On Saturday, October 7, he walked to the wharf at Menominee to take passage north on the steamboat *Dunlap*. But the steamer did not arrive. After waiting several hours, he decided that it was not going to stop. It surprised him. The *Dunlap* had never failed him before. He learned later that the captain had decided the smoke was too thick to allow a safe docking at Menominee.

101

The priest rode his horse back to Peshtigo that evening and passed the word that Mass would be said at his house the following morning. He prepared a temporary altar in one of his rooms and put the tabernacle from the church there. After Mass was over on Sunday morning, he placed the Blessed Sacrament in the tabernacle and prepared to leave for Marinette, where he planned to chant vespers and preach an evening sermon.

Several parishoners called on him that afternoon and protested his plan to go to Marinette. "There seemed to be a vague fear of some impending though unknown evil haunting the minds of many," he wrote. "Nor was I myself entirely free from this unusual feeling. It was rather an impression than a conviction for I saw that things looked much as usual and arrived at the conclusion that our fears were groundless — without, however, feeling much reassured thereby." The deciding factor in his change of plans was the realization that the Catholics at Marinette would not be expecting him, having known he'd intended to go to Cedar River, so they would not be planning to attend vespers. Father Pernin remained in Peshtigo, spending the afternoon at his house next to the church.

Toward evening, as the smoke increased, the temperature rose. Some of those who were in Peshtigo remembered feeling occasional puffs of hot air some hours before there was any sign of approaching fire. Later, before the line of advancing flames could be seen, some survivors remembered that the wind came in gusts almost hot enough to burn the skin.

Late that afternoon, Father Pernin felt increasingly uneasy. The sky was dark with smoke. The air was still, with the feeling of impending change that comes when a storm is approaching. But many Peshtigo residents were touched with none of the foreboding against which he was struggling. "The passing and repassing in the street of countless young people bent only on amusement — laughing, singing and perfectly indifferent to the menacing aspect of nature — was sufficient to

102

make me think that I alone was a prey to anxiety and to render me ashamed of manifesting my feeling," he said.

During the afternoon, one of the parishoners, "an old Canadian," asked for the priest's permission to dig a well close to the church. The water would be needed by the plasterers, who were scheduled to start work Monday morning. Besides, if fire should break out, the well would supply water to fight it. Father Pernin had doubts whether such work ought to be done on a Sabbath, but the Canadian pointed out that he was too busy with his regular job during the week to dig the well then. The priest told him to go ahead, and the pit was dug. Even in this time of drought, the water table was close enough to the surface to make digging to it a matter of only a few hours' work. When the job was done, the old man said he wouldn't sell a well like that for a good sum of money. "If a fire breaks out," he added, "it will be easy now to save our church."

Father Pernin invited the Canadian to join him for supper, then sent him home. About 7 P.M., the priest took a walk around the neighborhood. The wind was beginning to rise. It blew in brief gusts, subsided, then blew again. It worried him. He stopped to see an elderly widow, a Mrs. Dress, who was equally concerned. She had told her children to take precautions, to be ready to fight the fire if it came. But they had only laughed at her, she told the priest.

Father Pernin continued his walk. At one point, the wind began to blow hard. He noticed some dead tree trunks blaze up "as if the wind had been a breath of fire, capable of kindling them into a flame by its mere contact." He joined several other men in throwing water on the dead trees. Once they were no longer a danger, he went back to his house. It would not do to alarm people by letting them see that their priest was worried. He decided to stay indoors and keep his fears to himself.

The wind was blowing stronger now. He could see above the cloud of smoke a vivid red reflection. Suddenly, he heard a distant, muffled sound—a kind of dull roar. It galvanized him into action. His uncertainty was gone. Now that the danger seemed real, he quit being afraid. In fact, he felt a sense of great relief. He ran to where his horse was stabled and turned the animal loose in the street so it would have a chance to save itself. He grabbed up a pickax and began digging a six-foot trench in the sandy soil of his garden. A vigorous man, used to such work, the task should not have tired him, but somehow it was a strenuous one. The atmosphere was oppressive. It was hard to breathe. Only the feeling of impending catastrophe kept him working rapidly. The crimson reflection in the sky to the southwest was rapidly enlarging. Between each stroke of the pick he could hear a sound which he thought resembled "the confused noise of a number of cars and locomotives approaching a railroad station, or the rumbling of thunder, with the difference that it never ceased, but deepened in intensity each moment."

While he was digging, he could hear drunken shouts from the saloons, where lumberjacks and railroad workers on their regular weekend spree were paying not the slightest attention to the danger roaring through the woods toward Peshtigo. Father Pernin decided later that the roisterers had displayed thoughtlessness and folly in equal measure. But at the moment, he was too busy digging to spend time thinking about it.

His garden was near a house occupied by the Tylers. He described them as "an American family" to distinguish them from the foreign-born who made up a majority of his congregation. The Tylers were having a small gathering of friends. He could see them through the window. He could also hear them, particularly the laughter of some of the women. They seemed to find the priest's activity with the pickax quite amusing. About 9 P.M., the guests went home, and Mrs. Tyler came out into the yard to see what Father Pernin was up to. "The actions of the priest always make a certain impression," he noted in his account of that evening. "Even on Protestants."

104

"Father, do you think there is any danger?" Mrs. Tyler asked him.

"I do not know," he told her. "But I have unpleasant presentiments and feel myself impelled to prepare for trouble."

"But if a fire breaks out, what are we to do?"

"In that case, madame, seek the river at once."

Mrs. Tyler had joined in the laughter earlier in the evening. But the priest's advice, reinforced by the sky's glow, made her change her mind. Soon after their conversation, Father Pernin saw her and the family heading toward the river. He learned later what had happened to the guests who had visited the Tylers that evening. There had been eight of them at the party—Daniel McGregor, a railroad man, and his wife; Daniel's sister, Jennie McGregor; Nellie Marshall; Ira Washburne; Mr. and Mrs. William Thompson and a Mrs. Phillbrook. Before the night was over, all were dead except Washburne and Mrs. Phillbrook.

ELEVEN

•

John Cameron, a Civil War veteran with a beard like Ulysses S. Grant's, had once climbed a tree near Green Bay and looked off to the north. As far as his eye could reach, there was nothing but an unbroken sea of white pine. It was an inspiring sight for a man who made his living from trees and a comforting one—with such vast resources it seemed obvious that those who warned that the woods were not an inexhaustible resource must be wrong. He had just returned from a walk up the river to look for likely places to send the lumberjacks when the ground froze. Toward evening of October 8, he sat on the steps of the Peshtigo Company's boardinghouse where he and the other roomers had eaten a hearty dinner, ignoring the ashes that drifted through the open windows into their food.

Over the treetops to the southwest of the village, Cameron now could see the red glow of a forest fire on the horizon. He was familiar with such sights and he was not particularly worried, although he kept a shrewd eye on the glow. The wind was rising. Cameron didn't like the look of things. Still, there seemed no immediate cause for action and

106

he continued to sit on the steps, keeping his own counsel. Then he heard a low moaning sound—soft, deep, far away. As he stared toward the forest that surrounded the small town, the noise gradually changed to a sullen roar. Years later, sitting on the deacon seat of a logging camp, Cameron could describe the sound so graphically that a young logger listening to him would shiver and glance nervously out the window at the woods. The wind continued to rise. The trees made dry, rustling sounds. Some of their remaining leaves swirled down. Then the wind died again. The silence returned, except for that strange roar to the southwest. It was growing louder and more menacing. Still Cameron sat there, waiting to see what would happen.

Then a whirling slab of fire came down from the dark sky to land on the sawdust street. The ember seemed too large to be carried by something as insubstantial as the wind. He rubbed his eyes and looked again. It was still there. Then came another, and another. Cameron leaped up. He gave a yell of warning and fear and defiance as fire rained down on Peshtigo. The pine sidewalks blazed up. The top of a house leaped into flame. Seeming close at hand, the booming crash of great trees falling was heard over the crackle of the flames. Cameron ran for the river.

Earlier that Sunday, the smoke filtered the sun's rays to bathe the town in a sickly yellow light. It made familiar objects look strange. Peshtigo lived the final hours before its death in a kind of ghastly haze. Those who were there that afternoon told how the air was full of smoke and ashes and how, after a brisk wind in the middle of the day, the air became still, with no breeze stirring. Some went to church that Sunday evening. Other Peshtigo residents, according to a contemporary account, spent their last evening "in the pursuit of pleasure or the gratification of their own lusts." That morning two hundred railway workers had swung down off the railroad cars that had brought them from Peshtigo Harbor. They were Chicagoans for the most part. They expected to go

107

north into the woods to lay rails the next day for the North Western Road's line toward Marinette, but today was a holiday. Most of the men were already well full of whiskey when they arrived in Peshtigo. They headed for the saloons to reinforce their supply. Churchgoers saw them lurch along, shoving each other off the plank sidewalks and emitting what were described as horrible blasphemies. The drinkers went their accustomed ways and the honest folk went home to heavy Sunday dinners. Everyone was conscious of the danger in the woods. But Peshtigo had fought off other fires. If another came, they felt, the town would fight it off again.

By evening, when the danger became apparent, one account has it that both "the virtuous and the vicious were seeking the God-given boon of sleep." Some of the drunks were sleeping, no doubt, and a surprising number of the respectable householders were in bed by 9 P.M. Among those who were wide awake was T. A. Hay, a jeweler who had recently moved his shop to a building on the west side. He and other responsible citizens had done their best to be ready to protect the town. They had placed barrels and tubs of water on street corners. They had turned out so often to fight fires during the last few weeks that they had begun to think of themselves as expert firemen. On the night of October 8, a number of them were on guard in a swampy area to the west of the village. Hay was among them. He and the other volunteers had armed themselves with shovels and pails of water. Despite previous fires, enough dry underbrush remained in the area to make falling sparks dangerous. The men were ready to throw dirt or water on any small blazes that might spring up.

The first indication that this night was going to be different came when Hay and the others saw a fireball sail through the air from the burning woods to the southwest and strike the top of a nearby tree. The fireball—perhaps the burning top of a pine—fell to the ground in a shower of sparks. It set a brisk little blaze that the men extinguished with

108

difficulty. Hay decided to get a closer look at the burning woods from which the fireball had come. He and Elder Beach followed a new street that was being cut through from the village to the Oconto Road. They walked about a quarter of a mile, keeping a wary eye on the tall trees on either side of them. The wind was blowing hard. The pines were swaying alarmingly. Now and then one would come crashing down. The farther the men walked, the more alarming the outlook seemed. The roar of the wind and fire increased. The smoke made it hard to breathe. Hot sand blew into their faces. They soon decided they had gone far enough—perhaps too far. They headed back toward their companions. On the way, Hay stopped several times to pull his coat up around his face with his back to the wind, fighting for breath. Once as he stood there trying to get something in his lungs besides smoke, a hemlock crashed down just in front of him. The woods were aflame on both sides of Hay and Beach by now. The fire was coming toward them from behind. The narrow opening ahead of them was filled with smoke. They were nearly blinded.

They managed to get back to where the other men were waiting with their pitifully inadequate weapons, the shovels and pails. Soon after Hay and Beach returned, the men agreed the situation was hopeless. They began running toward the village to save their families. Hay followed. He had no family to worry about, but he wanted to rescue some of the valuables from his shop. The roaring sound that had startled Cameron and brought householders to their front porches was loud in his ears. It sounded like the approach of a fast-moving train, which made it seem like a bizarre foretaste of things to come. Only a ghost train could travel over a right-of-way whose tracks were not yet laid.

While Hay and the others were running full speed toward the village, other residents noticed a deer come bounding in from the forest and stand for a moment on a street near the river. Village dogs peered at it but made no move to attack. Some of those in Peshtigo that night remembered another instance of how the approaching disaster had changed the order of things among animals. They saw the housecats gather, as though at a secret signal, and glide down the sawdust street, glancing now and then over their shoulders. Cats are independent creatures, each a law unto itself. But that Sunday night they traveled in a pack, like wolves.

The rumbling noise increased and with it came the rapid ringing of the bells of the Congregational and Catholic churches. Women hurried onto their porches to see what was happening, then ran inside the houses to snatch children from their beds and wrap blankets around them against the night air. Men behaved in various ways. Some ran toward the danger, determined to fight it, leaving wives and children behind. Others snatched up a few valuables, while their families fled without them.

Great tongues of flame were visible above the tree tops to the southwest. Burning coals began to drop from the dark sky. Within a few minutes of the first alarm, the wind was blowing so hard that it was difficult for a man to stand. A number of families slept through the ringing bells and shouts and confusion. Their first realization of danger was when their houses burst into flames around them. "Some were burned to death within a few feet of the river, some in their houses, some in the woods and some on the roads attempting to escape," Franklin Tilton wrote. ". . . Within half an hour, and some say within ten minutes, of the time the first building caught fire, the entire village was in flames. The great sheets of fire curled and rolled over the ground like breakers on a reef."

One of the saloons with sleeping quarters above it was located near Father Pernin's church and residence. All day it had been crowded with noisy revelers.

"Perhaps they had passed the holy time of Mass, drinking and carousing there," the priest reflected later. "Towards nightfall, the greater part of them were too much intoxicated to share in the anxiety felt by the more steady members of the community." While Father Pernin had been out digging the

110

hole in his garden that afternoon, he had noticed several drunks lounging around the saloon's veranda. "Their intoxicated condition was plainly revealed by the manner in which they quarreled, wrestled, rolled on the ground, filling the air the while with wild shouts and horrid blasphemies," he wrote. It is impossible to know how many of the men who were on their regular weekend spree in Peshtigo might have lived if the disaster had occurred when they were sober. But it is likely that the toll was higher than it would have been if the fire had not arrived at the time of a weekend spree.

Father Pernin hurried back and forth between his house and the trench he had dug, filling it with trunks, books, church ornaments, and other valuables, then covering them with a foot of sandy soil. Meanwhile, his housekeeper was running about distractedly. She filled a basket with crosses, medals, rosaries, and the like and carefully placed it on the steps of a nearby store. She bustled back into the house and came hurrying outside carrying a canary cage. The wind wrested the cage from her grasp. The terrified woman called to the priest to run for his life as she herself fled toward the river.

Father Pernin was not quite ready to follow her good advice. He went into the room where he had held makeshift services that morning. He picked up the tabernacle that held the Blessed Sacrament and started to open the locked container. In his haste, he dropped the key on to the floor. There was no time to look for it. He caught up the tabernacle and carried it to his wagon, deciding it would be easier to haul it to the river than to carry it in his arms. Running back into the house to look for his chalice, which had not been returned to the tabernacle, he saw clouds of sparks here and there in the room. They blazed up with sounds like gunpowder exploding. Outside the door, in a cage attached to the wall, his pet bluejay was fluttering wildly, beating against the bars and squawking in alarm. Father Pernin decided there was no time to let the bird loose. He called for his dog, which was hiding under his bed. The animal normally came to him, wagging its

111

tail. But now it ignored his voice entirely and continued to cower there.

Starting to get his lightweight wagon from the yard, the priest put his hand on the gate to open it. At that instant, the wind gusted. The gate, planks and fencing were swept away. Father Pernin was thinking in a manner which he afterwards described as childish. If he had been in full possession of his senses, the danger might have paralyzed him. As it was, he saw the gate flying off in the wind as if by magic and thought: "The road is open. We have only to start." And so he started, putting himself between the shafts of the cart and hauling it along the road, taking the place of the horse which he had turned loose to try to save itself. With each step, the wind tried to pull the wagon from his grasp. "It was almost impossible to keep one's eyes open, to distinguish the road or to recognize people, though the way was crowded with pedestrians as well as vehicles crossing and crashing together in the general flight. Some were hastening toward the river, others from it; while all were struggling alike in the grasp of the hurricane. A thousand discordant, deafening noises rose on the air to-gether—the neighing of horses, falling of chimneys, crashing of uprooted trees, roaring and whistling of the wind, crackling of fire as it ran with lightning-like rapidity from house to house. All sounds were there except that of the human voice.

"People seemed stricken dumb by terror. They jostled each other without exchanging look, word or counsel. The silence of the tomb reigned among the living. Nature alone lifted up its voice and spoke."

The priest had hoped to find someone to help him pull the cart, but no one volunteered. The problem of making his way along the road was complicated by the number of other vehicles trying to go the opposite way—even though those who were heading west were going directly away from the one likely place of safety, the river.

As Father Pernin struggled forward, he passed the saloon where there had been so much shouting and horseplay not long before. Now the place was silent as death, and it was true

112

that those who remained inside it were doomed. A little farther along the road, the priest stumbled. Glancing down, he saw in the flickering light of the fire a woman and a young girl lying on the ground. He stooped and lifted the woman's head. She and her daughter were dead. He left them there and pushed forward, falling down a number of times, each time fighting back to his feet and grasping the cart shafts again to pull it toward the river. He felt something nuzzle his shoulder. He turned. It was his horse. The animal was trembling uncontrollably. The priest spoke its name and motioned to it to follow him. But like the dog, it refused to abandon present dangers for those unknown.

In an era when horses were so widely used, it may seem strange that so many of the refugees chose to use their own legs to try to escape. Generally speaking, however, the animals were of little value to those trying to save themselves from the fire. The experience of Anton Place, who ran a meat market in Marinette and owned a farm two miles south of Peshtigo, was typical.

Place had gone to his farm late in September to help harvest the crops. On October 8, he drove into Peshtigo with a wagonload of grain, bringing a boy along to help with the unloading. When he got to the village, he sent a friend back to the farm on an errand and lay down in the back of the wagon to sleep. The friend came back to shake him awake. "The woods is burning up, Place. Run for your life." Anton leaped onto the seat of the wagon and whipped up the horses, intending to try to get to Marinette. The wagon got across the bridge to the east side of the river, but by the time it had traveled a few hundred yards along East Front Street, Place could see fire ahead of him as well as behind. He and the boy jumped down from the wagon. Quickly, they unfastened the horses' harness to give the animals a chance to survive. Then they ran back to the river.

At the boardinghouse on Peshtigo's east side where Cameron had been sitting a few minutes before, men who should have known better ran inside to take refuge, along with

113

women and children who hoped that the building would be safer than the outdoors. They died there, their bodies burned to cinders and ashes. No one can ever be sure of who most of them were or how many perished—the estimates ranged from forty to more than two hundred. It is known that some had been staggering along the board sidewalks not long before, enjoying their Sunday drunk, which may explain why they chose such an unlikely refuge. But many of those in the boardinghouse were sober citizens who felt the big building would be safe. They paid with their lives for guessing wrong.

Nearly everyone in Peshtigo had given thought in advance to what he would do when the fire came. Many had told themselves that, if worst came to worst, they would make for the river. Now they poured toward it from east and west. On the way, they saw men and women fall to the ground, their clothes in flames, with no one willing to pause long enough to beat out the fire.

One man noticed pretty Helga Rockstad as she ran down a blazing plank sidewalk, her blonde hair streaming out behind her. Her hair leaped into flame. Helga crumpled to her knees. The next morning the man who had seen her die without being able to help her came back to look at the spot. Nothing was there except two nickel garter buckles and a tiny mound of ashes.

J. G. Clements, the young house painter who had promised his mother-in-law to take care of his new bride if danger came, kept his word a few hours later. When the clang of church bells brought them the first warning of danger, Clements leaped out of bed and gathered his wife into his arms. He started to carry her to the river. The road was a nightmare of jostling humans, animals, and wagons. Clements was soon gasping for breath. His wife clung to him, faint from the smoke and the realization that death threatened a sudden end to their three-day marriage. Looking desperately around, Clements saw a man alone in a buckboard, fighting hard to keep his frightened horse under control. The man had started

114

away from the river toward his home to try to rescue his family. But with most of the traffic heading toward him, he had decided it was hopeless. Clements put his wife into the buckboard and helped its owner turn the horse's head toward the river. The girl reached out to help her husband climb aboard, but he shook his head. There was no use burdening the horse any more than was necessary, he told her. The buckboard headed for the river, with Mrs. Clements lying in it and her young husband running along behind. They had gone only a short distance when he stumbled and fell. He lay flat on the dirt road. His wife shouted to the driver to stop. "If we stop, we'll die," he told her. She started to leap out of the buckboard. The stranger grabbed her arm, holding her with one hand while he urged on his horse with the other. The girl struggled with him. He refused to let her go to the aid of her husband, and to her death. When they reached the river, she was unconscious. The cold water revived her. She stood in the river as the town went up in flames around her, weeping for the bridegroom who had promised to give his life for her.

The experience of another Peshtigo husband is mentioned in numerous contemporary accounts of the fire, but none mentions his name. All agree that when the crisis came he ran home, took a firm grip on his wife, and started with her for the river. They hurried along with the others, blinded by the smoke but making good progress until they stumbled over something in the road—a body, perhaps. In falling, the man released his grip on his wife's arm. Picking himself up, he groped around for her. He grasped her waist and pulled her along with him to the river. They plunged into it. He turned to say something to her about how lucky they were to be alive. The smoke cleared momentarily. In the light of the fire, he could see clearly for the first time since he had stumbled and fallen. "My God," he said. "You're not my wife. I've saved the wrong woman." It was too late to go back. His wife was one of those who died.

The Catholic Church and the priest's house across the

street from it were near the corner of Oconto and Ellis Avenues, about two-and-a-half blocks west of the river. It was ordinarily a few minutes' walk, but that night it seemed endless to Father Pernin. When he finally came within sight of the river, the buildings along the west bank were on fire. The wind was blowing great billows of flame out over the water. He had planned to cross the bridge to the east bank, but by the time he got there the structure was on fire. The priest quickly realized it would be foolhardy to venture out along the span, which was filled with men, women, children, horses, and cattle. He decided to go downstream below the mill dam, where the water would be shallower and where the shore sloped gradually down to the stream. But the way was blocked by a wall of flames from nearby buildings. The Peshtigo Company sawmill, located across the river near the bridge, and the large company store nearby were on fire. The flames were blowing across the water.

Pernin thought of himself as a man of logic and he behaved accordingly. If he could not descend the stream, he would ascend it. He headed up the riverbank above the dam, where the water was deepest. He expected the bridge to fall at any moment, and he wanted to be out of the immediate vicinity when it did. He had dragged the cart with the tabernacle on it this far. It was as much as could be expected of him. He pushed the wagon into the water as far as it would go. As he stood there on the riverbank taking stock of the situation, the wind lifted the smoke momentarily, as though raising a curtain. He could see the scene clearly.

"The banks of the river as far as the eye could reach were covered with people standing there, motionless as statues, some with eyes upturned towards heaven and tongues protruded. The greater number seemed to have no idea of taking any steps to procure their safety, imagining—as many afterwards acknowledged to me—that the end of the world had arrived and that there was nothing for them but silent submission to their fate."

116

Father Pernin was not the sort to stand around and wait. If the Lord wanted him, he would obey. But until he had definite word, he intended to assume this disaster was of earthly origin. His priestly robes flapping in the wind, he began hopping about the riverbank, pushing people into the water. "I am wet," one of the men protested, springing back on shore. The priest was too out of breath to argue. He grasped the fellow around the waist and dragged him back into the water.

One of those standing in the river near the priest was Hay, the jeweler. When he had returned to the village, he had run into the Cavoit building and unlocked the door to his shop. He filled a basket with jewelry and hurried outside again. By then the west side of the building was on fire. Hay ran toward the river. His hat blew off. The wind hurled him against a water barrel. As he clung to it, he saw a man running through the smoke. A large wooden box, carried by the wind, struck the man in the back, knocking him down. He lay sprawled on the sidewalk, either unconscious or dead.

The river was close by, but in the few minutes it took the jeweler to reach it he saw and heard other things that haunted him the rest of his life. Women and children screamed for help, and there was no one to help them. In the smoke-filled darkness, lit fitfully by the flames, he caught sight of several people as they fell to the ground. Others would run for a few steps, then throw themselves to the earth to catch a breath of air before rising and stumbling forward again. Hay saw a child, perhaps four years old, run down by a team of horses that was out of control. He told of seeing a middle-aged man, a child under each arm, dragging his wife along the board sidewalk by her clothing after she had collapsed.

The jeweler started across the bridge. Before he had gone far, someone shouted that it was on fire. He elbowed his way back to shore. As he stepped off the bridge, a gust of hot air, filled with smoke and sparks, took his breath away. He dropped his basket of jewelry. Dr. Kelsey, who was nearby,

117

followed his example by throwing away an armload of books he was carrying. The two men plunged into the river, ducking under to extinguish their burning clothing. Hay found a place beside a large pine log. Standing in water up to his shoulders, he took off his wet coat and draped it over his head. It was three hours later when he felt it was safe to wade back to shore. Ten feet from the riverbank, he came upon the body of a man who had died only a few steps away from the water.

With the humans who scrambled down the riverbanks had come dogs and cattle. Some of the people standing in the water were knocked off their feet by the cows, to be swept to their deaths under the falling timbers of the blazing bridge or against the wooden dam that also caught fire.

Burning logs floated down the river from the supply kept near the woodenware factory. The logs moved swiftly in the current, bumping against some of the refugees. Amid these floating torches came a cow, swimming along where the river was deep, its eyes wide with fear. Clinging to one of its horns was a young girl. Carrie Heidenworth, who was five years old, had run to the river and waded into the cold water, although she could not swim. In the excitement, she got beyond her depth. As she went under, she reached out for something to cling to. The cow blundered by just then. She grasped one of its curving horns. The cow kept swimming. Carrie hung on tight. Some of those who saw the cow and its burden jumped to the conclusion that Carrie was a woman, not a small girl. That is how she was described in some accounts. But Carrie lived for many years to vouch for the story of her rescue by the cow.

The animal eventually swam near enough to shore so that a man grabbed the little girl. She was glad to abandon the cow. The cow, it can safely be assumed, was equally glad to relinquish her rider.

TWELVE

•

Not long after Father Pernin arrived at the river, the Peshtigo Company's woodenware factory began burning, sending flames high into the air. As the wind picked up, the roof blew off and a great cargo of burning tubs and wooden buckets exploded through the open top of the building, soaring high in the air in flaming arcs to fall into the river. Nine-year-old Amelia Slaughter, clinging to a log near the bridge, looked up in wonder at this fireworks display, then ducked as the blazing pannikins descended around her.

Even those who were standing in the water up to their necks were not safe. The flames darted over the water. Some refugees had been foresighted enough to bring coats or quilts with them, but lost them in the confusion. Father Pernin saw several such articles floating past and fished them out to cover the heads of some of those who had clustered about him, thinking there might be added safety in being near a man of God. The wraps dried quickly in the intense heat and had to be dipped repeatedly in the water.

"The river was brighter than by day," the priest said in his account of that night, "and the spectacle presented by those

119

heads rising above the level of the water—some covered, some uncovered—the countless hands employed in beating the waves, was singular and painful in the extreme. So free was I from the fear and anxiety that might naturally have been expected to reign in my mind at such a moment that I actually perceived only the ludicrous side of the scene at times and smiled within myself at it.

"When turning my gaze from the river, I saw nothing but flames; houses, trees and the air itself were on fire. Above my head, as far as the eye could reach into space . . . I saw nothing but immense volumes of flames covering the firmament, rolling one over the other with stormy violence as we see masses of clouds driven wildly hither and thither by the fierce power of the tempest."

As the fire nearest them died down, the refugees in the river became aware of how cold the water was. The priest could hear his companions' teeth chattering. He decided to move a little way toward shore to see if it was safe to leave the river. He had scarcely lifted his shoulders out of the water before a man shouted a warning. "Father, you are on fire." He ducked back under, convinced that it was better to be chilled than to burn. A woman standing nearby asked him, "Do you think this is the end of the world, Father?" He told her he did not think so. They lapsed into silence.

Some families lived too far from the river to seek its shelter, or were cut off from it by the flames. Plowed ground—any garden plot—was considered the next most likely refuge. Sometimes safety was found there. The members of three Peshtigo families, for example, spent the night in a plowed field owned by James Johnston. There were twenty-one women and children and only a single large quilt to shelter them from the embers that swirled down out of the gale. The twenty-one lay close together, the younger ones on top of their mothers, so the quilt could be of some value to the entire group. The fathers, though knowing it was death to do so, stayed in the open, wetting down the flimsy cloth shelter with water from buckets they had brought with them. The clothes were burned from the men's bodies. In the morning, they were all dead. But the twenty-one women and children under the charred quilt survived. Part of a coat belonging to one of the men was found. In a pocket were a pair of women's shoes—the dead man's wife had not had time to put them on when they fled from their bed into the night.

The residents of the east side of Peshtigo had a natural refuge closeby—a low-lying piece of ground between a bluff and the riverbank. Normally, "the flats" was swampy, but in the dry summer and fall of 1871 the swamp had disappeared. With the river closeby and the low bluff giving some protection from the east, the flats seemed a good place to seek out when the fire came.

Because the fire approached the village from the southwest, families in the eastern half of the village had a few minutes more warning. Fred Shepherd, eight years old, looked out of the front window of his family's house. The west half of the town was in flames, but the houses on his side of the river were still untouched. His father, William, a native of Washington County, New York, had migrated to Wisconsin with his parents in 1844, four years before it became a state. He worked as a railway postal clerk for thirteen years before moving to Peshtigo. He had been promoted to assistant manager of the Peshtigo Company only a few months before the fire. The Shepherd family was prosperous enough to afford a maid, Amanda. That is, Fred remembered her as the maid, although Amanda probably thought of herself as the hired girl. On the night of the fire, Amanda and her young man had gone to church. Fred and his father were in bed by 7 P.M. Fred's mother and younger brother were visiting Mrs. Shepherd's parents in Ogdensburg, New York. An older boy was with his paternal grandparents in Racine, Wisconsin.

Fred was awakened by a sharp rapping at the window. One of the workmen had come to arouse his father. Shepherd climbed into his clothes and left, telling his son to go back to

121

sleep. The boy waited until his father was gone, then leaped out of bed to see what was going on. He walked out into the yard. Amanda and her friend were standing at the gate, looking toward the west. Great tongues of flame were visible in the distance.

When Fred's father got to the sawmill about two blocks away, he began issuing orders to the crew assigned to protect the building. The company's fire engine was made ready. Buckets were filled. The men had plenty of experience with this sort of emergency. Each knew his task. Then the wind came sweeping in on the town, bearing burning brands from the woods, raining down sparks, filling the lungs with smoke. Shepherd gave the order to abandon the mill. "Save your families," he told the men. Many of them lived on the west side. Their rush to get across the river brought them running headlong into the first stream of refugees who were fleeing in front of the flames, contributing to the bottleneck on the bridge.

After standing briefly with Amanda at the gate, Fred had gone obediently back to bed. As the fire got closer, the girl came running into the house and told him to get up again. While he was dressing, he could see that the west side of Peshtigo was on fire. Looking out of another window, he saw that the company boardinghouse directly to the north of his home was still untouched by flames, but the wind was blowing so fiercely that the building seemed to the boy to be rocking on its foundations.

His father arrived then. Shepherd ordered Amanda and Fred to go to the flats while he and her young man stayed behind to try to save a few valuables. Feverishly, the men dug in the sandy soil to bury the household silver, a gun and Shepherd's violin. The violin had been given to him by a Union soldier who had dug it up from a hiding place on a Georgia plantation while General William T. Sherman's troops were marching.

Fred was supposed to see to his dog, a water spaniel

122

named Ned, but in the excitement he forgot. Fred and Amanda ran out of the house by the back door, which was farthest from the fire, and made their way across the street toward the low-lying land just east of the river. The wind was so strong that it threw the boy against a fence. He picked himself up. With Amanda clutching his hand, they clambered down the slight bluff to the flats. His father and Amanda's friend soon joined them. A half hour later, so did Ned. The dog apparently had jumped through an open window and come to seek its master.

Several hundred refugees took shelter in the flats that night. Some of the men were foresighted enough to bring buckets and some women brought quilts as protection from the heat and falling sparks. By carrying water from the river in the wooden pails and keeping the blankets and outer clothing of the refugees wet, many were saved. The terrain helped. It was noticed, not only in Peshtigo but elsewhere in the burned-over area, that the danger often increased in direct proportion to the altitude—the lower you were, the safer you usually were. Sometimes a small child, a few feet shorter than his parents, survived while the adults died around him. Sometimes those not too proud to grovel on their faces lived, while those who stood erect perished. The air in low-lying places seems to have been safer to breathe while Peshtigo was burning, making the flats a sanctuary while death was stalking the slightly higher ground to the east.

The fire reached the buildings on the east side of the river about 10 P.M. The boardinghouse caught only a few minutes after the Shepherd boy saw it shuddering in the wind. At 10:05 P.M. it collapsed upon those who had sought shelter there. That was the time recorded on a pocket watch carried by Dan McGregor, who had been visiting Father Pernin's neighbor earlier in the evening. The watch was found by men rummaging through the ashes. Another watch, which had been in the pocket of McGregor's brother, Duncan, stopped at 10:10, but Dan's was probably the one with the correct time,

123

since he had been conductor of the Peshtigo Harbor railroad. Most of the fifty Norwegian immigrants, who had just arrived to start a new life were inside the boardinghouse when it collapsed. So were the wife and nine children of Donald Roy McDonald, superintendent of the woodenware factory.

The building had three stories, which made it as tall as the two largest hotels in town, the Peshtigo House and the Forest House, both of which were on the west side of the river. A long, narrow building on East Front Street, the boarding-house was not far from the eastern end of the bridge. Just behind it was another building, which may have served to accommodate the overflow when the main structure was crowded. Immediately to the north of the boardinghouse was the company store. The assumption that the boardinghouse would be spared by the fire was described by one observer as "a strange hallucination." The company's fire engine had been brought up from the woodenware factory. The stream of water had hardly begun to wet down the boardinghouse when the hose burned through. Moments later, the building burst into flames. McDonald had taken his family there in the belief that they would be safe on the east side of the river, behind the barrier formed by the stream. "Stay here, no matter what happens," he told his wife, Margaret, as he left her there. The next day, McDonald poked through the ashes of the building, hoping his wife had disobeyed him. But she had not. The ten members of his family were part of what one account called "a heap of indistinguishable calcined bones and charred flesh . . . giving no clue to sex or number."

Those refugees who had gotten to the low-lying ground east of the river saw the flames from the boardinghouse, but there was nothing they could do to help the victims. They had to concentrate on keeping from being burned up themselves.

The clothing a person had chosen to wear might make the difference between life and death. Fred Shepherd was one of the lucky ones. He had put on heavy clothing, giving him protection from the heat and flying embers. His father was

124

even better off. He had brought not merely one overcoat but two. Thomas Burns, foreman at the woodenware factory, came running up, dressed only in trousers and a shirt. Shepherd handed him his spare overcoat. Burns accepted it gratefully and put it on. "Now if I only had a hat, I'd be all right," he said. Fred's spaniel had been taught to fetch its master's hat. Possibly the animal recognized the familiar word, for Ned went trotting off and came back with a hat and deposited it at Shepherd's feet. Burns picked up the gift and went away feeling safe.

In some accounts of the fire, written by survivors and by persons who visited the scene soon afterward, it was made to seem that the conflagration appeared almost without warning. For those who were asleep when it roared down on the village, this must have seemed the case. But in retrospect it would seem that those Peshtigo residents who were awake should have noticed signs of approaching danger. By early evening of October 8 the air grew quite warm, with occasional hot gusts. By 8:30 P.M., the glow against the sky to the southwest showed that a forest fire of considerable dimensions was burning there. When the wind began to blow hard from that direction at about 9:30 P.M., it should have been plain that the village was in mortal peril. By then, there was still time to get to the river. But few Peshtigo residents realized that this fire was going to be so much worse than others that had preceeded it. It was not until nearly 10 P M that panic set in. Within half an hour, the village was destroyed.

Some of those who fled from the flames had particular difficulties, such as David Maxon and his wife who were ill at their home near the woodenware factory. Maxon was up and about, trying to care for the five children, but when he looked out the window and saw what was bearing down on them, he forgot he was sick. He ordered his wife out of bed and, with the children following, they started for the river. On the way, Mrs. Maxon collapsed. Her husband grabbed her by the shoulders and dragged her the rest of the way. Once she and the children had reached the water, he ran back to his house, snatched up a feather bed, and carried it through the smoke and confusion to where his wife was waiting. He put the feather bed in the river near shore so it was partly under water, and lifted Mrs. Maxon onto it. He and the children took turns splashing water over her and themselves, saving all their lives. The wind was described by survivors as everything from a gale to a tornado. There is no doubt that it was strong enough to pick up a man and hurl him through the air, for G. J. Tisdale survived to tell about it. He was inside the three-story Peshtigo House when the hotel caught fire. He ran out the east door. As he stepped off the porch, the wind caught him and a few moments later he found himself sprawled on the ground some distance from the building. He picked himself up and ran for the river. Several times along the way he was knocked flat by the wind. Before he reached the water, he was showered by wind-blown sand that was so hot it burned his skin. Once in the river, the heat was so intense that he could keep his head above water only for a few seconds at a time. He remembered seeing logs floating in the river catch fire and burn down to the water line.

Trout Creek, which empties into the river in the village, was deep enough despite the drought to provide safety for some of those who lived near its banks. Among them was Frederick Nelding. After the Neldings were married in Chicago, he had come to visit his sister in Peshtigo for a week or two, believing that after a long trip west to settle with his bride in Texas he would never see his sister again. The visit continued longer than he had expected, and before he was ready to go, his wife became pregnant. Nelding decided to buy a lot next to his sister's house, build a cottage there and forget about his plan to head for the West.

Mrs. Nelding was seven months pregnant on the night of the fire. She went to bed early but could not sleep. After a time, she noticed a glow outside the window. Hurrying to look, she saw the nearby fences on fire. She roused her

126

husband. He grabbed his best suit and his wallet and ran to the door. When he opened it, the wind was too strong to close it again. With his wife following him, he ran outside, where most of the neighbors had gathered to debate whether they ought to run for the river. When they saw several families coming from that direction, it was agreed that it would be better to head for the creek, which was only half a block away.

A board fence blocked their path. Nelding ripped off several boards, then stood aside to let his wife and the other women go through the opening. By the time his turn came, the fence was burning fiercely. The suit and wallet he was carrying caught fire. He had to leave them behind as he ducked through the fence and ran for his life. He and the others stood in the creek until morning, ducking under or throwing water over each other to keep from burning up.

Nelding lived on the western outskirts of the village, as did John Mulligan, the railway crew boss. Mulligan's house was one of the first to catch fire. A former prizefighter, he told his wife to climb onto his back and he set off for the river—rushing "like a quarter horse through the flames," according to an admiring account. Mrs. Mulligan, who was clad only in a nightgown, snatched up a shawl as her husband carried her out the door of her house. By the time they got to the river, the nightgown was burned off her and only a torn and singed remnant of the shawl was left. But Mulligan was in no mood for false modesty. Once they were safe, he held up the tattered shawl as a token of their triumph.

Mulligan's feat of galloping through the burning town with his wife on his back was spectacular, but a man identified only as a "Peshtigo mechanic" was more effective as a rescuer. He was credited with saving three women and half a dozen children by dragging them to safety. But he was not satisfied. He later remarked sadly that other lost children had run about "with open mouths and uplifted hands till struck down by flame . . . and I could give them no help."

The stories of many of those who ran about in a panic

127

that night are not known, because they did not survive to tell them. J. W. Filiatrault, manager of a clothing store, was an exception. He began by behaving sensibly enough. With the fire approaching, he decided to save what he could and then run for it. He tossed his trunk into a well, threw several bolts of yard goods on top of it, then began to cover the cloth with handfuls of sand. But the fire moved faster than he had expected. Turning to see it nearly upon him, he decided to cross the river to the east side of town. He got across the bridge all right and kept on running furiously, with no notion of where he was going. He continued up the street until the smoke forced him to seek shelter. He threw open the door of a house. A young man was there, standing uncertainly in the kitchen. "Water," Filiatrault demanded. The youth pointed to a table. Filiatrault grabbed a tin cup, took a hasty drink, then stood for a moment, catching his breath. The young man said not a word. The clothier suggested it would be a good idea to leave, particularly as by now the house was on fire. The young man shook his head. Filiatrault insisted. He finally persuaded his host, who led the way out the back door. This proved to be a mistake. They were forced to climb over two fences to get out of the yard. This delayed them to the point where Filiatrault felt panic rising within him again. Blinded by the smoke, he ran here and there, his hands over his face to keep his whiskers from catching fire. In the confusion, he heard a shout: "Run for the river." It was the first sensible suggestion he had heard since his flight had begun. He went stumbling off in what he hoped was the right direction. Then he heard someone splashing in the water. He followed the sound until he felt the river around his ankles.

Filiatrault had only himself to worry about, but in many of the homes there were children to try to save. A family named Dix, for example, had five, and Mrs. Dix found herself increasingly alarmed as she watched the glow of flames in the southwest. Her husband was in the woods near the village, standing guard against the fire. ·She walked over to the home

128

of a neighbor named Jacobson to ask what she should do. "There is no danger," Jacobson told her. Mrs. Dix was not entirely convinced, particularly as the smoke was so thick that she could hardly find her way back to her house again. The air was hot. She was glad to get indoors. She turned up the wick of the kerosene lamp and tried to read, but she could not concentrate on the words. Most of the family valuables had been kept in trunks for the last two weeks, ready for flight. She put aside her book and packed up the rest, growing more worried about her husband.

By now she could hear some of the neighbors going past, heading for the river. She grimly thought Dix must have been burned to death by now, so it was up to her to save the children. But then her husband arrived. He told her the fire was almost on his heels and they must make a run for it. The older of their two daughters took two of her brothers and started ahead. Mrs. Dix grabbed up the baby from his crib, wrapped a quilt around him and started off, her younger daughter following. Dix lingered to try to save what he could. The mother caught up with the other children on the bridge, which had begun to burn. The wind had blown away the baby's blanket, and he was gasping for breath. The mother and children got across the bridge somehow, then stood uncertainly, wondering which way to go. Two young men came along. "You better get away from here, Mrs. Dix," one of them said. "The mill is on fire. You'll burn up if you stay here."

She led her children out onto some logs that were below the bridge, but then she heard a shout that the fire was coming their way, so she and the youngsters scrambled back onto shore. Her husband arrived just as the wind picked up the entire family, then dropped them sprawling on the sandy ground. When Dix got his bearings again, two of the children were missing. "Where are they?" he demanded. His wife pointed to an opening between two warehouses. The buildings were on fire, but Dix ran between them, snatched up the children and got safely back to the river bank, where the family plunged into the water. Somehow, Dix had managed to hang onto his hat and he used it to dip up water to pour over his wife and children. A blanket came floating past. He fished it out of the water and wrapped it around them. The blanket's owner came wading along, looking for it. He demanded his property back. But Mrs. Dix clung to it so stubbornly that the owner finally let her keep it.

Conditions gradually improved for those in the river. It was no longer necessary to keep ducking under the surface or to splash water over their heads to keep from being burned. On his side of the stream, Father Pernin again moved cautiously toward shore. This time, he found it was safe. He seated himself on the bank, his feet dangling in the water. Then he was seized with a convulsive chill, and a young man threw a blanket over him. The crisis was finished. After five and a half hours in the river, what the priest described as "this compulsory bath" was over.

The river had not been a safe refuge for all those who reached it. Some who could not swim had ventured too far from shore. Others were knocked off their feet by floating logs and swimming cattle. But without it, it is unlikely that more than a small percentage of Peshtigo's residents would have survived.

Father Pernin recorded that it was 3:30 A.M. when he left the water. He stood by a pile of burning embers to dry his outer garments. This was accomplished readily enough, but his underwear was still wet and he found himself shivering. There seemed to be nothing to do about it—it would be unseemly for a priest to take off his underwear in public. Stretching full length on the ground, which was still hot enough to comfort him, he took off his shoes and stockings and put the soles of his feet on the hot sand. His chest ached. His throat was swollen. He could scarcely talk. He saw several men lying nearby, their bodies resting on red-hot iron hoops that were all that was left of tubs and buckets destroyed

130

in the fire. He was too exhausted to crawl over to see whether the men were dead or alive. His eyes were nearly swollen shut. He had not been conscious of the pain before, but now that the danger was over it seemed intense. Toward morning, someone suggested he move away from the river to where a group of survivors had assembled, but he could not see well enough to walk. Someone took him by the arm and led him to where the others were. It was like the gathering of survivors after a battle—some safe and uninjured, some only slightly hurt, others close to death.

One of the most severely burned was an old woman who had been afraid to go into the river for fear of drowning. She had compromised by crouching on the bank, only her legs in the water. The upper half of her body was severely burned and she lay on the ground, moaning. She asked for the priest. Father Pernin did his best to comfort her. But he was handicapped by being scarcely able to see or speak, besides feeling "so exhausted and depressed myself that it was difficult to impart courage to others." The woman soon died.

The worst of the fire was over in about an hour. In that short time, the village was wiped out. Except for a small house on the Charles Schwartz farm a little west of town, the only remnant of a structure remaining was part of the unfinished home on the east side being built for Superintendent W. A. Ellis of the Peshtigo Company. The basement had been dug and the flooring laid above it. Perhaps because the lumber was still green, this was spared. The house was completed after the fire. It still stands. It used to be occupied by one of the survivors of the 1871 disaster, Will Dolan, who enjoyed taking visitors into his basement and pointing out the charred timbers above his head.

After the danger had passed in the flats, young Fred Shepherd found the corner of a wagon box that had escaped the flames. He crawled in and fell asleep. When he awoke it was daylight. In spite of his heavy clothing, he was numb with cold. A blacksmith shop had been located nearby. It was gone now, but the stock of coal the smith had laid in for the winter was still burning. Fred headed for the fire. As he walked toward it, he could see against the eastern sky the silhouettes of a long line of refugees walking or hobbling along East Front Street toward the glow of the coal fire. Some were fairly well clothed. Others were naked except for charred tatters of clothing. A number were wearing nightgowns. They gathered in a circle around the burning coal, holding out their hands to it.

"Have you seen my wife?"

"Have you seen my husband?"

The boy listened.

"My children—have you seen them?"

"Has anyone seen my mother?"

The questions went on and on, over and over, in cracked and despairing voices. They found few answers. After a while, the boy could stand it no longer. It was still cold, standing there in the October dawn. But he walked away from the fire and those voices that were asking questions, fearing what the answers would be.

Fred's father walked through the village as soon as it was light to see what could be done. When he came back, Fred asked him, "Can I go and look?" Shepherd shook his head. "Stay here," he ordered. Later, the boy understood why he was forbidden to see what had happened to his town. Many of his playmates were lying dead in the streets.

Donald Roy McDonald, the gray-haired neighbor whose family had died in the boardinghouse where he had told them to remain, stood staring at the ground. One of the McDonald boys had been Fred's best friend. Later, when he told about that night, he could not remember the dead boy's name, except that everyone had called him "Doughnut."

A woman and two children still lay on the ground there in the flats, covered with a blanket. Long after the fire had passed and the danger was over, she kept crying out: "We're burning up. Throw water on us." No one paid any attention.

132

She kept calling, lost in the nightmare from which the others had finally awakened. "Throw water on us. We're burning up." Fred's father picked up a bucket. He filled it at the river and he walked back to empty it onto the blanket. The woman lay silent at last.

•

THIRTEEN

Not everyone who ran into the company boardinghouse that night perished. The adults—perhaps from a subconscious conviction that the company that had built most of the town would save them if they put their faith in one of its most substantial buildings—stayed there until it was too late to flee. But a twelve-year-old boy named Peter England was wiser.

Peter was one of nine children of Mr. and Mrs. William England, who had come from Massena, New York, the previous year to carve out a farm in the woods along the road that ran from Peshtigo to Oconto. One of the sons, Harvey, was married. The other children ranged in age from Parce, who was seventeen, to a baby still too young to walk. When the first glow of the flames appeared to the southwest, all the Englands except Parce fled from their log house and joined other refugees from the farming area in heading for the village two miles away. The family started out riding in a wagon drawn by oxen. But they came to a place where a tree had blown across the road, blocking the way, and were forced to abandon the wagon and continue on foot.

In the confusion they found in the village, the family

became separated. Peter, carrying five-year-old Edwin on his back, made his way across the bridge. He and his brother were barefoot. The sandy soil was hot under his feet. With his young brother still clinging to his back, Peter ran into the boardinghouse.

He must have stayed near the door, with a farm boy's shrewd understanding that a refuge sometimes turns into a trap. When the building caught fire, he ran outside—Ed was still on his back. As he ran, plaster from the doomed building fell on his bare heels.

The boardinghouse was only a short distance from the bridge. Peter scrambled down to the river and he and his brother waded into the shallows and sat there, only their heads above water, until it was safe to leave.

Meanwhile, at the farm Parce stayed in the clearing next to a barrel half full of water, holding a blanket over his head. Now and then he dunked the blanket in the water, then huddled under it again. When morning came, he started down the road toward town. It seemed to him that he was the only human left alive. His parents, his brothers and sisters could not have lived. As he came to the outskirts of the village, he saw that Peshtigo had disappeared. He walked numbly on, expecting to find nothing left of his family but their corpses.

But the Englands had survived, except for the mother, Marion, and the baby she was carrying when she became separated from the others. The bodies of the mother and child were never found—or, at least, never identified. Harvey England's young wife was also alive, but her newborn baby was dead. During the night, while the town was being destroyed about her, she had given birth to the child on the river bank.

Three or four other babies were born that night in Peshtigo, possibly more. The turmoil and panic brought on premature labor. One of the mothers was a Norwegian, unable to ask for help because she spoke no English. She is said to have died after having given birth. One account

135

indicates her baby was born in the little shanty on the Schwartz farm just west of the village that for some unaccountable reason escaped destruction. Another report indicates that it was another woman who found shelter there.

Tilton is the authority for the latter story. The woman, who lived in one of the Sugar Bush settlements, started to drive to Peshtigo with her children as the fire approached but found the road blocked by a fallen tree. Cutting one horse loose, she mounted it, ordered the children up behind her, and arrived safely at the river bank, where her child was born. Then, according to Tilton, she made her way with the newborn baby to the building on the Schwartz farm. It seems possible that both this woman and the Norwegian woman might have been given shelter there only after the fire, once it was realized that this was the one building standing in the vicinity—Ellis' uncompleted house would not have been of much use. During the disaster, few had time to worry about anyone but themselves or their families, but after the danger had passed there would have been a return to normalcy and a willingness to help a new mother find whatever refuge the stricken countryside still offered.

As we have seen, though, even during the fire some found the courage to help those weaker than themselves. Among those few was a young man named John Cox, who helped a girl, Kate Guillfoyle, find safety in the river. Even with the town burning around them, John noticed Kate was pretty, and Miss Guillfoyle felt a natural gratitude to the youth who had saved her life. It was an unlikely night for a romance to start, but start it did. Within a few weeks the couple were married.

Another young man was less successful. As he led his girl toward the river, she panicked. She broke loose from him and screaming hysterically ran back toward her home. At the top of a little rise, she stopped short. He could see her standing there, silhouetted against the flames. Then her clothing blazed up and she sank to the ground. In a few moments, she was dead.

136

A number of Peshtigo residents—sixty-eight, according to one account—fled to a corn field near the village. They stayed together there, hoping that being in the clearing would save them. The heat was so intense from the burning forest around the field that a boulder five feet high was cracked in two. All of those who sought safety there perished.

Many families, like the Englands, became separated that night. It was hours and sometimes days before survivors knew which of their relatives had lived or died. Charles Albrecht, a carpenter, was working at the harbor when the fire approached the village. His wife and two of their three children were in their house on Emery Street, west of the river. The third child, nine-year-old Louise, was staying with Mrs. Friedrich Aust, a farm woman who lived in the Lower Sugar Bush. Since her husband was away cutting hay near the harbor, Mrs. Aust had asked the Albrechts to let the girl stay with her for companionship—with all the talk of forest fires, she hadn't wanted to stay in the house alone. Trout Creek ran near the Aust farm. When the fire threatened the house, Mrs. Aust and Louise ran to the creek. It was nearly dry, but they found a place where there was a pool of water. This seemed as safe a place as any that night, but Mrs. Aust was terrified for her husband's safety. She wanted to find him and warn him of the fire. A neighbor, Job Place, came along just then. He grabbed her shoulders and held the hysterical woman in the water until the danger was past.

As his wife had feared, Aust did not survive. His death was blamed on gas that was supposed to have accompanied the flames. Aust lies buried in a small cemetery along a brook that is now called Bundy or Bunday Creek, within sight of tourists going north along United States Route 41 through Peshtigo.

Louise Albrecht's mother, although worried about her absent daughter and husband, set about saving herself and the two younger children, Mary, who was six, and Louis, a baby. By coincidence, she found refuge in the same small stream

137

that Louise was sitting in a few miles away. She and the children stood in Trout Creek, at a spot near where the Peshtigo High School is now located. The water was fairly deep there, a few hundred feet from the creek's junction with the river. Mrs. Albrecht's only mishap occurred on the way, when she tripped on a tree root and broke the heel of her shoe.

The harbor area was east of the path the fire took, so Albrecht was safe enough. As reports of what had happened to the village reached him, however, he was in despair over the probable fate of his family. He came walking up from the harbor, peering into the faces of the dead. But he was among the lucky ones, for his wife and children were safe.

Many families who lived through the fire had similar moments of agonized suspense before the members found each other again. In the cases of the Lars Hanson and August Jacobson families, who shared a double house near the river, the confusion was compounded because the Hansons and Jacobsons had not constrained themselves to family allegiances while fleeing the flames. When the danger became obvious, the two fathers and Jacobson's son, Charles, ran from house to house shouting in Swedish and Norwegian: "Fire! Gather your families and run to the river." Meanwhile, thirteen-year-old Hilma Jacobson grabbed the arm of five-year-old Aagodt Hanson and ran toward the water. Terrified and in tears, the children fell into the excavation pit on the west bank where a railroad turntable was being built. A man heard their cries, took time to help them out, and they continued to the river. Charles Jacobson and his seven-year-old brother, Gus, set off by themselves, no one knew where. Mrs. Jacobson, running along with assorted Hansons and Jacobsons, took off her gold wedding ring and tied it in a corner of a shawl. In the confusion, the shawl slipped from her hand. There was no time to stop, but even after she was in the water with the others the thought of her lost wedding ring brought tears to her eyes. When the worst of the fire was over, there was a more pressing worry than the ring—no one knew

138

the whereabouts of Charlie and Gus. With daylight, however, the boys were discovered floating on a log in the river.

A count of noses disclosed that every Hanson and Jacobson had survived. Mrs. Jacobson knew she should be thankful they were all alive after a night when so many had died. But she couldn't help regretting her decision to slip the ring from her finger and tie it in the corner of the shawl. Perhaps, she thought, the ring could still be found. The Hansons joined the Jacobsons in the search, retracing their steps as best they could, although every familiar landmark was now ashes. It was Mrs. Jacobson herself who found the shawl. The corner holding the ring was the only part of it that had not burned. She put the gold band back on her finger. Surrounded by Jacobsons and Hansons and with the ring safe, she was ready to start over again with every other possession burned to cinders.

The wife of Superintendent Ellis, writing to a friend not long after the disaster, told how she and her husband had first known something was wrong when they heard the frantic ringing of the bell in Father Pernin's church.

Ellis was a dignified-looking fellow, as befitted the chief local representative of the Peshtigo Company. At forty-three, he was nearly bald. To make up for this shortage of hair, he had a spade-shaped beard and luxuriant side whiskers. He had come to Peshtigo in 1857 to take charge of the company store and books. In 1871, he was not only the company manager and secretary but the community's postmaster. Despite all his titles and responsibilities, Ellis does not seem to have behaved any more calmly than less-important men that night—at least that is the impression his wife gave in her letter. When they rushed outside and heard "a terrible roaring, as of the rushing of mighty waters" from the southwest, he stood peering toward the sound. Little could be seen because of the smoke which made their eyes water. "What was to be done we did not know," Mrs. Ellis wrote. "We watched and soon saw a spark alight near the hen house. In a few moments a breeze

139

sprang up and a piece of fire the size of my arm dropped on the roof and fell off into great sparks. A little remained. Mr. Ellis went up and put it out. He had been down but a few moments when a terrible wind burst upon us, carrying two of those immense chimneys to the ground with a terrible crash. In a few minutes more the whole place was lighted up and then began the shower of fire and the simultaneous rush for life from every house. Mr. Ellis told us to leave the house and go somewhere."

The Ellis home, located on the river side of East Front Street near the corner of Birch, was the largest private dwelling in Peshtigo. A detailed drawing of the town completed only a few weeks before Peshtigo disappeared shows the Ellis house set back a hundred feet or more from the street, surrounded on three sides by groves of trees.

Mrs. Ellis does not make clear what her husband did after he told her to "go somewhere." it is likely that he hurried down the street to try to save the company buildings located about three blocks away. It seemed to Mrs. Ellis that the worst danger was on the opposite side of the river and that the east half of town might be saved. She sent her son, Edward, to rescue an old man named Oakes, who lived with his daughter, Nan, across the bridge.

After her son left, she went back into her house—the big house in the woods that was her pride. She picked out two of her dresses and two that belonged to her sister, hoping to save them. Then she hurried to the drawer that held her jewelry and other small treasures and took out a ring that had belonged to another sister, now dead. Before she left the doomed house, she blew out the kerosene lamps.

"I thought we would burn before we got out of the yard," she wrote. "The fire came onto us and all around us like snow. The hot sand and cinders filled our eyes and blinded us. We could scarcely keep our feet or keep from fainting. The air was so hot." Mrs. Ellis had run only a short distance before

140

the wind blew the dresses from her grasp. She went into the yard of a neighbor named Emery and crouched down. By then, houses were aflame on the east side of the river, as well as the west.

"It seemed as if everything caught at once. The fire and sand blew into our faces so that we were obliged to keep our heads covered as much as we could. We stayed there until Mr. Shepherd's house caught fire."

Like her neighbors, the Shepherds, Mrs. Ellis finally took refuge in the low-lying land along the river. Meanwhile, her son had roused Oakes and Nan. They made their way across the bridge while Edward lingered to see if a man named Bartels was all right—which member of that numerous clan is not clear. Young Ellis found Bartels in front of his house. Bartels told him he couldn't find his wife. "Ed went into the house," Mrs. Ellis continued, "and found his wife sitting on the bed, crying. He got her and the children into a buggy, told Bartels to drive across the bridge as fast as he could go. He did, and saved them."

Oakes and his daughter had reached a wooden fence near the company boardinghouse—Mrs. Ellis called it the "Big House"—and had stopped there, too exhausted to go any farther. Young Ellis, who "had all he could do to get by the Big House for fire," found the old man and Nan there. "Nan," he ordered, "you go ahead. I will take care of your father." He grabbed Oakes' hand and half led, half dragged him down to the flats. Mrs. Ellis, who had been considerably worried about her son's whereabouts, saw them coming. Oakes, she said, looked like a specter "with his white hair streaming in the wind and fire."

"I am proud of my boy for persevering that night," Mrs. Ellis wrote. "Nan says they both would have perished if it had not been for him. She had made up her mind to perish with him [her father] if no help came.

". . . What scenes of suffering were witnessed above the

bridge. Scores in the water, frightfully burned getting there, some drowning; others burning in the streets and by the warehouses, trying to get to the river.

"Mrs. Marshall lost her beautiful daughter, Nellie. What a blow to them. When they got as far as Mr. Emery's yard, they turned in there [toward the flats] and Nellie went right by. Her father went for her but went only half way to the store; had to turn back for the flames. Nellie fell but a short distance from the store. Probably in two minutes after she left her mother she was dead.

". . . I cannot describe to you that awful night. I hope no one on earth will ever witness another such scene."

By the morning of October 9, Peshtigo was a blackened waste. The iron portions of two locomotives, several brick kilns, the stone walls of the engine and boiler rooms of the woodenware factory, the blackened timbers of Ellis' new house—these were all that remained of Peshtigo, except for a few railroad-car wheels and steel train cars.

Bodies of humans and animals were lying where the fire had caught them. Men, women and children were naked, their clothing burned off. Some of the bodies, according to one witness, had "shriveled up to two-thirds their natural size." The dead were generally lying face down. The arms or legs of some had been burned off. One boy, the son of a man named Tanner, was found in a kneeling posture, his head bent down on his hands, as if in prayer.

On November 12, 1871, when Mrs. Ellis wrote her letter, she and her family were staying in Peshtigo Harbor, but she was planning to go back to Peshtigo "in a few weeks." Already, the rebuilding had begun. Ogden, who was said to have lost three million dollars worth of property in the fires at Peshtigo and Chicago, had ordered that the town be restored.

FOURTEEN

•

After it had destroyed Peshtigo, the fire roared on north. Directly in its path were the twin lumber towns of Marinette and Menominee along the Wisconsin-Michigan border. Residents there and in Menekaune, a Wisconsin community since absorbed by Marinette, had no suspicion of the horrors that had visited Peshtigo only six miles away. But the glow of the approaching flames told them that danger was heading their way.

Marinette, named for the French-Indian "queen" who had married a pioneer settler, and the smaller community of Menekaune appeared to be in the most danger. Menominee had the river for which it was named between it and the fire. If its residents had known how easily the flames had jumped across the Peshtigo River they would have realized that this barrier might not be sufficient. The force of the wind associated with the fire that night is indicated by the fact that pieces of boards identified as being from Peshtigo were later found among debris in the Menominee River, having been carried for six miles through the air.

Editor Noyes had recently bragged that "more horses and

buggies are owned and used at the mouth of the Menominee River than at any other point of its size in the west." The two communities were prosperous centers of the lumber industry. Marinette had about 2,500 residents. Menominee was roughly the same size. The river's natural channel was only four feet deep in places, but work had been begun the previous summer to deepen it to twelve feet to improve the port's competitive position in lake shipping. A narrow wooden bridge connecting the two communities had been built four years before. Despite their prosperity, neither village had a fire engine. Menominee bought one the next year, as did one of the local lumber companies, having been persuaded the night of October 8, 1871, that modern fire-fighting equipment was not a wasteful luxury.

Three steamers were in the port when the fire approached. One was the little ship that had failed to pick up Father Pernin the day before—the *George L. Dunlap*. It was owned by the North Western Railroad and shuttled back and forth between the end of the rail line at Fort Howard, Wisconsin—now part of Green Bay—and Escanaba, Michigan, with several stops along the way. The other steamboats in port that Sunday were the *Union* and the *St. Joseph*. Their presence provided a means of escape from the approaching fire. Women and children were put aboard the three vessels and were joined by a few men. The steamers headed out into Lake Michigan.

Thomas Hawley, captain of the *Union*, estimated that three hundred refugees crowded aboard his ship that night, and the other two steamers took their share. Captain Hawley allowed the *Union* to drift down the channel toward the lake, using his engines only to keep the wind from shoving the vessel against the Michigan bank of the river. The captain explained later that the channel was so narrow and crooked and the smoke so thick that he did not dare steam down it for fear it would run aground. Fires were burning on both sides of him before he reached the river mouth, but Hawley took his steamer through unscathed. He later liked to claim that the

144

trip was just as dangerous and daring as when Union gunboats had run past Rebel batteries at Vicksburg.

Once their families were safe aboard the ships, the men who remained in Marinette and Menominee prepared to do battle with the fire. As it happened, they were lucky. If the full strength of the fire that had swept through Peshtigo had roared down upon them, many of them would have died defending their towns and the lumber mills. An accident of geography saved them.

North of Peshtigo, the fire came to a line of sandy hills—hogback eskers forty or fifty feet high, left by a glacier that had drawn back ten thousand years before. The hills have since been whittled away by road builders and other users of glacial sand, but in 1871 they formed a natural barrier. It diverted the wind and forced the fire to skirt around both sides of the hills' thinly covered slopes in search of fuel. After the fire divided, the main portion swept along to the west of the hogback hills, missing most of Menominee and much of Marinette. It then continued into the sparsely populated country to the north. The lesser wing of the fire—a mighty blaze, nevertheless—went to the east of the hogbacks. It headed north toward Menekaune, which had been built around a fine new mill owned by a company called Spalding, Houghteling & Johnson.

A Menekaune druggist who doubled as a physician, J. J. Sherman, and the sawmill manager, H. P. Bird, had ridden their horses out into the woods earlier that Sunday to take a look around. For the last several weeks, a fire had been burning about two miles south of the village. They wanted to see if it was getting dangerous. They found that it had burned only a short distance along a road that ran east and west about a mile south of Menekaune—closer than the last time they looked, but not close enough to worry them. "It will take a long time to get to Menekaune at this rate," Bird said.

"It would be well to watch it, nevertheless," Doc Sherman told him.

It was agreed the druggist would stay there and keep an

145

cyc on the fire while Bird returned to the village and found another man to stand guard. After the sawmill manager left, Sherman busied himself by setting backfires along the road, hoping to create a burned-over strip between Menekaune and the fire.

Sherman continued with this task until about three o'clock, when he was joined by Charles Laughrey, proprietor of the hotel in Menekaune, and by James D. Smith and several other men who had been setting backfires to the southeast. The group talked things over and, according to Sherman's recollection later, decided that "we had got it pretty safe." They agreed to leave two men to watch the fire and put out any sparks that might blow across the road toward Menekaune. The others went home for dinner. Toward evening, Sherman persuaded Peter S. Downie and another man to go out to the road and watch the fire all night. Sherman and his family attended church for the second time on that Sunday, then returned home and went to bed. But Mrs. Sherman was too worried to sleep soundly. When the wind picked up, she shook her husband's shoulder and asked him if the fire might not overpower the guards in the woods and endanger the village.

"I being only partly awake, I told her I guessed not and again fell asleep," Sherman wrote. "But soon she aroused me again with the exclamation that the atmosphere felt hot and oppressive, and that she was going to get up, and in doing so fully aroused me and I got up, too."

Sherman and his wife peered out of the window. What they saw made them decide to get dressed. Mrs. Sherman chose her best dress. "If the town is going to burn," she told her husband, "I might as well try to save a good dress as an old one."

Sherman decided not to put on his Sunday suit, however. Expecting to have to fight fire, he dressed accordingly. "In a short time, a bright illumination sprang up in the southwest," according to his account. "The wind increased to a gale.

146

Sparks began to fall in the streets. We could see the fire approaching with the speed of a race horse."

A neighboring dwelling belonging to August Lindquist burst into flames. Sherman decided his own house was likely to catch next. He aroused his three children and the hired girl. He yelled for his stable man and ran down to the barn to harness the horses and hitch them to a wagon. While the stable man was getting the team ready, Sherman turned out the rest of his livestock—another horse, a cow, and eleven hogs.

Meanwhile, other houses had caught fire, including one belonging to a family named Briggs and a new building being constructed by a man named Archibald.

"I decided that the whole south point would burn over and that if I kept the horses trammeled with harness and wagon they would burn, too," Sherman continued. "So I stripped the harness off and let them go, having first locked the barn so they would not go back in there and burn up.

"We put what we could on my wagon and drew it away by hand; also my buggy, into which I put my medical library, and a buckboard wagon in my charge belonging to Mr. Stearns of Peshtigo. In the meantime, our hired girl and our oldest daughter, aged twelve years, and youngest, aged two, came down and asked me what they should do." Sherman ordered them to go out on the narrow wooden bridge that connected Menekaune with the Michigan shore. Meanwhile, the other child, a boy of nine, was helping his mother try to save some of their valuables.

Soon after the hired girl and Sherman's two daughters left, his house and other buildings caught fire, together with the dwellings on the street along the river bank, buildings on an offshore island, and the bridge connecting the mainland with the island. Among the burning buildings on the island were the homes of two brothers named Philbrook, their shop, stables, and shipyard, and a warehouse and docks belonging to Sherman.

Mrs. Sherman and her son, with numerous other re-

147

fugees, fled to a point of land along the river. Charles Johnson, one of Sherman's employees, hitched three wagons together with a team in front, and this makeshift caravan hauled some of the family possessions out onto the peninsula.

The sawmill foreman, Mike Curry, and a crew of his men were fighting the fire at the south end of the village. Other workmen carried furniture into the new mill's boiler house. This building was considered fireproof. Besides, it was located on an island separated from the mainland by six hundred feet of water.

The fire continued to move closer. The company's large barn caught. Then the barn and stables behind the Exchange Hotel. Curry's house went next, followed by the company store and boardinghouse and several adjacent buildings. Finally the mill itself caught fire. "The flames burst the slates from the roof and the whole magnificent structure was a mass of fire," Sherman wrote. "The solid two-feet walls of brick composing the end of the boiler house next to the mill, with its double iron doors, were no barrier. . . . The roof, composed of iron framework covered with heavy slates, melted away as though it were composed of paper. And the Menekaune mill, which had so recently cost over a hundred thousand dollars, was reckoned among the things that were."

A smaller mill on the north point was soon in flames, along with houses and other buildings near it. On the south point, several hundred persons were hemmed in by the fire, their backs to the river. But the fire veered around this somewhat dubious refuge.

Desperately worried about his two daughters, Sherman tried to go in search of them but was forced back by the heat. He waited impatiently for an hour or more, pacing nervously up and down. Then he tried again and was forced back a second time. Finally, he managed to make his way up the road that ran alongside the Wisconsin bank of the river. Most of the familiar buildings were gone, including Father Pernin's church.

148

He walked all the way to Marinette without seeing his children. Then he met a friend, Leonard Guild, who shouted to him, asking him if he knew where the Sherman girls were.

"No," Sherman told him.

"Well, I do, and they are safe. They are on Philbrook's vessel in the middle of the river. Go right back and let them know where you are, for they think you are burned."

After the hired girl had taken the two children out on the bridge, Sherman later learned, she soon decided that the wooden structure was not a safe place to wait for him. She started across the bridge, intending to take the children to their uncle's house in Menominee. But several hundred other persons were trying to cross the river. Some were in buggies or were pulling carts full of household furnishings. All was darkness and confusion, and the hired girl soon realized she could never force her way to safety. It was then she saw Philbrook's schooner and took the children there.

S. V. D. Philbrook, one of the brothers who owned the Menekaune shipyard, was a man of courage who kept his head that night. A small schooner named the *Stella* was tied up in the shipyard awaiting repairs. When the danger from the fire became obvious, several dozen Menekaune residents came running down the dusty street and jumped aboard her. Several of the men whipped out knives and started to cut the schooner loose. Philbrook ordered them to put away their knives. They ignored him. He picked up a handspike. "The first man to cut them lines gets this here spike across his head," he shouted. Since the men knew the shipyard owner as a man of his word, the pocket knives were folded and put away.

With Philbrook standing guard, the schooner stayed tied to the dock until numerous other refugees got aboard, including Sherman's daughters and a number of other women and children who had been on the nearby bridge. The fire was so close that some of the ropes had begun to smoke before Philbrook gave the order to cut the *Stella's* lines. Pushed by the same wind that was driving the fire northward, the schooner drifted out into the Menominee River where it grounded on a sandbar a safe distance from the flames.

Thanks in part to Philbrook and his handspike, not a single life was lost in Menekaune. Sherman listed the other losses: thirty-five houses, three stores, two sawmills, one planing mill, a sash, door and blind factory, two hotels, ten barns, and several cows and pigs.

Marinette, a little to the west of Menekaune, lay in an area between the two wings of the fire that had separated at the sand hills. The town's location gave its residents a ringside seat for the big disaster. One of them, A. M. Fairchild, jotted down his impressions soon after the fire:

"At about 9 o'clock a strange sound burst upon our ears, coming from the southwest. . . . At first it seemed a great way off, but gradually grew nearer and nearer until, as if by magic, a sea of flame rolled in upon us and mountains of fire rose up around us. Rushing furiously forward, the flames would leap high in air, then dive to earth again, seemingly meaning to leave nothing unscorched or living . . . here and there bursting forth and spreading as fast as eye could discern until it seemed that the whole heavens were on fire and the earth to be but a vast pit of fire wherein all must perish. How frightful, yet how grand, how indescribably grand was the sight!"

The citizens of Marinette seem to have behaved much like their neighbors in Peshtigo—most ignoring the danger until it was nearly upon them. The billiard room in the basement of the Dunlap House was busy early in the evening. The sinful were in the saloons that Sunday evening and the godly went to church. Men stood around on street corners talking, feeling no special alarm about the danger. The smoke was thick, but that was nothing new. The lumber companies ran Marinette, however, and each of them had crews standing by. Isaac Stephenson and his fellow timber-kings were preparing to save the town if the woods fires got out of

150

hand—the town, but particularly the mills which were the town's chief reason for being.

Stephenson lived on the west side of town, the part of Marinette which was in the greatest danger. When he got word that the fire was heading that way, he acted quickly. Like a feudal baron under siege, he sent bearded couriers galloping to ask for help from his fellow nobility—his brothers, Samuel and Robert, on the Michigan side of the river, A. C. Brown, part-owner and superintendent of the N. Ludington Company mill, and other mill owners. Gathering the combined crews that responded to this summons, Stephenson decided the best way to protect Marinette was to put the men to work saving his own house. It was the key to keeping the fire away from that part of town, as he saw it. Others in the neighborhood would have preferred to concentrate on saving their houses, which seemed equally valuable to them. But Stephenson was calling the signals and his house was saved.

Brown, meanwhile, was not idle. He leaped upon his horse and rode around like a general, directing men and teams. A. M. Fairchild, full of admiration for the mill superintendent, testified that Brown's voice "could be heard loud above the roar of the fiery tempest, telling men what to do and how to do it."

Thanks more to the fact that Marinette was not in the main pathway of the fire than to the efforts of its defenders, the village escaped with the loss of fourteen buildings. Among them were the sash, door, and blind factory of Bagley & Curry and a mill and boardinghouse belonging to a man named McCartney.

The river mouth was perhaps a thousand feet wide, but sparks from the Spalding mill in Menekaune blew across the water and caught what was known as the Gilmore mill on the Michigan side of the stream. Farther up the river, where the westward wing of the fire was pushing northward, a large wooden dam burned to the water's edge. The fire then roared on up the river valley for about twenty miles, killing several

151

persons and burning a mill owned by T. Cole & Company, five miles north of Menominee. This mill was located in the middle of a large clearing, but the heat was so great that the wooden structure caught fire and panes of glass, stored on the open ground, were melted. The workmen jumped into a pond and were saved.

Settlements were scarce on the Upper Michigan peninsula north of Menominee, but the easterly wing of the fire managed to find one at Birch Creek, which consisted of twenty homestead farms and perhaps one hundred residents, mostly recent immigrants from Germany. It was around midnight when the families there awoke to find the forest ablaze around them.

Phineas Eames, one of the Birch Creek farmers, had noticed that the smoke was increasing toward evening, but he, too, was so accustomed to such things that he gave the matter little thought. His house was in a twelve-acre clearing. Even if the woods should burn, he believed he would be safe. He sent his wife and children to bed and lay down on a lounge in another room, planning to keep an eye on things.

Shortly before ten, he roused himself and walked outside his cabin. There was no wind. The smoke was even heavier than before. It made him uneasy, but he decided not to alarm his family. He lay down again, but did not sleep. He heard the clock strike eleven. By that hour, the fire had destroyed Peshtigo and much of Menekaune and its eastern portion was moving up the peninsula toward him and his neighbors. Looking out of the window, Eames saw a group of people moving across the clearing, carrying a lantern. He woke up his family and told them to get dressed. The visitors turned out to be a family named Blauvett, who had decided Eames' house would be safer than theirs because it was in a larger clearing. The women and children from the two families waited inside the cabin. The men walked outside to stand guard. Several weeks later, Eames set down an account of what happened next: "All at once I saw a bright light

152

approaching. In size [it was as] large as a half-bushel measure, and as it came toward us it appeared like a ball of fire, approaching from the southeast. I saw it pass directly over my house to the northwest, just high enough to clear the house. The night being so very dark, as it passed over it dazzled our eyes. I watched it out of sight. All in the house saw the same light . . . from the windows. Next we heard a tremendous explosion. . . . The ground shook and trembled beneath our feet."

Then they heard a low rumble and the wind began to increase. The air became warmer, with now and then a puff of wind that was uncomfortably hot. "Suddenly," his account continued, "my house took fire overhead. . . . As I looked, my large barn was also on fire, the fire crawling along like a snake, on top of the barn, on top of the house, in the tops of the trees . . . and yet no fire on the ground."

There was a ridge west of the house. Exactly why the men decided to head for it is not clear from Eames' story. It is possible that there were fewer trees there or that they had some notion of getting above the fire. At any rate, Blauvett and his family ran on ahead. Mrs. Eames was carrying the youngest of their three daughters, who was still a baby. She suddenly stopped part way across the clearing and told her husband that their young son, Lincoln, had been left behind in the house. Eames ordered her to go on and he ran back to the cabin. Making a rapid search of the rooms with the building on fire around him, he found no sign of the boy. When he ran outside again, his wife was standing where he had left her. He took the baby from her. Just then, Lincoln came running up. "Papa, I'll be burned up. What shall I do?" Eames told the boy to hold tight to his hand. He ordered his wife to take hold of the collar of his vest so they would not become separated. They hurried along toward the ridge. "The heavens seemed one vast wave of fire," he said, and he could see as well as if it had been noon instead of midnight. The wind was blowing hard enough so that tall pines bent before it.

153

A few yards before they reached the top of the ridge, Lincoln let go of his father's hand and bounded away toward his sisters, who had gone on ahead with the neighbor family. At that moment, Eames said, there came "a wave of living fire, completely enveloping us in its embrace." He fell to the ground. His wife fell across his feet. All three of them — the parents and the baby — were on fire. In agony, Eames let go of the child and drew his feet from under his wife's body. He prayed for death. But he soon was able to climb to his feet, and he staggered forward a few steps, stopping when he nearly stumbled over the body of a child. It was burned beyond recognition. He supposed it was Lincoln. He could hardly see by now, for the smoke was thick and his eyes were painfully burned. He groped his way forward, calling out. His oldest daughter came to him. She told him her sister, Mary, was alive and led him to where the younger daughter was huddled on the ground with Mrs. Blauvett and two of the Blauvett children. Blauvett was gone with the rest of his family, no one knew where. Eames told everyone to lie down on their faces, hoping the air would be better next to the ground.

When the firestorm had swept over them, Eames found that the two pairs of trousers he had been wearing were burned completely off and the leather of his boots was "burned to a crisp on my roasted feet." The other five who remained alive of the two families — Eames' two daughters, Mrs. Blauvett, and two of her children — were also nearly naked and all were in agonizing pain. Eames was "fearfully burned from the top of my head down to the soles of my feet."

The body Eames had supposed was Lincoln's was one of the Blauvett boys. Lincoln was dead, but he seemed to have been untouched by the flames. Mrs. Eames and the baby were also recognizable — their faces had not been burned, but their bodies were charred.

Eames realized there was no use waiting there for help, which might not come for days. Menominee was seven miles away, but the group started toward it. Large trees had blown down across the road, making it nearly impassable. They walked for five miles before coming to a house that had not burned. It belonged to Judge Ingalls, but the judge wasn't there. His caretaker, "an old Frenchman," took them in and got word to Sherman, the Menekaune druggist and physician, who rode out to give them first aid. Sherman put Eames to bed until morning, when a team was sent out from Menominee to carry the six injured Birch Creek survivors the final two miles to an improvised hospital.

In all, twenty-two persons out of the population of one hundred died at Birch Creek the night of the fire. Twenty of the dead were residents of the settlement. Two were traveling salesmen who had the bad luck to have chosen this remote spot to spend the night.

So far as is known, the Birch Creek casualties were the Peshtigo fire's last human victims, although its eastern wing continued for another fourteen miles along the creek. The rains of October 9 finally extinguished it.

FIFTEEN

•

The Chicago fire and the two-armed holocaust that burned its way up the two sides of the Green Bay were not the only major disasters to occur in the upper Middlewest on October 8, 1871. A series of forest fires on the lower peninsula of Michigan devastated an estimated two million acres of timber, ruined several lumber towns, and sent lumberjacks and homesteaders fleeing for their lives. These fires had no direct connection with the fires in Wisconsin, but the same conditions were responsible: drought, human carelessness and a change in the wind.

What the settlers called "pasture-maker" fires had been set as usual that summer in the Michigan woods, as in Wisconsin, clearing the land for farming by burning the trees and underbrush. In spite of the drought, some settlers went ahead and set their pasture-makers, which often got out of hand. As in Wisconsin, the danger of these fires spreading was obvious that fall. Residents of the little sawmill towns turned out periodically to fight them. When a strong southerly wind started up that Sunday in 1871, settlements along both the

156

Lake Michigan and the Lake Huron sides of the state were wiped out.

The Michigan fires began to spread several hours earlier than those in Wisconsin. It was 3 P.M. when fire emerged from the woods near Holland City, a Dutch settlement near the east shore of Lake Michigan across the lake from Milwaukee. Holland had about three thousand residents. It had been settled twenty-five years before by a Protestant religious sect led by the Reverend A. C. Van Raalte. The Dutchmen had strict rules about such things as keeping the Sabbath, but they worked hard the other six days of the week. In a quarter of a century, they transformed the wilderness settlement into a thriving community. Once the Dutch had the town built, they were joined by numerous outsiders who wanted Holland to resemble every other Michigan hamlet, and who rather looked down on the settlers from Europe.

When the forest fire threatened to wipe out the town, a resident named George Howard tried to organize a fire-fighting crew. He claimed later that when he handed spades to fourteen Hollanders and told them to throw sand on the fire, they refused. It was the Sabbath. And so they stood by, free from sin, according to Howard, while the fire ate its way into the community. By nightfall, Holland's women and children were evacuated aboard a train for Grand Haven. One aged widow was overlooked and died when her burning house caved in. By daylight, according to one local citizen, "not a hitching post remained." This was an exaggeration. About a third of the homes were still standing. But the fire did destroy 73 business places and 243 houses.

Among them was the expensive home of M. D. Howard, which was filled with elegant furniture and contained a grand piano that was the family's pride. When it became obvious that the house was doomed, Howard sent his wife and children outside. Then he walked through the house, visiting each room, bidding his home good-bye. Just before the building caught fire, Howard took a final look around, squared his shoulders, and walked out the front door for the last time. "Come," he told his wife, and they and the children stepped off down the street, meeting their disaster with dignity. Howard took his family aboard a lake tug.

One hundred fifty miles to the north, the lumberjacks at Manistee had to postpone plans for their customary Sunday spree. Another of the series of fires that were destroying vast quantities of Michigan timber came toward the town from the south. The shanty boys were joined by clerks from the stores, saloon keepers, and other townsfolk and did their best to save the town. With nothing but shovels and buckets of water to fight a forest fire, they were only partially successful. Part of the village was saved, but more than two hundred homes were burned.

Lansing, the state capital, was also threatened by woods fires, fanned by the brisk southerly wind. Students at the State College of Agriculture hurried to the rescue. With faculty members joining them, they were divided into squads, so that when one group of boys was too weary it could rest for a while and a fresh batch of students was ready to take its place. By keeping up a constant battle with the flames from Sunday until Monday night, the students and the townsfolk who came to help them were able to save Lansing.

The hero of a backwoods settlement in Central Michigan's Gratiot County was a bearded Englishman named Jacob Laird, who had been in the Union army. Determined to save the small sawmill owned by Case & Turner, he ordered a series of shallow wells dug around it and placed barrels filled with water between them. Wetting down the mill roof as the fire approached, he lifted up his voice in defiance. "Come ahead," he yelled. "I'm ready." The flames took up the challenge. As the fire roared out of the woods toward the mill, everyone but Laird fled. He stayed on, working like a madman, fighting the blaze with water and shovelsful of dirt, pausing only long enough to curse the fire and defy it to try to get him.

158

The hair was burned from the man's head, his beard and eyebrows were singed, his woolen shirt was scorched. But he won. Thanks to his stubborn efforts—or perhaps to a lucky shift in the wind—he saved the mill. His employers were properly grateful. They not only doubled his wages but bought him a new suit of clothes.

The Reverend E. J. Goodspeed, a minister who compiled a history of the fires of October 8, liked to sermonize in later years about what happened to another defiant backwoodsman, a blasphemous sawmill operator in the western Michigan woods. The fellow was a rough and wicked man of large frame and generous impulses, to hear the reverend tell it. When fire came close to his mill, he and his two brothers did their best to fight it off. Finally they saw it was no use. The mill operator ripped off a few hearty oaths and told his brothers to go home. "Nothing more can be done," he shouted. "God can do as he damned well pleases."

It might have made a better text for a sermon if lightning had struck the wicked fellow down. Instead, it began to rain. First a few drops, then a downpour. Goodspeed enjoyed describing what happened next—how the contrite sinner dropped to his knees there in the mud, tears mingling with the rain on his weatherbeaten face, and tried to express his thanks for the miraculous rescue of his mill. But it had been a long time since he'd done any praying. The words wouldn't come. He sprang to his feet. He waved his hat. He gave a mighty shout: "Hurrah for God! Hurrah for God!"

The rain that the reverend's favorite sinner called down from heaven was not reported elsewhere, at least not in time to save such flourishing Michigan villages as Forester, Richmondville, Forestville, White Rock, Elm Creek, Sand Beach, and Huron City.

A revenue cutter, the *Fessenden*, picked up a sailboat on Lake Huron containing Isaac Green, described as the principal owner of Forestville, together with his family and about twenty others. The *Fessenden* brought them to shore, then

159

went hunting for other refugees. It picked up seventeen along the lake shore. By the time the little ship returned to Port Huron, two of the seventeen had died of their burns.

At Huron City, a Huron County community, R. B. Hubbard watched the fire approaching and despaired of saving his livestock. He loaded his gun, filled his pockets with extra shells, and walked to his barn. Then he shot the horses and cows one by one to save them from suffering.

Huron County occupies the tip of a peninsula between Saginaw Bay and Lake Huron. It was a lumbering area. Its small communities were mostly located near the lake shore. At one of them, White Rock, the residents put up a stout fight against the fire but finally were forced to flee. Most of them tried to find safety in the clearings at first, but when the fire became too hot there they took to the lake. A Detroit visitor named Brady later said he had stayed in the cold water for eight hours, lying part of the time on a log with the waves breaking over it. "About him were men up to their waists in water and holding children in their arms, women but poorly protected by their clothing from the chill of the water, which was their only security against the burning heat," according to a contemporary account. "The inhabitants, of course, saved almost nothing. Not only were their houses, fences, barns and stock destroyed, but their furniture and clothing and even the deeds by which they held their farms, and their insurance papers."

Once the fire had subsided, the White Rock refugees emerged from the lake to face another problem—there was no food or shelter within miles. They remained along the shore until Monday afternoon, when a steamer named the *Huron* arrived and took them aboard. The *Huron* continued down the shore to pick up more refugees at Forestville and Cato. There were too many for the little ship. It left some behind and hurried to Port Huron to deposit its human cargo, then returned for the others.

Inland residents of the area were in even greater danger.

160

John Kent, for example, lived with his wife and two young daughters, one of them less than a year old, on a farm near Forestville in Huron County, about five miles from the lake. The smoke had been thick for weeks. On some farms, chickens sickened and died from it. But Kent stayed with his family on his homestead, believing he might save it, since the house was in the middle of a considerable clearing. He filled barrels, tubs, crocks, and anything else that would hold water. He placed the containers around the outside of the house, ready to extinguish any sparks or embers that blew his way from the burning forest.

The first to leave the household was the cat, who stalked off into the woods. The dog left two days later. Kent considered this an ill omen, but he refused to follow the animals' example.

The fire appeared on the outskirts of the farm about noon of October 8. Kent and his wife hurried off to try to beat back the flames. They were so busy dealing with the fire in the woods that they failed to notice another blaze which crept across the field behind them. Then they heard a scream from one of the two little girls left behind in the house. The parents started back, but the smoke was so thick they could not find the cabin. Frantically, they stumbled around, as in a nightmare, the frightened screams of the children they loved sounding in their ears. They were in the farmyard that each know so well, but their eyes and lungs were filled with smoke, the landmarks were all hidden, and in their haste to reach the trapped children they became increasingly confused, running now this way, now that. It was not until they heard the crash as the roof fell into the burning dwelling and stifled the girls' screams that they knew where the house had been.

Some days later, Kent talked to a Detroit reporter. "I tell you, mister," he said, "it made us crazy. The fire was all around us except to the west—house gone, barn burning, hay and everything destroyed. There was only one thing to do. I got hold of Mary and plunged through the fire and smoke

161

until we got to the Lake Road, and then we had hard work to keep ahead of the fire before reaching the water.

"It was awful, sir, to hear that screaming from those burning children. And it was dreadful to go away and leave them roasting there."

The lake ships pulled in at every little village that had landing facilities. At each there were refugees waiting. At Forester, a Sanilac County community on Lake Huron, the *Marine City* took aboard a man who asked for a ride as far as Lexington, where he hoped to get provisions for twenty-five families. He had walked from a house where they had taken refuge six miles away. The house was the only one still standing in the vicinity, he said, and he was the only man among the twenty-five families who was able to go for help. The others were suffering from fire blindness, burns, or exhaustion. There were two days' rations in the house.

Some of those who fled from the fire took to the lake in smaller boats. One such party consisted of nine children and two adults from Rock Falls, a small settlement on Lake Huron. There was a strong offshore breeze. The boat's owner was unable to bring it back to land. For three days it drifted, the waves breaking over the sides. No one had thought to bring along anything for bailing out the water, but a man's boot and a woman's shoe were used, and the craft was kept afloat. One child died from exposure before the boat drifted to the Canadian shore near Kincardine, Ontario.

In a small community in west central Michigan with the grand name of Paris, about twenty refugees were able to survive the flames and heat by lying down in a roadside ditch. Among them was a grandmother with her three-month-old grandchild. The baby's mother, a Mrs. Seymour, had become separated from the child. After the fire was over, the baby gave unmistakeable evidence of being hungry. None of the women who had fled to the ditch was prepared to take the mother's place, but one of them managed to catch a cow that had survived the fire. Someone found a tin pan and the cow

162

was milked. But the wind was still blowing hard and the air was so full of sand, cinders, and ashes that the pan of milk was not fit for a baby. The women sat on the edge of the ditch and debated what to do. Finally one of them hit upon a solution. She took a mouthful of the vile-looking mixture in the pan, put her mouth to the baby's and filtered out the sand and ashes through her teeth as she fed the child in what the chronicler described as an "original manner."

From the standpoint of timber ruined, the fires in Michigan that Sunday were among history's most destructive. The death toll there, however, was surprisingly light. No one knows the exact number—a settler on a lonely farm, a trapper or "land looker" in a wilderness camp might burn to death with no one ever likely to add his name to the casualty list. The total accepted as official in Lansing was ten deaths, but this is obviously far too low. A better guess would be that from one to two hundred died in the Michigan fires.

William A. Howard, writing to Alexander H. Rice of Boston to appeal for help for the fire victims, estimated that fifty bodies had been found near the eastern shoreline of Michigan, and he believed that a considerable number of others had died without their bodies being found. He made no estimate of the toll on the western side of the state or in the central part.

The area burned followed the Lake Huron shoreline from near Port Huron on the Canadian border to the Saginaw Bay, extending back into the countryside for a considerable distance. On the west, the fire that had ruined Holland and other woods fires along the Lake Michigan shore extended for one hundred ten miles to the north of the Dutch settlement.

A committee appointed by Governor Henry P. Baldwin for the relief of the eastern shore reported that twenty-three townships had been entirely or nearly burned over, with another eighteen townships partially destroyed. The blackened area on that side of the state included fourteen thousand square miles, according to the committee. In some places, it

163

reported, boats trying to rescue residents of shore communities had to wait for nearly two days before the smoke lifted enough for them to dock. The committee told Governor Baldwin that from three to four thousand survivors in the region near Lake Huron were left destitute.

In later years, survivors of the Peshtigo fire often complained that the Chicago fire on the same day got all the publicity but the several forest fires in Michigan were even less known to the rest of the world.

Extensive as it was, the Michigan burn was much less deadly than its counterpart in Wisconsin's north country. The fact that the Michigan fires got out of hand in the afternoon while those in Wisconsin became dangerous after dark probably helps explain why casualties were much lighter in Michigan. Fires in the Wisconsin communities came when many families were in bed and when weekend revelers were often too drunk to make clear-headed decisions. The darkness added to the confusion and terror. A man who has awakened to the realization that his town is burning around him is less able to meet the crisis than one who has to face a similar danger at noon when he has full possession of his faculties.

SIXTEEN

●

In Peshtigo before dawn the morning after the fire, John Mulligan found a blanket to replace the nightgown that had been burned off his wife's back. Then he set off on foot to Marinette. He sought out Isaac Stephenson.

"Can you get us something for the folks in Peshtigo to eat?"

The lumber baron was exhausted from a night spent helping to keep the fire from destroying Marinette. He looked at the muscular boss of the railroad crew in surprise.

"Why, what is the matter at Peshtigo?" he asked.

"My God! Don't you know? Not a stick of the village is standing."

Anton Place, the Marinette meat market proprietor, who had chosen October 8 to haul a load of grain to Peshtigo, returned to where he'd left his wagon. The wagon was nothing but ashes and a few scorched bits of metal, but Place found one of his horses. He and the boy who had shared his adventures climbed on its back and rode through the devastated countryside to Marinette, arriving about the same time as Mulligan. Place shouted to the men standing in front of the

Dunlap House that Peshtigo was wiped out and its survivors needed help.

Once Marinette residents were convinced that their own losses were minor compared to those a few miles to the south, they reacted promptly. Ike Stephenson dashed off messages to the governor and to the mayors of several Wisconsin cities, asking for help. He entrusted them to Captain Hawley, who agreed to send them as soon as he could get to a telegraph office. The nearest one still operating was at Green Bay, and the captain had to finish unloading the refugees still aboard his ship before he could set sail. By the time the *Union* was empty of its overnight passengers, survivors from Peshtigo were beginning to straggle into Marinette and Menominee. Some were anxious to take passage to Green Bay—or almost anywhere away from Peshtigo. Captain Hawley took them aboard, including a number of the injured, then pointed the prow of the *Union* toward Lake Michigan. His steamer groped its way down the river through smoke still so thick that two men had been stationed on the dock to drop a heavy plank whenever a ship approached so its captain would know he was close to the landing.

Stephenson knew it would be some time before help could be expected from the outside world, and he had no notion of waiting. He sent Mulligan across the river to Menominee to tell his brothers, Robert and Samuel Stephenson, to send men, teams and supplies to Peshtigo. Robert was an owner of the Ludington, Wells & Van Schaick Company, and Samuel was co-owner and manager of another lumber mill, the Kirby Carpenter Company. Ike Stephenson helped arrange to have the Dunlap House converted into a temporary hospital before he set off for Peshtigo to see the disaster for himself.

It was Monday evening before Captain Hawley and the *Union* got to Green Bay to send the telegrams to Governor Lucius Fairchild and the mayors of Milwaukee, Oshkosh, and Fond du Lac. He brought Green Bay and the rest of the state the first definite news of what had happened in Peshtigo twenty-four hours before, although rumors had been circulating. Beginning with George Watson, refugees from the region east of the bay had been arriving in the city with reports of widespread havoc on the Kewaunee-Door County peninsula. It was also known in Green Bay that some sort of extensive fire had taken place on the west side of the bay, and there were reported to be numerous casualties there. But such newspapermen as Tilton were aware of the rule of thumb that early estimates should be cut in half to allow for normal exaggeration. It was not until several days had elapsed that he and other Green Bay residents realized that the first reports had only hinted at the unprecedented proportions of the disaster.

Before Captain Hawley's arrival, Green Bay citizens had been more interested in reports from Chicago than in the talk about fires on their own doorstep. The telegraph line linking the city with the south brought word of the disaster two hundred miles away before details of the far more deadly fire nearby were available. "Chicago was the pride of the west," Tilton wrote. "It was typical of western enterprise and energy, and it was a sad day indeed when its magnificent marble buildings and its millions of wealth melted away as the frost-work on the window panes. All business was comparatively forgotten here [Green Bay] and no one cared to hear aught but the news of the fires. The telegraph was monopolized by its recital and the presses of the city were taxed to their utmost in printing extras containing the fearful news. Our own kindred calamity made us feel more deeply the sufferings of our Chicago neighbors."

Even after Captain Hawley arrived, there was no realization in Green Bay of the extent of the disaster at Peshtigo. The captain's estimate of the death toll there was fifty or sixty, and those of the survivors he brought with him were not much more accurate. Actually, the fires on both sides of the Green Bay killed at least twelve hundred persons. The Chicago fire, which remains far better known than the north country

167

disaster of the same day, caused about two hundred fifty deaths — about one-fifth as many.

The Wisconsin fires that together are called the "Peshtigo fire" set a mark that has not been equalled by any such disaster in North America. The Peshtigo fire killed twice as many persons as the Iroquois Theater fire and panic of December 30, 1903, in Chicago. Its toll far exceeded that of the 1942 Cocoanut Grove fire in Boston and the 1944 circus fire in Hartford, Connecticut. Its closest rival is the fire which broke out in 1904 on the excursion steamer *General Slocum* that was carrying Sunday-school children up New York's East River. One thousand thirty persons were killed.

The exact number of dead in the Peshtigo fire is not known. A relief official, Colonel J. H. Leavenworth, spent nearly three months trying to compile a list of its victims, then gave up the task as impossible. The late Stewart Holbrook made an educated guess at the total, based on research for his book, *Burning an Empire* (Macmillan, 1943). His estimate was 1152, on the assumption that 600 died in Peshtigo, 255 in the three Sugar Bush settlements, 75 in the Kewaunee County and Door County communities, 22 at Birch Creek, and 200 in the isolated cabins, logging camps, trappers' huts, and other places remote from official statisticians. This is a good, conservative guess. It may be somewhat low, but it is probably closer to the actual total than the estimate of 1500 dead which is used by most current reference works. It seems likely that the 75 deaths Holbrook allotted to the peninsula settlements were only half of the actual total there — Williamsonville alone accounted for nearly 60. The other totals seem close to the mark, although they may err on the side of conservatism.

Walter Heath, a Peshtigo hotel man who had jumped from the burning bridge and swum to safety, said a few weeks after his escape that 752 bodies had been buried in the Peshtigo vicinity and many other victims had been entirely burned up so that there was nothing left of them to bury. "The

168

names of half the dead will never be known," Heath told a visitor. "They are buried all over Peshtigo. The boards that mark their graves are marked 'two unknown,' 'three unknown' and so on."

Heath's estimate for the Sugar Bushes and Peshtigo was 1000 dead. It was only a guess. In the case of many transients—lumberjacks and others—there was no way of telling whether they had died or had simply drifted off to a safer part of the vast forest.

It is probable, in fact, that the total number of dead in the Peshtigo fire, including those killed on both sides of the bay, was between 1200 and 1300 and that another 100 or 200 were killed the same day in the similar forest fires in Michigan.

Father Pernin had begun to recover his old spirit by the time the first reports of the extent of the devastation were brought to those still huddled on the river banks. He suggested there was a ready-made refuge at Marinette, where he had a new church, presbytery and schoolhouse.

Monday morning, a large tent was erected to shelter the women and children and those men who were most severely injured. Father Pernin believed it was supplied by the Peshtigo Company, but other accounts indicate that the Marinette and Menominee mill workers sent by the Stephenson brothers had brought it. At any rate, as soon as the tent was up one of the priest's friends suggested he go into it. He did so, stretching out on the bare ground in one corner. He testified later that he had tried to take up as little space as possible, but the man in charge of the tent ordered him out, "accompanying the rude command with a perfect torrent of insulting words and blasphemies."

The priest did not have the strength to argue. He simply rolled himself over, passing under the edge of the tent, and was outside again. Months later, however, he was still indignant. His evictor had a coarse and brutal nature, he declared, and seemed "inaccessible to every kindly feeling,

169

though he manifested a remarkable interest in the welfare of the ladies and would allow none but them under his tent."

First had come the fire, then the chill; now there was hunger. What Pernin wanted most was a cup of hot coffee or tea. He had to settle for cold cabbage, the only edible food that could be found. This indicates that the first among those who had come from Marinette to help had not thought to bring along food. About one o'clock Monday afternoon, however, several wagons did arrive with provisions, including coffee. The priest recognized one of the drivers as a parishioner. He asked him how Marinette had fared.

"Thank God, Father, no one perished, although all were dreadfully alarmed. We have had many houses burned. All the mills and houses from our church down to the bay have gone."

"And the church?"

"It is gone."

"The presbytery?"

"Burned."

"The new schoolhouse?"

"Burned, also."

And so Pernin knew then that he had lost two churches instead of one, as well as two houses and a school. His plan to use the buildings at Marinette to shelter some of the Peshtigo survivors had to be abandoned. One of his Marinette parishoners invited him to stay at his home, so along with others who felt able to travel, the priest climbed aboard one of the wagons as it headed northeast.

Most of the early relief for Peshtigo came from nearby towns. Railroad and logging crews that had escaped the fire walked across the stricken countryside to do what they could to help. They found that of the two thousand persons who had been in Peshtigo the night before, no more than seven hundred remained. Hundreds were dead. Others had reached safety near the bay. As Monday wore on, half-naked strag-

170

glers, their hands and faces blackened from crawling over charred logs, returned to find their town had disappeared. Some survivors who had fled before or just after the fire never came back. Many, however, spent Monday walking sadly around Peshtigo, peering into fire-blackened faces. Some bodies had no mark of injury on them, but most were horribly burned and many of the dead were unrecognizable. Some had disappeared, except for a few ashes that the wind soon dispersed.

Some survivors remembered seeing the bodies of several Swedish workmen who had fallen next to the ditch they had been digging to keep the fire at bay. But when a burial detail went to the ditch to find the workmen, nothing was left there but ashes and the metal from their axes and shovels. The fire that had killed them had apparently returned later in the evening to cremate their remains.

"The ravages of the one night's tornado left unmistakable traces on every hand," wrote a visitor who traveled to Peshtigo a few days after the fire. "Through the solid growth of timber a clean swath of blackened stumps and roots marked the course of the fiery tempests. The roads were cumbered with roasted cattle and frequently with the carcasses of bears and deer, while the ditches and cleared fields were strewn with smaller game and wild birds."

He had come along the road from Marinette that connected the two communities. "Nearing the vicinity," he continued, "sadder relics were found, for those who penetrated eastward through the wall of flame met equally fierce flames in the clearest places. Remote dwellers on the high roads . . . with their families safely packed on their great farm wagons made northward through the highways for security. But the flames engulfed them in the heart of the woods and the fragments of stout vehicles, burned to the irons, now strew the road hither from Marinette, the last town on the northern Wisconsin border.

"The high road enters Peshtigo from the north through a

171

break in the encircling belt of woods, where the pretty Episcopal [actually, the Congregational] Church stood—the last to burn in that fatal place. Even before this was reached, a putrid hecatomb of dead cattle cumbered the wooded street.

"Among the pines, scores lay—not burnt, but smothered to death. Through this underbrush, thirty bodies of men and children were picked up, more or less injured by fire. In a great many instances the human remains were distinguished from animals by the teeth alone. One horror-stricken relative recognized the relics of his nephew by a penknife imbedded in an oblong mound of ashes.

". . . With one of the men who passed through that night of destruction, I wandered over the pretty, rising plain where Peshtigo had spread its thriving stores and handsome houses. Save where the houses were built with cellars, which was very rare, there is no trace of former habitation. Here and there are metallic remnants of sewing machines and cracked stoves. The hardware and drug stores leave almost the only reminders of things that were—a blackened mortar stands idly in a wild confusion of melted glass and lead, with the pestle ready for a new decoction.

"Two or three men with troubled faces were moving about, putting up a shed for the relief committee. They answered civilly and sadly that they had been in the fire, but saved themselves and nearest kin. They should have starved to death if the outside world had not stepped in, and now hoped to be shortly on their feet again.

"They despaired of the bright, cheery little town ever being as it was but complacently 'reckoned' if the scared ones didn't drive newcomers away with their silly stories, a new people would make a new Peshtigo.

"If you ever walked over the ground where a camp had been burned—and there are few that served during the war that have not—you found there as much semblance of a substantial city as now marks the spot where Peshtigo's two thousand people carried on the business of life a few days ago.

172

On the bank of the river, fish killed by the lusting flame are still to be seen. . . . Crossing the frail remnants of the bridge on timbers charred and fragile, my neighbor said:

"'It was as like the Judgment Day as I can imagine. Friend Hansen, with his wife and four children, believed firmly that it was. And while the fire rained down, he began to walk composedly up and down his parlor with his family about him, and I have never seen him since.'"

Another man who visited the scene said it was hard to explain to anyone who had not been there how intense the heat had been. He compared it to the flame concentrated on an object by a blow pipe, but said even that would not explain some of the phenomena.

"For instance, we have in our possession a copper cent, taken from the pocket of a dead man in the Peshtigo Sugar Bush, which will illustrate our point. This cent has been partially fused, but still retains its round form and the inscription upon it is legible. Others in the same pocket were found partially melted, and yet the clothing and the body of the man were not even singed. We do not know how to account for this unless, as is asserted by some, the tornado and fire were accompanied by electrical phenomena.

"The house, barn and fences of Mr. [L. H.] Hill of the Upper Sugar Bush were burned and Mr. Hill and his family all lost. By the side of the family was a narrow alley, just wide enough to drive through. In this alley stood a wagon, and while the barn and fence were entirely destroyed, the wagon box was not even singed.

"Alf Phillip's house in the Upper Sugar Bush was destroyed, but the family escaped. They state that two opposite currents of air apparently struck the house, which was sixteen by twenty-four feet, and carried it bodily into the air—they think about one hundred feet. In the air, it burst into flames and in a few minutes was entirely destroyed. The house was not on fire when it left the ground."

Survival sometimes seemed to have been mainly a matter

of chance. The fire might spare one cowering group of refugees while every member of another group a short distance away was burned to death. It was Father Pernin's theory that a "torrent of fire passed at a certain height from the earth, touching only the most elevated portions" so that "no one could meet it standing erect without paying the penalty of almost instantaneous death." This generality was not always accurate. Some of those who hugged the ground, burying their faces in the dirt and digging their fingernails into the sandy soil in terror, died as quickly as those who stayed on their feet and ran until the fire brought them low.

A Menekaune man named J. Harris, described as "chief messenger of the [Wisconsin] house of representatives," made an inspection of some of the burned-over region and reached his own conclusions as to why so many persons had perished in the Sugar Bush settlements. He unrolled a map and pointed out that many of the deaths occurred in densely wooded areas from three to five miles from the nearest place of refuge, the Peshtigo River.

"The fiery tornado came upon these people with such fury and so suddenly that there was no escape," Harris said, "and this fact accounts for so many families being swept away." Harris concluded that "the wonder is that so many escaped alive, and many of those who did escape were saved by throwing dirt on each other to keep from burning."

Among the numerous descriptions of what Peshtigo was like after the fire is one from James Monahan, a Peshtigo Company mill worker, who had lived with his wife at Johnson's boardinghouse on the west side of town. Like so many others, they saved themselves in the river. A few days later, he told of what he saw when daylight came on October 9: "Here and there over this great field of ashes lay the blackened corpses of the dead and the carcasses of animals. The stench rising that morning was so powerful that we could not bear it. The smell of burned flesh was so sickening that many of the women, after escaping from the river, fainted."

174

Survivors were astonished at how little was left of some of the victims. At one place, it was said, three adults produced among them only enough ashes to fill a two-quart measure. All that was left to show where one boy died was a slate pencil, a pocketknife, a few teeth and bone fragments—"all of which," it was noted, "could be held in the palm of the hand."

On Tuesday evening, October 10, Father Pernin felt well enough to go back to Peshtigo. He took passage on a steamboat that pulled into the harbor landing the following morning. He visited injured survivors who had been given shelter there, then climbed aboard a railroad car which was taking a party of men to Peshtigo to continue burying the dead. The company's two locomotives had been destroyed by the fire, so the car was pulled by horses. The improvised train had to stop some distance from the village because the tracks had been destroyed beyond that point. The group continued on foot.

When Father Pernin reached Peshtigo, he looked about him. Nothing remained of the houses, trees and fences except a few blackened posts.

"Wherever the foot chanced to fall, it rested on ashes," he wrote. "The iron tracks of the railroad had been twisted and curved into all sorts of shapes, while the wood that had supported them no longer existed. The trunks of mighty trees had been reduced to mere cinders, the blackened hearts alone remaining.

"All around these trunks, I perceived a number of holes running downwards deep in the earth. They were the places where the roots had lately been. I plunged my cane into one of them, thinking what must have been the violence of that fire which ravaged not only the surface of the earth but penetrated so deeply into its bosom."

It was hard to tell where the streets had been. After some difficulty, Pernin found the site of his house. Where his bedroom had been was the charred body of his dog. The priest

175

then retraced the path he had taken when he fled to the river. On the way, he found what was left of his horse, so disfigured by the fire that he had difficulty recognizing the animal. He apologized for mentioning his horse again. Those who had owned such a fine animal, he suggested, would understand.

He met a man who was still seeking his lost children three days after the fire. "If I at least could find their bones," the man told him. "But the wind has swept away whatever the fire has spared."

Although this was Wednesday, children were still hunting for parents, brothers for brothers, husbands for wives, fathers for sons and daughters. "But I saw no women amid this scene of horror, which it would have been almost impossible for them to contemplate. The men I met, those sorrowful seekers of the dead, had all suffered more or less in the battle against wind and fire. Some had a hand burned; other an arm or side. All were clothed in blackened, ragged garments."

Father Pernin felt the need for solitude to sort out the things that had happened to him and to the town. He walked alone down the road that led toward Oconto—the road he had taken toward the river on Sunday while others had been fleeing in the opposite direction. He had not gone far before it was plain that there was no escape here from the grim reminders of the tragedy. "I saw much more than I would have desired to see," he said.

After continuing a little farther, the priest turned back and made his way to where his new church had been. Nothing remained but the steeple bell and a mound of ashes. The bell had been thrown about fifty feet from the church when the steeple toppled. Strangely, half of it was intact. The other half had melted from the intense heat, the metal spreading over the sandy soil, then congealing. It occurred to Father Pernin that the bell must have clanged as it fell, "the last sound in the midst of the hurricane." Then he moved to the nearby graveyard where he performed a funeral service for a young

176

man from his parish. "Never was burial service more poverty-stricken nor priest more utterly destitute of all things necessary for the performance of the sad ceremony," he said. "Nor church, nor house, nor surplice, stole nor breviary. Nothing save prayer and a heartfelt benediction."

When the ceremony was over, he walked to the river to see what had happened to the tabernacle he had tried to save on Sunday night. He noticed that the charred beams of the bridge had been hastily joined together to allow passage across the river. A parishoner came hurrying up to meet him.

"Father, do you know what has happened to your tabernacle? It is a great miracle." The priest followed the man to the river. He found that the cart had tipped over on its side, but the tabernacle had landed on a floating log and was undamaged. No man to remove such evidence of divine intervention before every member of his parish could see it, the priest left it on the log for two days. The Catholics, he said, generally regarded the saving of the tabernacle as indeed miraculous.

He did not open the container until he sent it to Marinette, where he intended to say Mass. Then he found the "consecrated host intact in the monstrance while the violent concussions the ciborium must have undergone had not caused it even to open. . . . The flames had respected the interior as well as the exterior, even to the silky tissue lining the sides."

Before leaving Peshtigo, the priest hunted for other belongings he had lost in the river. The search was made easier when it was decided to open the charred wooden dam which had backed up the water under the bridge to a depth of about fifteen feet. The water was allowed to go downriver so bodies of persons drowned in trying to escape the fire could be recovered. Some reports indicated there were twenty such bodies. When the dam was opened, Father Pernin was able to find his chalice, which had floated out of the cart when it overturned.

177

In the days immediately after the fire, boards were hauled by wagon from the harbor sawmill so rough coffins could be hastily hammered together. John T. Bagnall, who had come to a Sugar Bush farm two months before with his wife and daughter, was one of those who helped pick up the dead and construct boxes to hold them. Some victims needed full-sized coffins. Their bodies had not been burned, and it was assumed they had suffocated. Other remains, of course, were nothing but ashes and charred bones. Bagnall sometimes put as many as five members of a family in a single casket.

After the ash-strewn streets of Peshtigo had been cleared of everything identifiable as human, the men walked farther afield. Bagnall found one fire victim, a young girl, lying next to a log. Her body had not been burned. Even her lovely curly hair was untouched. Bagnall stood looking down at the child, thinking how easily his own baby daughter might have met death when the great fire came. The dead girl looked at once peaceful and very lonely, with no one to claim her body. On an impulse, Bagnall stooped and cut off a lock of her hair. He carried it with him in his wallet for the rest of his life. When he looked at it, the unknown child was not quite forgotten.

After he had finished helping bury the dead, Bagnall and his wife and baby moved back to their former home in Jacksonport, Door County. After his daughter grew up, he told her he had seen so many terrible sights that he couldn't stand living in the Peshtigo vicinity any longer.

The lumberjacks who survived the fire knew that a number of men—timber cruisers and the like—had been in the woods the night of October 8. If they were dead, they deserved proper burial—if nothing more than a shallow grave under a pine with their calked boots hung from a branch. So the bearded men in mackinaws tramped across the blackened land where the forest had been thick, searching for friends or strangers.

It is certain they did not discover all of those who were trapped in the woods when the fire came, but they knew the

178

most likely places to look and found some of the victims. One of those discovered was a young logging camp foreman. As a search party was passing by, his body came crashing to the ground from high in a tree. It was as though the dead man had been waiting for them before relinquishing his perch. He had climbed into the pine and been roasted there, wedged in the crotch of a branch.

The foreman's body, found six days after the fire, was one of the last to be identified by the lumberjack searching parties. After a week, it was felt, any fire casualty who had been alive would either have found help or succumbed. The others—the unknown dead—would have to be left without burial.

It was thirty years later when the body was found of someone who may have been a Peshtigo fire victim. The "petrified man" was discovered in a swamp in the township of Porterfield near the Peshtigo River. It was quite well-preserved. No one recognized the man, but it was assumed he had perished while fleeing from "the big fire of '71." Some enterprising resident acquired rights to the body and tried to charge admission to view it. He got few takers; after three decades, the fire was half-forgotten history.

SEVENTEEN

•

It was the morning of October 10 before Ike Stephenson's telegram was delivered to the office of Governor Lucius Fairchild in Madison, bringing the first word to the state capital of what had happened in the north woods counties. But the governor was not there to receive it.

The day before, Fairchild had learned the details of the Chicago fire and hᵃd decided it was up to Wisconsin to go to the aid of its neighboring state. A forty-year-old Civil War veteran who had commanded an Iron Brigade regiment before a cannonball at Gettysburg tore off his left arm, the governor immediately began issuing orders. Before Monday was over, a relief train had been organized. Fairchild and virtually every other high state official, including most members of the legislature, got aboard it and went to Chicago's aid.

Only an elderly clerk was on hand to open Stephenson's seven-word telegram: "We are burning up. Send help quick." His hands trembling, the clerk stuffed the telegram into his pocket and hurried to the executive mansion. He handed it to the governor's young wife.

Strictly speaking, she had no authority to do anything

about it. But to Mrs. Fairchild, this was no time to be concerned about legal niceties. She put on a cloak and hat, ordered her carriage, and drove to her husband's office. Then, according to the recollections of her daughter, Mary Fairchild Morris, she "took charge of everything and everybody—and they all obeyed her."

Someone remembered that there was a freight car loaded with supplies for Chicago on a siding in the railroad yard. "Send it north instead," the governor's wife ordered. No one was disposed to argue with her. The railway officials issued the necessary instructions. Meanwhile, Mrs. Fairchild inspected the freight car. It contained food and clothing. Knowing Wisconsin's fall climate, she decided blankets were equally necessary. Servants and clerks were sent to the houses of her friends, and soon carriages, buggies, and wagons began converging on the freight yard, bringing bedcovers snatched from trunks and closets. The railway men had considered the car completely full, but the women, knowing there is always room for something more, stuffed blankets and quilts into the car. A few hours after the telegram had arrived the relief shipment was on its way to the end of the railway line at Fort Howard, with the railroad giving it priority over all other traffic.

This done, Mrs. Fairchild called a meeting of Madison residents and told them what was needed. By nightfall, another collection of supplies—food, clothing, and bedding—had been loaded onto a train and started on its way north.

Meanwhile, telegrams had gone to the governor and other state officials, who began hurrying back from Chicago. On Wednesday, Mrs. Fairchild was able to give up her self-imposed position of acting chief executive and go back to her proper role as a helpless woman in a world run by men.

While the dead were being buried in Peshtigo and the other stricken communities, surviving residents of the region concentrated most of their efforts on helping the living. Houses which remained unburned were thrown open. Neigh-

181

boring towns sent help. This emergency assistance was later supplemented by aid from more distant places, but at first the north country was largely on its own.

Isaac Stephenson led one of the Marinette relief expeditions. He noted that in an area twelve miles wide, including the village of Peshtigo, "every form of life was obliterated." Where the forest had been, "gaunt and disfigured tree trunks stood like sentinels of death under the low-hanging pall of smoke." In the area between Marinette and Peshtigo, he said, the fire's path was clearly marked "and varied little in width for the entire distance."

On the day after the fire, hundreds of survivors walked or were carried by horse and wagon to nearby communities. Some of the most seriously injured went to the hospitals established in the Dunlap House hotel in Marinette and the Kirby House in Menominee. The Dunlap was then owned by Ike and Andrew Stephenson and their fellow lumber baron, August C. Brown.

Converted into a hospital for fire victims, the Dunlap House was put in the charge of Dr. Jacob May of Fond du Lac. One of his assistants was Dr. Ben R. Hall, whose father, Jonathan, had been a pioneer physician in the area. Young Dr. Hall had just finished medical school, so his work with the Peshtigo fire casualties was his introduction to a medical career. Dr. May was a meticulous physician who kept records in a cardboard notebook and a small leatherbound book. He recorded the names of sixty-four persons he treated at Dunlap House, eleven of whom died.

A newspaperman who visited the Dunlap House talked first with "an American, who has with him his wife, babe and five other children." In the next bed was "an old German who lost his wife, daughter, son and eight grandchildren.

"In another bed," he continued, "an old lady is dying, the only one left of a family of ten. The next three beds are occupied by the Hoyt family, or what is left of them, some half dozen having perished."

182

Dr. May's records indicate that many of the patients were moved from the hotel to what was called the Merryman Hospital on October 25. This was a temporary hospital established in connection with A. C. Merryman's boarding-house to relieve crowding at the Dunlap House. Under the direction of Dr. B. T. Phillips, Merryman sheltered numerous fire victims. Dr. Phillips, a Civil War veteran, had been graduated from Rush Medical College in Chicago in 1869 and gone to Fond du Lac to practice. He kept the improvised hospital in operation until May, 1872. Toward the end of its existence, there were grumblings about men who took advantage of their status as survivors of the fire and were lolling around in hospital beds or eating at the hospital mess when they ought to have been out working. By closing the place, such malingering was stopped. The injured were encouraged to hobble off and make a living.

About sixty fire-orphaned children were housed in a barracks built behind the Presbyterian Church in Marinette. Some families were also accommodated there, and the building was partitioned off to give them some privacy. Stoves were provided for the family groups. The orphans ate in a dining hall attached to a cookhouse, as did transients. J. C. Manning of Peshtigo was in charge.

Peshtigo's only physician, Dr. J. F. Kelsey, had survived in the river. The next morning, he went to the harbor instead of staying and doing what he could for the injured. He came under considerable criticism for that. His defense was that he was in need of medical assistance himself and had his aged mother to take care of. The mother, whom he took with him to the harbor, died there of her burns a few days later.

Several days after the fire, it was estimated that several hundred injured were in hotels, boardinghouses, and other improvised hospitals in Green Bay and nearby communities. Half of those at the Dunlap House were ambulatory by then, it was reported, but "burned ears, faces, hands and feet were common to nearly all. . . . There were women with great burns on the sides and limbs, with faces as black as kettles and hands like claws, burned to the bones. . . . Little children are sadly maimed in their feet and faces."

One newspaper reporter who interviewed some of those at the Dunlap House said that most suffered even more "from hurts of mind than body."

"I have a sad memory," he continued, "of a poor widow who lost her crippled boy who went on crutches and a sprightly little girl who fell between the burning logs. They were all of her family." The widow, he went on, could still hear the screams of her children and expected to hear them calling to her forever from out of the nightmare she had lived through.

The cabins which were still fit to serve as shelter from the chilly Wisconsin autumn were generally crowded with several families. "I saw one with four men, five women and sixteen children, two of them suckers," a Green Bay visitor wrote. "They had just received an outfit of clothing—warm stockings, knit hoods, thin shawls, thin gaiters and light-colored dresses for the women and girls; old-fashioned hats, bursted boots, thin jackets and summer coats and pants for the men and boys. There were some occasions of laughter, but none of ridicule. All were glad and surprised at getting what they did."

By far the greatest loss of life had occurred in the Peshtigo area, but the damage was extensive all along the west shore of the Green Bay and in the lower half of the Kewaunee-Door County peninsula. A traveler who visited the latter area estimated that at least four hundred farms south of the Sturgeon Bay had been ruined. They were "left desolate—stripped of every improvement. Fences, barns, dwellings, implements, furniture, wagons, harness and crops—all went up in a whirlwind of fire. It will take thirty years, in that cold, hard soil, for their timber to grow again.

"In the aggregate, their losses must foot up to one thousand dollars a family. Farmers may have saved half of

184

their teams, that were let loose in the woods, and a third of their stock. But they have no hay, straw, grain or feed of any sort, not even the chance of browse in the woods. Nearly all, with large families, have lost their last cow and pig.

"In a ride of nearly six miles, on nearly a straight line, I saw but three hens and a fanning mill—the only farm implement left in town. In the Belgian settlement of Red River, sixty-two families were burned out in a row. Not a house, not a shed, not a coop, not one fence rail left upon another. The families had fled, almost naked, and breadless, to the few cabins in the outskirts that were saved. . . . One large-hearted old farmer was keeping eighty-odd cattle belonging to his unfortunate neighbors.

"Without stopping to consider the ways of providence or the uses of philosophy, these simple-minded people seem to have understood the art of helping one another."

G. W. Young of Forestville, Wisconsin, told authorities what he had seen in the town of Brussels: "The only living thing found was a pig, burned so badly he could neither see nor walk. The people perished from suffocation before the flames reached them, so dense was the smoke."

Kewaunee County, in the southern portion of the peninsula, was generally burned over. The townships of Ahnapee, Pierce, Kewaunee, Casco, and Carlton were hit hardest by the fire.

Those who lived along the western shore of the Door County peninsula generally escaped the worst of the fire. At the Little Sturgeon Bay, only a few miles north of where the Williamson family and employes underwent their ordeal, a dock and sawmill belonging to F. B. Gardner of Chicago was untouched. Gardner, for whom the township was named, was described as being on "the sere and yellow side of sixty" but still "busy as a bee and earnest as a tumblebug, trying to roll up a little more property." Gardner was apparently not in the vicinity when the fire threatened his $100,000 holdings at Little Sturgeon, which also included shanties for his workmen, storage buildings, and a shipyard. The superintendent, a man named Baptist, rallied the hired hands. With the bay at their back to supply water, they managed to keep the fire from their employer's property.

Scofield's Mill, near Dycksville in the Kewaunee County township of Red River, also escaped. There was a pier there, besides a store and other buildings clustered around the sawmill, so relief steamers could tie up. Scofield furnished three teams to carry supplies from the first barge to arrive, hauling them to a nearby warehouse. A small group of hungry refugees was waiting. "There were four or five men and eight or ten Bohemian women and children, ready to pack off the supplies to their neighbors where they had temporary homes," a man aboard the rescue vessel noted. "The women were of large girth, with stout arms and broad faces, frowzly hair and *wooden 'understandings'* [shoes]. The men made directly for the flour and pork barrels, while the women fastened to the clothing bundles. The younger fry went for an open apple barrel and were in the midst of a general revel as our boat gave the signal of departure."

On one remote farm, a young girl survived the fire only to die of starvation before help came. Hunger was common in the days immediately following the disaster, although many of the survivors managed to forage for themselves, grubbing in the fields for turnips, potatoes, and other root crops. In the Belgian settlement of Brussels, two hundred survivors shared four loaves of bread on the morning after the fire.

After boatloads of supplies began arriving at Kewaunee and Door County ports, messengers were sent inland in buckboards loaded with provisions or hiked through the devastated countryside on foot to tell backwoods families where provisions could be obtained. The supplies provided were mainly sacks of flour small enough to be carried on a man's back, together with bacon and salt meats. One visitor claimed that within a week "there was probably not a hungry person in all that stricken and almost impenetrable region."

186

Xavier Martin by then was living in Green Bay, having been elected county register of deeds some years after explaining to his fellow Belgians the importance of voting. As soon as news of the fire reached him, he jumped onto a horse and headed for the Belgian settlements to see what he could do to help his old friends. When he arrived at Dycksville, he found that several tugs loaded with provisions, clothing, and tools had arrived there from Green Bay, so he took charge of the distribution of the supplies. Later, he rode over much of the burned area, which he said began in Glenmore township southeast of Green Bay and extended through all the Belgian settlements to the Little Sturgeon Bay. Martin guessed that the fire had left five thousand persons homeless and destitute on the two sides of the bay.

In a communication to the Milwaukee Relief Committee, which sent him as a special agent to bring help to the fire victims in Brown, Kewaunee, and Door counties, George Godfrey related what he had seen in a day spent walking through a brisk snowstorm in the vicinity of Ahnapee, located in the northeast corner of Kewaunee County on the Lake Michigan side of the peninsula:

"The pathway of the great fire presents a heart-sickening appearance. From two to five miles wide in places and extending north and south indefinitely, as far as I could see, forests, fences, barns and houses were swept away. Farming tools and household furniture carried out into the fields fared no better than those left in the house. Pumps in the wells were burned off to the ground. . . .

"In one spot in the town of Brussels, some thirty-six persons were found and buried. Other more isolated instances were discovered. In one place, three or four children were found on their hands and knees, with their heads against a large stump, dead in this position. In most instances, the victims had apparently died without a struggle, probably killed outright by the first hot breath they inhaled."

Godfrey estimated that 100 had died in the townships of

187

Lincoln, Brussels and Forestville alone. He told the Milwaukee committee that he had the names of 170 persons in the Kewaunee County township of Lincoln who were homeless and destitute. In Forestville, he said, he had found 12 families totaling 60 persons who were in need of help.

A Lincoln township farmer, Eugene Naze, had a barn which had escaped the fire. It was being used to store relief goods which were arriving by way of Green Bay. Godfrey said nine or ten wagonloads of flour and other provisions, together with some clothing, had arrived October 29, the day prior to his report. Some supplies had reached Naze's barn earlier and refugees in the vicinity were "tolerably well supplied" with food and cast-off clothing, he added.

"But the cry is for blankets, quilts and bedding," Godfrey told the Milwaukee committee. "Hay and feed for the surviving cattle are absolutely necessary. In order that the people may help themselves, they must preserve their cattle. Boards to cover the log cabins which they are now putting up are indispensable. Stoves to warm them and cook their food are lacking. These, with all their utensils, must be supplied.

"Most of the inhabitants, astounded and bewildered by the calamity, were about to flee from the country. But upon learning that relief was coming they have plucked up courage and are going to work to repair, as far as they can, the great damage and get upon their feet again."

Some of the food sent to help the survivors arrived in the form of cooked provisions—housewives realized there would be no stoves available on which to cook.

The treasurer of the Milwaukee committee was Alexander Mitchell, that city's wealthiest resident, whose grandson, General Billy Mitchell, would gain recognition as an exponent of air power. Used clothing came into the Milwaukee office from as far away as Maine and California. Money needed to purchase food, building materials, livestock, tools, and hay was harder to find. The committee praised the "spontaneous liberality of a sympathizing people, especially our women."

188

But this liberality consisted in some instances of sending clothing of little value to anyone, even a Peshtigo fire victim. A farmer who had lost everything he owned might find a top hat and swallowtailed coat a little better than nothing, but he wasn't sure how the cows would react when he wore such an outfit to milk them. A Philadelphia woman sent a silk gown. The women guests in the Fifth Avenue Hotel in New York decided to do something for the refugees out West and got together a box containing embroidered underwear, ribbons, laces, kid slippers, toilet boxes, and dainty gloves. Even such impractical outpourings of generosity, however, were an indication of how the nation's sympathy had been aroused by the fire.

One woman sent along the entire wardrobe of her dead baby, which had been put tenderly away as a reminder of her heartache. She decided that helping some homeless Wisconsin baby would be a more suitable memorial. In Wisconsin's Walworth County, a woman who was to be married the following month packed up her entire trousseau and sent it to Peshtigo.

"Some said I was foolish to send articles I had embroidered," she explained some years later, "but I never regretted parting with my outfit. I thought some woman would realize there was love and sympathy in the gift."

•

EIGHTEEN

The Wisconsin fires worked their destruction in a period lasting from about 7 P.M. until an hour or two after midnight. In general, their paths were from southwest to northeast along the two sides of the Green Bay.

The fires on the western side of the bay began just north of the Green Bay city limits. A small settlement called Mill's Center, located in Pittsfield township north of Green Bay, was completely wiped out, and the fire destroyed adjacent timberland. Suamico, immediately east of Pittsfield along the west shore of the bay, was also heavily damaged.

But the fires, which burned over the territory between Green Bay and Oconto, and the bigger one which swept out of the southwest toward Peshtigo were probably separate entities. This helps explain why Oconto escaped almost unscathed, while the village a few miles to the north was erased from the earth. One man who rode over much of the burned-over area on the western shore of the bay shortly after the catastrophe said that the "tornado" which wiped out Peshtigo and then continued north toward Menekaune, Menominee, and Marinette began about six miles north of Oconto.

Authorities do not agree on the fires' exact dimensions — there was no way to discover them except by tramping over the entire region, a task no one considered worth doing. By piecing together various accounts, it is apparent that the fires on the west side of the bay burned an area about sixty miles long and ten to fifteen miles wide, totaling from six hundred to nine hundred square miles. On the east side of the bay, mostly on the Kewaunee-Door County peninsula, the burned-over region was roughly fifty miles long and perhaps five miles wide, adding another 250 square miles. The paths of the fires were irregular, with the extent of the destruction varying from partial to total, depending on vagaries of wind and topography.

The coincidence that the great Chicago fire took place on the same day, coupled with the primitive communications available in the north woods wilderness, resulted in the Peshtigo fire gaining little attention outside Wisconsin for some time after the unprecedented disaster occurred. By the time the details reached the Eastern seaboard, the Chicago fire was no longer providing fresh copy for the newspapers, so they were glad to give full play to the previously ignored events in the northern forests. With one or two exceptions, the Eastern newspapers did not send reporters to the scene. But their accounts, cribbed from Milwaukee and Green Bay papers, aroused the sympathy of their readers.

In Boston, among other places, a relief committee was formed to help the destitute in distant Wisconsin. Some weeks after the fire, the Boston committee's representative journeyed out to take a look for himself. By then, he said, the Milwaukee committee had received so many donations that it had divided them with its counterpart in Green Bay. The Bostonian estimated that four thousand persons were entirely without means and must be aided until the next summer's harvest. The men could find work in the woods, he said, but assistance was needed for their families and for the women and children left without a male breadwinner.

191

Governor Fairchild's estimate, based on a personal inspection tour and a report from state relief agents, tallied with that of the Bostonian. He declared that three to four thousand persons needed help until the following summer. Food and clothing were coming in from various parts of the country and the supplies were reasonably adequate, he added, but unless money was provided to buy seed, tools, and grain for the animals, the farmers would not be able to make a fresh start on the burned-over land and support their families. What was needed, the governor specified, was flour, salt, cured meats, bedding, blankets, baled hay, building material, light farming implements and tools, boots, shoes, clothing, log chains, axes, nails, glass, and "everything needed by a farming community that has lost everything."

Most of the donations were funneled through Green Bay. Fairchild's political enemies claimed that the relief committee there "passed out bread with one hand and campaign literature with the other." This may have been nothing more than sour grapes over the fact that the Republicans, as the party in power in Madison, were in a position to build up valuable stores of gratitude among the fire victims which might be helpful in future elections.

The governor decided it was not necessary to call a special session of the legislature to deal with the calamity. The expense of such a session, he said, would be as much as the amount the state would be willing to provide to help the fire victims. He felt it would be better to go ahead and provide the relief and let the legislature give its formal approval at its next regular session.

The final total of the relief fund administered by the state was $141,568.49. Much of this came from private contributions rather than state funds. The contributions came from as far away as Peru, but most of the money was raised in Wisconsin.

The Milwaukee and Green Bay relief committees and some of those organized in smaller cities operated independently, at least at first, and concentrated mainly on keeping the refugees from starving and supplying them with clothing and blankets.

The federal government was not asked for money—in those days, President Ulysses S. Grant would have been surprised at any such request—but the U.S. Army came through nobly. It sent 200,000 rations of hard bread, bacon, and beans, as well as supplies of blankets and clothing.

Relief depots in Green Bay and Milwaukee kept records indicating they had helped 7187 persons from 1534 families. In Green Bay and its neighboring community, Fort Howard, many private homes were opened to the fire victims. According to one Green Bay man, "the old, hopeful, generous spirit of the war was revived." The Turnverein Society, a social and gymnastic club organized by German immigrants, turned over its brand new three-story hall at the corner of Walnut Street and Monroe Avenue to the Green Bay committee. The building was transformed into a temporary hospital in the charge of Dr. H. O. Crane.

Relief from outside the state was slow to arrive, but when it came it was relatively generous and some of those who brought help went to considerable trouble. The Reverend H. T. Fuller, former pastor of the Peshtigo Congregational Church, made the long journey from his new pastorate in St. Johnsbury, Vermont, to bring five hundred dollars in cash and thirty-five boxes of used clothing collected by his New England congregation.

Some of the second-hand relief supplies may have been contaminated. An outbreak of smallpox shortly after the fire was blamed on germs carried in clothing or bedding. It is possible, of course, that the disease came from some other source—possibly the railway worker with smallpox whom Dr. Kelsey had ordered out of town. At any rate, one of the first houses to be rebuilt in Peshtigo had to be pressed into use as an isolation hospital. A man named Clark, who had survived the disease some years before, was put in charge. Those

193

patients who managed to get plenty of whiskey recovered, according to one local observer of the remedial methods used.

Once the most pressing problems of burying the dead and assisting the survivors were taken care of, many of the lumberjacks went back to their regular routine in the forest. Among them was John Nelligan, who worked for Sargent and Bransfield on Little River, a tributary of the Oconto River, during the winter following the fire. As a swamper, clearing roads through the woods for the logging sleds, he frequently came across carcasses of animals killed by the fire. Some of the deer's legs were burned off. It was Nelligan's guess that less than half of the wild animals in the path of the fire had been able to escape.

The Peshtigo River had been alive with pickerel, bass, sturgeon, suckers, and other fish. Each spring before the fire, farmers had driven down to the banks with poles and nets. By evening they had had a wagonload of fish to take home, where it was salted or smoked for use the following winter. But that fall of 1871, after the great fire had passed, the streams in the burned-over area were full of dead fish and for weeks afterward the water tasted of lye.

The area where Nelligan worked that winter was some distance from Peshtigo, but he said he did not see a green pine all winter and from handling so much burned wood he became "as black as an Ethiopian." He added with some satisfaction that the loggers saved much good pine lumber that otherwise would have been destroyed by worms which infest fire-damaged trees.

Some of the timberland was so devastated that there was little left to salvage. One pinery outfit, Woodruff & Company, seeded three hundred acres of former forest with timothy and clover. The first year's hay crop was so encouraging the company ordered more acreage seeded. Within ten years, the tract had grown to a thousand acres. A herd of fifty Jersey cows, one hundred head of purebred Cotswold sheep, and

194

twenty-five horses found fine pasturage there, along with a stock herd of 150 cattle.

Superintendent Ellis, who had been in charge of relief efforts in Peshtigo, was also in charge of its rebuilding. It had been decided at the Chicago headquarters of the Peshtigo Company that the town should be brought back to life. The company wanted to open its lumber camps as usual, for there was enough timber to be salvaged even in this stricken region to make it worthwhile to send out the crews of lumberjacks.

No one could have blamed the company or Ogden, its president, if Peshtigo had been written off—the company estimated its monetary losses there and in its pinery holdings at $1,100,000, not over a tenth of it covered by insurance, and Ogden had taken even worse losses in the Chicago fire. The decision to rebuild the town and reopen the camps was greeted by the refugees at Peshtigo Harbor with enthusiasm. This meant that those men able to work could have jobs to support themselves and their families. Ellis put carpenters to work putting up temporary buildings to house the workmen in Peshtigo while the mill there was rebuilt.

The company's example was soon followed by others, including Nicholas Cavoit. He had not lost three million dollars as Ogden had, but he had lost his sawmill, his house, and a building housing a meat market and Hay's jewelry shop. But he got a supply of boards, grabbed a hammer, and went to work. When his new house was finished, he nailed a sign on it proclaiming it was the first home built in Peshtigo after the fire.

Rumors spread after the fire that the Peshtigo Company had taken advantage of the situation by charging refugees for relief goods. Captain J. P. Moore, the company representative at the harbor, issued a statement calling this a foul slander.

Because the harbor area had escaped the fire, the sawmill there was able to turn out the lumber needed to rebuild the town. Within a remarkably short time, the town was springing up from its ashes. "During a visit to the village of Peshtigo we were almost deafened by the noise of building," a visitor wrote. "Already there are about twenty buildings erected and others in the process of erection on the site of the old village. Real estate is changing hands and the people of that once thriving little village are determined to put themselves into shape for business again at once." Haste was necessary. The long Wisconsin winter was nearly upon them. No one could exist in the cold weather ahead without shelter.

The North Western Road got busy with its rebuilding, too. It took only a little more than two months for the railroad to replace its burned ties and complete laying the rails from Fort Howard to Peshtigo. The first train arrived there December 11. By December 29, the railway had pushed on as far as Marinette.

Even before the railroad was completed, the telegraph line was replaced between Green Bay and Peshtigo along the North Western right-of-way. For the first time since it had been destroyed in the smaller fires that preceded the big one, the wire linked the town with the outside world again.

As the railway approached Marinette and that city made ready to celebrate the long-awaited arrival of train service, some familiar problems arose. The railway workers joined the lumberjacks in making Saturday nights and Sundays difficult for the townsfolk who wanted more peace and quiet. The *Eagle* resumed its campaign for a jail: "A calaboose where drunken offenders and rowdies that make the night hideous with their unearthly yells can be lodged safely ought to be erected at once," Editor Noyes wrote. "The advent of the railroad makes this and like adjuncts of modern civilization necessary." Noyes also suggested a 10:30 curfew on drinking each night. The proposal was considered too absurd by the saloon keepers and their customers to be worth discussion.

At Peshtigo, a new hotel was being built by A. B. Phillips a little west of the site of the old Peshtigo House. It was to have two stories. The Peshtigo House proprietor, Levi Hale, was planning a new hotel nearby.

T. A. Hay moved his jewelry business to Marinette and put on display the knife Warren Church used to cut his throat. It was an ordinary jackknife, made somewhat interesting by the dried blood still noticeable on the larger of its two blades.

Bodies were still being found here and there several weeks after the fire. Someone got around to climbing down into a well belonging to John B. Drees at Peshtigo to investigate a report that nine persons had died there. He found two bodies.

In Peshtigo's rebuilding, the saloon keepers did not lag behind. "Whisky holes are getting thick again," the *Eagle* noted on December 30. "Many of them are an intolerable nuisance and ought to be abated."

There was much hardship among the farm families after the fire, but for those who survived the long-term results were not altogether unfortunate. The fire had cleared their land for farming with a terrible efficiency. "Thousands of good tillable acres were added to the farming tracts already under cultivation," Xavier Martin wrote, referring to Kewaunee and Door counties on the east side of the bay. "Nearly all the marketable timber having been burned or destroyed, it followed that the lumber and shingle mills which had been destroyed by the fire were not rebuilt, and this alone was a great loss to the people.

"There was nothing left for them to do but to turn their attention strictly to farming, which they did. From that time on, farming, stock and wool raising, butter and cheese making were the main occupations of the Belgian settlers."

This was equally true of other rural settlers. Within three years, Martin said, the farmers were better off than they had been before the fire. Cheese factories were springing up in the little settlements, replacing the sawmills and shingle mills. Steam threshing machines appeared, along with a much-needed invention, a machine that could pull stumps from the fields.

"Some settlements, such as Rosiere and Graniez, have

taken down their fences," Martin wrote a few years after the fire, "and it is a beautiful sight in summer time to see fine crops of wheat, rye, barley and oats covering fenceless and stumpless fields. The wilderness begins to look like the fields of Belgium."

"In fact," he said, "the settlements were becoming so modernized that many of the young Belgians had abandoned wooden shoes."

NINETEEN

•

In the weeks after the fire, some faltering attempts were made to explain why it had been so much more deadly than others that had taken place within the memory of those who lived in the north country forests. The destruction of Peshtigo, it was said, was the result of a hurricane or tornado which sent the flames sweeping through the village and surrounding countryside. Some of the deaths were blamed on marsh gas or some other mysterious emanation from the fire. There was frequent mention of dark, balloonlike objects rolling in from the night sky and causing whatever they touched to explode into flame.

The report made by the Boston relief committee's representative was fairly typical. It was handicapped hardly at all by the fact that the Bostonian had been in Massachusetts when the fire occurred. He based his conclusions on talks with numerous eyewitnesses. On the night of October 8, "there were currents of air on fire," he said. "The atmosphere seemed saturated with inflammable gases from the pitchpine forests which had been burning for weeks. The heat was far greater than that of any ordinary conflagration, melting iron and bell metal at a distance of many rods from any buildings."

199

One Sugar Bush resident, watching from the pond where he had taken refuge, told of seeing a dark mass of smoke and fire descend out of the sky in the middle of a clearing and burn up six members of the Lawrence family.

Father Pernin said he was told by a number of persons that they had witnessed a "large black object, resembling a balloon, which revolved in the air with great rapidity, advancing above the summits of the trees toward a house which it seemed to single out for destruction. Barely had it touched the latter when the balloon burst with a loud report, like that of a bombshell, and at the same moment rivulets of fire streamed out in all directions. With the rapidity of thought, the house thus chosen was enveloped in flames within and without so that the persons inside had no time to escape."

Other accounts told of balls of fire hurtling out of the night. There were tales of cabins suddenly bursting into flame in the middle of a large clearing, a considerable distance from the burning woods. There were stories of a child who survived unharmed while the parents were burned to cinders a few feet away. There was an account of a young man whose body was found, seemingly untouched by flame. But his pocket watch had melted.

Some of the more imaginative stories were easy enough to refute. The belief that October 8, 1871, had been chosen as the day of judgment appeared less likely the next morning than it had when the world seemed to be on fire. The legend that the flames were so hot the rivers boiled can still be heard in Wisconsin, but the hundreds who spent the night standing in the Peshtigo and other streams were living evidence that this did not happen.

Some inaccuracies about the fire can be traced to writers who allowed their sense of drama to overcome any proclivity to remain factual. For example, a dramatic account has been published of how the Peshtigo telegraph office burst into flames just as the brave telegrapher was preparing to tap out a

200

plea for help, ignoring the well-documented fact that the wires connecting Peshtigo with Green Bay and the rest of the world had been destroyed several weeks before.

Some theorized in 1871 that the conflagration had been caused by a vast storm, a hurricane or a tornado, which had reached Antigua and the Virgin Islands on August 21 and the Bahamas on August 23 and was a veritable "besom of destruction." "Besom" is a fancy word for broom, and no one would dispute that the fire swept through the woods like one. But the notion that the October conflagration in Wisconsin — or Chicago, for that matter — could be blamed on bad weather in the Atlantic in August was not given much credence, even in 1871.

Faced with the overblown rhetoric then in fashion, it is tempting to suppose that some eyewitnesses simply let their imaginations run away with them in describing some of the phenomena they claimed to have seen. Visibility was hampered by the billowing smoke and the stinging, windblown sand. Such conditions, coupled with panic, could have made the burning crowns of trees seem like balls of fire sailing through the air or even, perhaps, like dark balloons that burst into flame on impact.

And yet, strange things do happen in fires as large as this one. Nearly a century after the Peshtigo disaster, the causes of what are termed blowup fires remain imperfectly understood. No scientist can stand calmly by, taking notes, when one is in progress. According to two California scientists who have studied such conflagrations, the energy released by a fire like this one may be greater than the output of "one average-sized atom bomb every minute."

"No wonder researchers have been stymied," R. Keith Arnold and Charles C. Buck added, "and direct control measures do not exist."

Some of those who saw the Peshtigo fire or visited the scene shortly afterward and then wrote descriptions of the weather conditions associated with it, used words like "tor-

201

nado" simply as a synonym for a very strong wind, without concerning themselves with the fact that a tornado is a quite specific sort of high wind.

In most of the burned-over region, there is no evidence that such a devastating whirlwind was associated with the fire. It seems probable, however, that a tornado did accompany the fire in portions of the Sugar Bush settlements and perhaps in Peshtigo. It is possible that such a whirlwind also occurred in some other places—Williamsonville, for example. This conclusion is based not only on the eyewitnesses' descriptions and those of men who walked over the ground soon afterward, but on recent studies of how huge forest fires behave.

If a tornado or tornadoes accompanied the fire, it would explain some of the tales told of houses being lifted into the air and of swirling "balloons" enveloping barns or cabins. In a series of fires such as those of October 8, 1871, such vastly destructive whirlwinds are to be expected—not as a primary cause of whipping up the fire, but as one of the fire's effects.

As noted earlier, one eyewitness said the tornado began six miles north of Oconto. J. H. Hauser, a Fond du Lac lawyer, estimated its starting point a little farther north—eight miles from Oconto and twelve miles south of Peshtigo, by his reckoning. To the south of where "the tornado began its terrible work of destruction," he said, the countryside was pretty well burned over and numerous houses were burned, but the devastation was less complete. Hauser drove through the region on the west side of Green Bay shortly after the fire. "It is probable that the tornado carried the fire along with wonderful rapidity," he wrote. "For mile after mile, not a tree of any size was standing. . . . The trees were blown down; the roots in many instances, after the trees had fallen, standing twelve to fifteen feet high, with rocks and dirt among them."

Father Pernin was less specific about the area of greatest destruction, but he said he had seen "whole forests of huge maples torn up, twisted and broken, as if they had been

202

willow wands," presumably in the Sugar Bush region. "A tree standing upright here or there was an exception to an almost general rule," the priest went on. "There lay these children of the forest, heaped up over the other in all imaginable positions, their branches reduced to cinders and their trunks calcined and blackened."

Like Father Pernin, others who visited the Peshtigo area after the fire mention trees uprooted and twisted as a boy might twist a weed stem. A number of other witnesses, however, make no mention of such evidence of tornadolike winds, although virtually everyone agreed that the wind was strong and a major factor in the fire's destructiveness.

Conditions varied considerably from one place to another in the burned-over region, as is to be expected in the light of modern research into the behavior of such great fires. In some localities, the fire behaved predictably enough so that residents were able to save themselves and, in some cases, even their buildings. In other places, the fire was of almost unimaginable proportions. It created conditions similar to those of the fire storms that devastated Hamburg and some other cities after Allied bombings in World War II. Such a fire storm is more accurately described as a fire tornado. It occurs under conditions where a high rate of combustion is combined with a low surface wind speed. Small but deadly whirlwinds are created, ten to twenty feet in diameter. Sometimes, for reasons which scientists still do not fully understand, these whirlwinds grow until they are as much as a half mile across. Their winds may reach a speed estimated at two hundred miles an hour. "Under these circumstances," the United States Forest Service reports, "everything combustible within the fire storm zone is completely consumed. Such was the case at Hamburg. Similar occurrences have been documented in forest fires both in the United States and Australia."

There is no scientifically precise information on weather conditions in the Peshtigo fire area. In 1871, the closest weather station was at Milwaukee, but even there, the information was scanty—record-keeping had begun only that year. The statistics that might be most pertinent to an understanding of conditions causing the fire's unprecedented destructiveness were not yet included in the bureau's records. Most notably, there is no information on the wind velocity and direction on October 8, 1871.

R. W. Harms, Milwaukee's present weatherman, does have yellowing records which show that the maximum temperature in that city increased from 66 on October 7 to 83 degrees on the day of the fire. The minimums also rose, from 43 on October 7 to 53 on October 8. Harms pointed out that this rise in temperature is a good indication that the wind had shifted so it was coming from the south and that it had increased in velocity. But there is no way of telling from the weather bureau files how strong the wind was in Milwaukee that day or how much conditions varied between southeastern Wisconsin, where that city is located, and the state's northeastern counties.

Harms' records show the amount of rainfall in Milwaukee that summer. They do not bear out the accounts of the Peshtigo area's amateur weather observers. September was a dry month in Milwaukee, with .57 of an inch of rain, but August had been wet, with 3.7 inches. Milwaukee had a minor shower on October 6 and another on October 9, with a real cloudburst on October 14. The statistics, however, do not disprove the reports of the drought's severity north of Green Bay. Rainfall often varies considerably from one part of the state to another. In view of the unanimity of the accounts of how dry the north country was that summer, it can be accepted that there was a serious drought and that the woods were unusually susceptible to fire. The reports came from lumberjacks, farmers, country newspaper editors, and others who take more than a casual interest in keeping track of the weather.

The only other pertinent statistics available at the Milwaukee weather bureau are the temperatures on October 9,

204

the day after the fire. The minimum was 61 and the maximum 81, indicating a warm fall day, similar to the day before. Temperatures are generally a few degrees lower in Peshtigo, which is 165 miles north of Milwaukee. Still, it seems likely that the survivors did not have to contend with particularly cold weather and that the numerous complaints of chills after the fire were caused by shock associated with the experience, coupled with the fact that those who had taken to the river were standing around in wet clothing.

Despite the absence of official statistics on the Peshtigo area rainfall, it is logical to accept the word of such residents as Noyes that the last rain before the fire came on September 5. In such a dry year, nearly everyone was looking anxiously for rain, and the *Eagle* editor would never have been able to face his cronies at the Dunlap House billiards room if he had made a mistake about a matter so important to his readers.

It does not seem to have occurred to anyone in the region, but it may have been more than mere coincidence that the small fires sprang up in the woods not long after the September 5 rain. This brief downpour could have prompted a lessening of precautions by rural settlers, railway crews, and lumberjacks who had been waiting impatiently for the drought to end so they could touch a match to the piles of slashings that had accumulated. At any rate, it is agreed that the small fires were smoldering here and there in the timberlands on both sides of the Green Bay. Ike Stephenson blamed the railway crews for them—"in our efforts to better our position, we unwittingly paved the way for disaster," he wrote. But the editor of Green Bay's *Advocate* made a more accurate analysis. "It would be easy to conceive that the line of fire northwardly from Green Bay and Fort Howard to Menominee was occasioned by the burning up of the debris of the woods on the railroad workings," Tilton wrote a few months after the fire. "But the fact is that it was confined to no such line, but sprang up on both sides of the bay in places remote from each other."

205

Despite such accurate appraisals, the misapprehension grew up that the Door County and Kewaunee County fires had been touched off by embers from the fires on the west side of the bay. It is clear that Tilton was right and that they were entirely independent, although occurring at the same time and from the same basic cause. Filibert Roth, a federal agriculture department map-maker who studied the region in 1897, came to the correct conclusion about the disaster's origin. He found that the Peshtigo fire—by which he meant the fires on both sides of the bay—was the result of numerous small fires which had been making headway in the forest for several weeks before they "broke out into the final and then perfectly unmanageable form." Roth was also correct in his assessment of the basic cause of the disaster. All or nearly all of the small fires "had their origin in carelessness," he said, adding: "It is more the carelessness of letting these fires go than of starting them which has resulted in enormous losses."

The cause of the carelessness was a part of the north country's history. When the white man discovered Wisconsin, there were something like five million acres of forest in the state, mostly in its northern two-thirds. Only a few people, such as the early conservationist, Increase A. Lapham, suggested that such a vast resource was not inexhaustible. Lapham headed a committee that made a report to the state legislature four years before the Peshtigo fire. By then, half of the five million acres of woods was gone. The wasteful methods being used to harvest the trees filled Lapham with dismay. "Man has too long forgotten that the earth was given him for usufruct alone—not for consumption, still less for profligate waste," he warned. "Usufruct" is a legal term—the right to use another's property without injuring or destroying it. The notion that this had anything to do with men's relationship to the inexhaustible forest resources of the north country was considered too absurd to be worth a second thought, and Lapham's warning was filed away and ignored.

It was recognized that one-fourth of the lumber was

wasted by the methods then employed. It was understood that forest fires caused by human carelessness were a perennial problem. But only a few north country residents understood that Lapham's warning had anything to do with them. Professor James Joshua Blaisdell, writing a few years later to describe how Wisconsin continued to squander its timber resources, told how settlers march into virgin lands like "the army of Tamerlane or Genghis Khan" and soon "learn, after many rough encounters, that the soil cannot be trifled with but, to be their friend, must be wooed into their alliance. The mountains withstand their onset. They cannot conquer the sea. They cannot contrive to stay the rivers and send them back to the hills they left behind.

"But the forests—the silent, princely, august, awful forests—are unable to resist them. And only late they learn that the perishing of the forests touched the heart of Nature and that the avenger is at the core. . . ."

Flame was the avenger. It turned out that the penalty for the misuse of the right of usufruct was death.

Filibert Roth discovered that the fires caused by human carelessness had exacted economic penalties in northeastern Wisconsin, too. In some regions devastated in 1871, farmers found good crop land or at least good pasture. But in others, Roth noted, nothing was left but large tracts of "stump prairies," bare wastes where the ground was sparsely covered by weeds, grass, sweet fern, and a few "scattering, runty bushes of scrub oak, aspen and white birch." Here and there, the map-maker saw thickets of young jack pine, a species of conifer that takes over when the soil fertility is too poor for more desirable varieties. Twenty-six years after the Peshtigo fire, he found that more than 80 percent of the burned-over area was still devoid of any valuable forest growth. Half of the sawmills of 1871 had vanished. Their supply of pine had run out.

The heritage of the fire persisted into modern times, changing the face of the land. Those who grew up in the

Peshtigo area in the years after the fire had to go a considerable distance from home to see a tree dating back beyond 1871. Mrs. Fay Stuart Dooley, who spent her girlhood in Peshtigo, recalls when what seemed like an ancient tree was cut down some years ago. The rings were counted in the hope that here, at last, was a survivor of the big fire. But no. The tree had not sprouted until 1873.

Modern students of such matters agree that the four largest forest fires which occurred in nineteenth-century North America had the same basic causes: many small fires, coupled with unusually dry weather. If the Wisconsin and Michigan fires of October 8, 1871, are considered **as a unit,** they were probably the most extensive of the **four—there is** no doubt they were the most deadly.

The death toll, particularly in the **Peshtigo** area, is the principal difference between the 1871 fire and those in forested areas before and since. Many of those who died that October 8 were homesteaders and lumberjacks, who were well-equipped physically and by experience to meet any danger they encountered in the forest where they had chosen to live. There must have been an unusual set of circumstances to account for the unprecedented loss of life. It seems likely that those who wrote in 1871 of a tornado of fire were not simply indulging in hyperbole. Similarly, it is quite possible that those who blamed marsh gas or some similar phenomenon for some of the loss of life were only partially in error.

Modern investigations of similar fires, including those made by the Forest Service, do not bear out the contention that marsh gas was to blame. A Forest Service spokesman said it was highly unlikely that marsh gas could have accumulated in sufficient quantities to cause or even add to phenomena called "flashovers," often associated with large forest fires. But just as a large fire can create its own tornado, it can provide its own supply of potentially explosive gases. When a forest fire is burning over a large area, combustion gases may become trapped near the ground at some distance

208

from the main fire. When these gases achieve the required mixture of fuel and air and are ignited by an ember, they may explode.

The small fires of September, 1871, prepared the way for the blowup fire that followed. Fires that burn surface vegetation without consuming the green foliage above them dry out the leaves of taller bushes and trees to the point where the greenery is highly inflammable and needs only a spark to set off a fire that will race through the crowns of the trees. Fires that have become established over a considerable tract of land without using up a significant proportion of the potential fuel can flame up all at once with a slight change in the weather. Radiated heat between two or more scattered fires may cause the combustible material between them to ignite—"area ignition" is the technical term. Given the proper conditions, the result can be a violent fire storm, created nearly instantaneously from what had seemed to be separate fires which were not in themselves particularly alarming.

Every fire has a convection column above it—a swirl of heated air rising rapidly. When two fires are in the same vicinity, their convection columns are often drawn together so violently that a single whirlwind of fire is created, frequently running considerable distances beyond the area where the smaller convection columns joined forces.

Despite the tantalizing lack of scientific data about weather conditions in the north woods prior to the October 8 fires, certain facts are known. Numerous accounts agree that the air felt oppressive and heavy. There seems to have been little or no wind until just before the advance of the fire—which would, in any case, have created its own windstorm.

No one can know with certainty what the atmospheric conditions were a mile or two in the air above northeastern Wisconsin that day. It is tempting to guess, however, that a layer of relatively chilly air—an inversion—lay above the doomed area. When such an inversion exists, the rise of a fire's convection column is held in check, causing it to burn sluggishly. But when the swirling, overheated air of the convection column breaks through the layer of heavy air above it, it is as if a furnace damper had been opened. The hot air rushes skyward. Cool air sweeps in from all sides toward the column of rising air. Whirlwinds develop. What had been a relatively small fire becomes with breathtaking speed a large and highly dangerous one. The heavy smoke that had hung over the area for several weeks would have tended to hold heat near the ground, resulting in clearly defined layers of warm and cold air and creating the classic conditions for such a breakthrough of the convection columns into the upper atmosphere.

According to scientists, four factors govern the behavior of forest fires—fuel, weather, topography, and burning pattern. Arnold and Buck pointed out in a modern evaluation of why fires go out of control that these four factors are often in such critical balance that only one need change to provide blowup conditions. "For example," they said, "a change in wind velocity alone, or merely the movement of fire from a closed to an open timber type, may be sufficient to set up a combination that will cause a quiet fire to flare up or run with devastating effects."

There was, in fact, a change in the wind on the evening of October 8. After sundown, it blew strongly from the southwest. The forest foliage was dry from the heat of small fires in the surface vegetation. The pall of smoke that hung over hundreds of miles of timber country may have helped create an inversion in the atmosphere overhead. The wind fanned the small blazes into bigger ones. Some of the bigger ones combined. And suddenly the situation was wholly out of control, with combustibles catching fire by area ignition well ahead of the line of advancing flames, with whirlwinds sweeping down on homesteaders in the Sugar Bushes and elsewhere, with a fire storm of awful power created in that burned-over area where the greatest losses occurred.

210

It is obvious that what happened to Peshtigo resulted from the mischance that a large number of humans happened to be in exactly the wrong place when the blowup occurred. Faced with a fire of this magnitude, nothing the residents could have done—short of mass evacuation in advance of the fire—would have been sufficient to save them. As it was, the death toll would certainly have been even greater had it not been for the river, which offered a chance of survival only a few blocks from nearly every house in town.

Even with modern scientific knowledge, transportation, and fire-fighting equipment, large forest fires can be deadly. To cite one of numerous examples, fifteen fire-fighters were killed a few years ago when flames jumped a road in the Mendocino National Forest and caught them before they could get away. This California fire was one of those which often act in "unexpected and unexplainable ways," according to a report made in 1958 by Richard E. McArdle, Chief of the U.S. Forest Service. He added that such fires "successfully defy all that man has learned about fighting them." These fires, it has been found, burn "with an intensity far out of proportion to apparent wind, fuel, moisture and other conditions."

George M. Byram, who began his career with the Forest Service in 1932, now heads a research unit established to study forest fire energy systems. Based on his studies of such conflagrations as the Chicago fire, the Cloquet forest fire in Minnesota in 1918, and a series of disastrous forest fires that broke out in Maine in October, 1947, Byram has found that catastrophic fires may create convection columns that rise to a height of about five miles. The energy generated by such whirling chimneys of super-heated air can twist off large trees, as can the more ordinary kind of tornadoes. Such fires frequently carry embers nearly a mile in the air, then drop them far ahead of the fire front—a discovery that explains how charred boards from Peshtigo were found in the Menominee River six miles away and how a piece of wood was carried through the air for seven miles before falling near a Lake Michigan vessel in the Green Bay.

By creating models of fire whirlwinds under laboratory conditions—using a wind tunnel and other research equipment—Byram has demonstrated the existence of a horizontal jet in the flame front of a wind-driven fire. He has concluded that this jet of fire, darting out horizontally from the advancing flames, is one of the principal factors to be considered in dealing with fires as huge as the Peshtigo. It is no wonder that to some of those trying to flee on that Sunday in October it seemed apparent that the very air itself was on fire.

There are three major classifications of forest fires— ground, surface, and crown fires. All three occurred in the north woods that fall. A number of accounts of conditions in the woods in September gave good descriptions of the first of these, the ground fires which smolder in organic material beneath the surface litter of the woods floor. A ground fire may go along quietly for weeks, eating away the peat and humus, without attracting much attention. But a change in the wind may fan it into the second main type of forest fire, that which burns the surface litter of the forest. This, in turn, can develop into the most spectacular of the three, the crown fire, which advances through the tops of the trees more or less independently of the surface fire.

An increase in the wind velocity is frequently one reason why a small, innocuous fire suddenly changes into a dangerous conflagration. But a big fire is perfectly capable of creating its own atmospheric turbulence. It seems likely, from studies made of later fires, that tornadolike winds resulted from conditions that existed in the Peshtigo area. An analysis made of several comparably large fires indicated that surface winds averaged only ten to fourteen miles per hour, except in the immediate vicinity of the fires. It is probable that this explains why only those close enough to the Peshtigo fire to be in danger noticed high winds, which apparently did not occur elsewhere in the region.

A forest fire as large as this one may reach a total rate of energy output comparable to that of a summer thunderstorm —or, as has been noted, even a series of atomic explosions. Showers of burning embers within a half mile of the main fire occasionally produce disastrous fire storm effects by igniting large areas almost simultaneously. When the embers are carried aloft by the convection column, the winds a mile or so above the ground carry them forward before allowing them to drift down to start new fires. This movement is generally on the advancing fire's right flank because the convection currents move in a clockwise direction.

The whirlwinds which occur in large forest fires are of several types. The most common is a small "fire devil," forming near the surface and moving in a rapid swirl over a small area. The larger whirlwinds are similar to a tornado, often originating a thousand feet or more above the ground and burrowing downward until they reach the surface.

No one yet knows what the updraft velocities in the hot central core of a fire's convection column may be. One guess is that it is something over eighty miles an hour—possibly quite a bit over. Huge bubbles of gases can sometimes be seen traveling upward in this column.

If fires of this nature are only partially understood now, it is natural that those who lived through the one in 1871 were baffled by some of the things that happened then. The accounts of such objects as wagons being reduced to ashes in the middle of a clearing, hundreds of yards from anything else combustible, can be explained by the flashover phenomenon that occurs when combustible gases explode. A fire storm, accompanied by a jet of flame shooting out of the main body of the fire and by tornadic winds, has such awesome power that it cannot be expected to behave like other, smaller fires.

Not all of the Peshtigo fire's descriptions can be accepted as true. The best explanation for such claims as Hauser's contention that "the earth trembled" as the fire advanced is that he was mistaken. No one else seems to have noticed an

213

earthquakelike phenomenon. Some of the other stories that came out of the fire are doubtless false. But even a skeptic can accept the fact that strange things did happen during the Peshtigo fire, if for no better reason than that during any such catastrophe unexpected things can be expected. After a tornado, a feather will be found imbedded in an oak, where it can be pointed out to newspaper cameramen. After a flood, a kitten will be found asleep in the upstairs room of a house that had been completely under water, and the kitten's fur will be dry.

And so it is quite possible that 720 brand-new axes in the Peshtigo Company's store were melted into a single metallic lump and that Mr. and Mrs. Samuel Slaughter's feather bed was found unscorched in a shallow well where they had thrown it. And that the hickory wood of the wagon tongue on the Black Hawk, the company's hand-operated fire engine, was not even charred at a point two feet from where the heavy iron at the point of the shaft was melted by the fire.

TWENTY

•

In the years after the Peshtigo fire, stories of the fire were told by the survivors to their families and friends, who in turn passed them along to others who would listen. There was, for example, the tale of Nettie Delano.

Nettie was three years old the night the fire came to Peshtigo, so when she talked about her experiences she was relying mainly on what she had heard from others. Her mother had died when Nettie was born, leaving several older children as well as her husband. It is said that Delano was a member of the Hudson River clan which later combined with the Roosevelt family.

When the town began to burn, the Peshtigo Delano gathered his motherless children and headed for the river. All was confusion. On the way between the house and the river, Nettie became separated from the others. By the time she was missed, it was too late for her father to go back and look for her. Leaving the water seemed like certain death.

The next morning, Delano searched for Nettie among the survivors and among the dead. She was nowhere to be found. It seemed that, like so many others, she had vanished that night. Still, Delano kept looking long after a more practical man would have accepted the certainty that his daughter was dead. Eventually, he found her—not in Peshtigo, but living with a family named Dunton in Oconto.

The child was too young to tell more than the barest details of what had happened. It appeared that when she became separated from the others she had stood by the side of the road—stood there among the careening carriages and the hurrying crowds of desperate people, smoke in her eyes and nose, the town on fire around her—and waited for her father to come back. Did she call out for him, this small girl caught up in a nightmare, or did she stand quietly waiting, full of confidence that nothing would be allowed to happen to her so long as she was good? No one remembered. She was still there, still waiting for her father, when dawn came. Someone saw her and asked her what her name was.

"Nettie."

"Nettie who?"

She did not know. Nettie was all she could remember. Someone put her in a wagon bound for Oconto, where families were opening their homes to refugees. She was one of a number of children without parents that morning. It was logical to assume that, like the others, she had been orphaned by the fire.

After her father found her, he asked the Duntons if they would keep her for another month while he established a new home. They agreed. When he came back for her, she seemed so contented with the Duntons that Delano decided she was better off with them than with him. He agreed to let them adopt her. As Nettie Dunton, she lived to be an old woman and one of the last of the Peshtigo survivors. Yet no one ever understood how she had lived through the fire.

Nettie's escape became one of the stories savored by the survivors in the years after the catastrophe. They liked to tell, too, of the Peshtigo man who was convinced that October 8 was the Judgment Day. He decided to watch for Gabriel from

216

a vantage point where he would have a good view of the wonders he'd heard his minister speak of. He ran to the middle of the Peshtigo River bridge and climbed up on the railing. He stood there, waiting and listening. When no trumpet sounded and the bridge caught fire, however, he decided to wait no longer. He jumped into the water and was saved.

Amanda Stuart had been eighteen years old the night of the fire. Her husband, John, owned six or seven teams of horses and worked each winter cutting logs in the woods for the mill in Peshtigo. In the fall of 1871, they had been married about a year. Their daughter, Sarah, was three weeks old.

The Stuarts had prepared for the possibility that the woods fires might get out of hand. They had put the family valuables in a "turkey"—a lumberman's pack—and Stuart had lowered it carefully into a dry well and put a wooden cover over the pit. The plan they had worked out before the fire had been to run to a plowed field if their home was threatened, but by the time they heard the blast of the factory whistle and the clang of church bells, this doubtful refuge was cut off by flames. They hurried instead toward the river.

The men who had been taking turns fighting the woods fires had agreed that those who were off duty would be responsible for saving the families of those working in the woods. So Stuart took time to stop at the home of a Mrs. Lovelace. He shouted to her to follow him. She ran outside. Then, to his deep disgust, she insisted on going back into the house and blowing out the kerosene lamp.

With Mrs. Lovelace following them at last, the Stuarts continued toward the river. As they ran past the company boardinghouse, a burning door from an upper floor flew past, close enough to singe Stuart's hair and one leg of his trousers. In the river, the young couple stood with only their heads above water, taking turns holding the baby. Stuart kept dipping water from the river on their heads. A calf was swimming nearby. It kept pushing its head up beside Amanda

217

and Sarah to get its share of the water. Great balls of fire whirled overhead from the burning pines. The bark on logs floating near them caught fire. Stuart splashed water on the timber, putting out the flames.

Mrs. Stuart's mother, Mrs. James Eamer, and her two sons headed for the plowed field near their home. Mrs. Eamer collapsed and died on the way. Her sons dragged the body with them. By the time they reached the field, it was on fire.

Amanda's older sister, Annie, and her husband, George McDonald, were among those who lived through the fire. The Eamer girls had married Scotsmen who had come from Canada. Mrs. McDonald was one of those who remembered having a premonition of disaster before the fire came. A bird had repeatedly flown against the window of her home. As everyone knew then, such things were certain signs of bad luck.

After the fire, Stuart and the other men were too busy helping the injured and burying the dead to go back to the well for some time. When he and Amanda went to see what had happened to their valuables, they discovered the wooden cover had caught fire and dropped embers onto the "turkey." It had burned. Only a few things were left—among them a pocket watch and a retractable gold toothpick, brought by a Stuart from the ancestral home in Scotland to provide a token of gracious living in an uncivilized land.

Mrs. Stuart continued to rummage through the fragments remaining in the well and came up with a scorched piece of her brown silk wedding dress. A five-dollar bill she had tucked into its pocket was still intact. With everything else gone, the money seemed like a small fortune. With a key-wound watch, a five-dollar bill, and a retractable gold toothpick, the young couple was ready to help rebuild the town.

Wesley Duket was six years old in 1871. He lived in a part of the Sugar Bush settlement that was later called Harmony Corners. When he was ninety-three, he still remembered what it had been like to be a small boy in the midst of the worst forest fire in American history.

"When the balls of fire started coming down that night," he said, "my mother and father took us down to the spring. We lay down on the ground. They wrapped us with wet quilts. A ball of fire hit the house and it burned. But my sister saved the sewing machine. She wrapped it in wet blankets.

"Next morning, my mother and father were blind. They recovered their sight later. We had a team of oxen. One ox stayed with us at the spring but the other ran away and was burned. We had a shed of colts. We could hear them thrashing as they burned. My brother wanted to open the door, but my sister wouldn't let him."

Wesley had been fond of a woman neighbor, a Mrs. Reinhart. In the morning, when the fire was over, he thought of her. He ran across the blackened fields to her house—or where it had been. It was burned and Mrs. Reinhart was dead.

Eighty-seven years later, Duket could still remember that moment vividly and the hurt he had felt as a boy of six, standing there in the farmyard looking down at what was left of the woman who had given him cookies. Most of the clothing was burned from her body. A fragment of shawl remained. He took the unburned corner of the shawl and put it in his pocket so he would always remember Mrs. Reinhart.

Among those who crossed the bridge before it burned were Mrs. Henry Merkatoris and her five children. The mother and her two sons and three daughters then waded into the river and perched on a log. One of the girls, who was five years old that night, grew up to become Mrs. Elizabeth Wilke and to tell how the air had been full of flames and the river full of animals and people. She remembered that in the morning there were numerous bodies along the river banks and in the village streets and how the family feared that Merkatoris, who had been in the woods with the men on guard there against fire, had perished. But he rejoined them after daylight came. Mrs. Wilke lived to be ninety-five. She still carried scars on

219

her hands and legs as a reminder of the night Peshtigo burned.

Some of the stories the survivors told had been passed along from one to the other until some of the details were vague. This was the case with the account of how a lumberjack saved a sick friend. No one remembered the names anymore, but everyone agreed the shanty boy had upheld the honor of the woods code that holds no man leaves a helpless companion when danger threatens. The friend was recuperating from typhoid fever and was lying in a bed in Peshtigo when the town began to burn. The lumberjack picked him up and carried him outside. He scooped out a shallow trench in the sandy soil, laid the sick man in it and covered him with dirt. Then the lumberjack fled. But he had delayed too long. The fellow with typhoid survived in his temporary sepulcher. The body of the lumberjack was found nearby.

In the tales the survivors told, there were a number of accounts of how fate singled out one fleeing human for survival while those around him perished. One example was the family of J. E. Beebe of Peshtigo. He, his wife, and four children ran for the river. Flames struck down both parents and three of the children. But the four-year-old daughter, who was only a few feet from the others, was entirely unhurt. Fred Guse, a cobbler, saw the child standing there next to the bodies of her family. He snatched her up and carried her with him to the river. With the child clinging to his shoulders, he swam out to deep water and the two of them stayed there, floating and swimming, until the worst of the danger was over. Then Guse waded into shallow water with the child. His face and neck were burned but the girl was still uninjured.

The rescue proved lucky for Guse. Mrs. Beebe had been the daughter of Governor Henry P. Baldwin of Michigan. When the governor came to Peshtigo to claim his granddaughter he heard the account of how she had been saved and gave Guse five hundred dollars, a sum generous enough in those days so the cobbler was able to set himself up in business in Chicago.

The story of the hermit who lived near Peshtigo is one of those in which it is hard to tell where fact ends and fancy begins. But it seems certain that there was such a fellow, if only because it is agreed his name was Schwartz—no one setting out to make up a story of a hermit out of whole cloth would give him a name like Schwartz the Hermit.

It was said that Schwartz had been a fine-looking fellow as a youth—in Prussia, that would have been, before he lost one of his eyes. He was in love with a girl there, but she chose a Prussian major instead. Convinced that mankind in general and womankind in particular were a bad lot, Schwartz sailed for the United States and tramped north into the Wisconsin wilderness about 1852. He dug himself a home in the side of a hill and went about being a hermit with Teutonic thoroughness and efficiency. Even as a hermit, he couldn't avoid prospering to the point where he began to acquire such things as chickens, geese, and hogs, along with a pet dog and cat. As his livestock increased, he expanded his burrow to accommodate them. By 1871, he and the animals were living cozily in a single dwelling, which appears to have been a sort of hut combined with the original excavation he had made.

There were stories circulating around Peshtigo that Schwartz was rich and had gold buried in the dirt floor of his combination house, barn, chicken house, and hog pen. It seems doubtful that this was the case, but it was believed so widely that after the fire searching parties headed through the smoldering woods to see what had happened to Schwartz. If the old man had burned up, they intended to do a little prospecting in the floor of his living quarters.

The searchers were greeted by the hermit, who was hale and hearty as ever. He had gathered his animals about him when the fire approached and hurried down to nearby Trout Creek. He assured the lumberjacks that he and his livestock weren't even singed. It was quite a disappointment to those

221

who had been hoping to seek their fortune in Schwartz's floor. Still, it was agreed that the fire had been beneficial in one respect. As far as anyone knew, this was the first bath old Schwartz had taken since he came over from Prussia nearly twenty years before.

Charlie House, a Milwaukee newspaperman, interviewed Mrs. Antone Grandow when she was ninety-five about her experiences as a girl of twelve, and he kept his notes of the conversation. She and her father had gone out to a log cabin near Peshtigo to go partridge hunting in the fall of 1871.

"It was so hot you couldn't hardly breathe," Mrs. Grandow told House. "There was smoke everywhere for three or four days there. Big pieces of black things floated through the air and you couldn't hardly keep clean of it."

"You were afraid?" House asked.

"I was afraid of it. I was only a little girl. It was terrible. It smelled hot and it hurt you to smell that air, it was so sharp. My daddy didn't go hunting because the smoke got in your eyes. The stuff in the air got to be like snowflakes, there were so many. And it blowed. I tell you it blowed. It blowed like anything."

The owners of the cabin had gone off to visit someone in Peshtigo. House asked if they came back after the fire.

"They never come back at all," the old woman said. "I never heard of them again, not in all these years. They was burned — but they was never seen dead, neither."

She remembered that before the fire a man came out of the woods carrying a box of what she called "draw line things," presumably surveyor's instruments.

"He was scared. The draw line things was very important. He said to us that he would sink the draw line things in the mud and if any of us gets out without dying he will know where it is. He said he don't think he can make it.

"We prayed and prayed and prayed. And then it come. And we prayed all the time until we got into the water and we prayed. But it was too hot and we went in the cabin and

222

covered us with wet blankets and clothes—a big pile of them, all wet."

"Do you remember how long you were in the cabin?"

"A long time. Then finally it went away. My daddy, he asked the man to look out for me and then he went off to get some help and some food because we was hungry. My daddy tried to get to Peshtigo but he come back and he sat down and cried because he couldn't find the way out. The roads, they was all covered deep with ashes and trees and my daddy got lost so he couldn't get out. We had to stay there until somebody came and helped us."

"Were you or the man or your daddy burned?"

"Our skins was all bright red and we had burned places on us from burnings things the wind blew on us. Daddy was the worst of all from going out into the hot woods."

"Was there something to eat in the cabin?"

"It was all et up when the fire came. They was some turnips in the garden and some carrots, I think. They was cooked in the ground. We ate them. We didn't have no water. The well was dried up and so was the river. The mud was baked hard. We didn't have no water. We found a poor cow, though, and we got a little milk."

"Do you remember any more?"

"I saw some big piles of burned people—you couldn't tell they was people. In Peshtigo, I think. Everything had dried up from the hot."

"The man with the draw line things—was he all right?"

"Well, he went away and said he would come back for the draw line things, but he never come back."

"And the draw line things?"

"They must be there yet."

There are a few stories of the fire's aftermath that tell of looters who preyed on the dead. John Nelligan recorded the case of one such scavenger who joined in the search for a man who had fled from Peshtigo carrying a considerable sum of money—three or four thousand dollars was the amount

223

mentioned. The missing man was found where he had died, overcome by heat and smoke. Blood had seeped from an injury and stained the currency, which could be seen sticking out of the man's pocket. The victim's brother was in the group that found him. He stood looking down at the body, his eyes wet with tears. The thief also appeared to be saddened by the sight, although his sorrow came from the fact that he hadn't found the dead man before the others got there. He knelt by the body, then reached over and took the money.

"I will just keep this for a remembrance," he said.

The brother was too filled with grief to grasp what was going on for a moment. Then he grabbed the cash and handed the con man a fragment of newspaper the dead brother had been carrying.

"Here," he said, "this will do just as well for a remembrance."

A favorite story told by those who lived through the fire involved a man who was found skulking about Peshtigo, looking for rings and other valuables among the dead. Several indignant men grabbed him. Their shouts brought others running. A jury was formed on the spot. It returned a unanimous verdict: Hang him, and the sooner the better. This was easier ordered than done. A proper hanging requires a rope. Because of the fire's thoroughness, none was available closer than Marinette. The guest of honor relaxed a little. But in pioneer country, there is always someone who knows how to make do.

"If we can't hang him with a rope," a lumberjack on the jury pointed out, "we can string him up with a log chain."

There were plenty of such chains in the vicinity, although there was a serious shortage of tree limbs from which to swing the culprit. But no one had ever tried hanging a man with a log chain before or even seen such a thing accomplished. While the crowd was discussing how best to go about this unprecedented method of execution, the victim continued to plead for mercy.

Perhaps it was his pleas, reinforced by the melancholy

224

scene of death and destruction. Perhaps it was simply too much trouble to lynch him without the proper equipment. At any rate, according to the account handed down by men who claimed to have been there, the fellow was told he could go free if he would get down on his knees and ask pardon for stealing from the dead. He lost no time in doing so and the lumberjacks and townsfolk turned him loose.

Some of the stories that came out of the fire are only fragments, with important parts missing. One of these is the incident involving a two-year-old boy, Frankie, whose father, Frank Jacobs, was described as a "Hungarian of Kossuth's party." Jacobs had lived in Peshtigo for eighteen years before the fire. On the night of the disaster, Frankie was in the care of his mother's sister, a young woman named Charlotte Seymour. She got beyond her depth in the river and was drowned. Jacobs could find no trace of his son for several days and had nearly given up hope when Mrs. John De Marsh returned to Peshtigo from Green Bay, where she had gone with other refugees aboard a steamer. She told Jacobs she had seen the blue-eyed, brown-haired boy on the ship. The man who was taking care of him had asked her if she knew the child. She told him she did, adding that she had not seen the parents among the survivors and thought they were probably dead.

Mrs. De Marsh had not asked the man his name or address, but she remembered he had said something about going to Chicago. With that clue, Jacobs appealed for help to the most important Chicagoan he knew, William Ogden. The millionaire took time to write a lengthy letter on Jacobs' behalf which was printed in the *Chicago Tribune*. It said the boy could speak only one word plainly—the name of a favorite uncle, Ike. "If asked where Ike is he will show, his parents think, an interest, and that he understands the meaning," Ogden wrote. "Frankie wore on the night of the fire a black and white checked flannel shirt, a red flannel dress and red, brown and white checked apron, with a band of purple-and-white check."

That is where the story ends. Whether the stranger saw

Ogden's letter and returned Frankie to his parents is one of the things that no one seems to remember, leaving the anecdote unfinished — leaving, too, the picture of a very small boy in a red flannel dress and checked apron somehow surviving an experience that killed so many others.

Another account of a seemingly unlikely survival was told by a Green Bay man who happened to be in Peshtigo the night of October 8. He grabbed up a pair of blankets and a bucket of water before he fled. Among the frightened refugees he saw a woman with two children who seemed uncertain about where to go.

"Come with me," he told her.

They followed him. When they came to a ditch near the road, he ordered the woman and children to lie down. He threw himself down next to them and shared his wet blankets with them. As they lay there, another woman came running along. Her clothing was half burned from her body. A large bundle was in her arms. When she saw them, she put the bundle down next to the Green Bay man in the ditch. He saw it consisted of a young child and an empty roll of clothing.

"Great God!" the second woman cried. "Where is my baby?"

The man jumped to his feet. A few yards away, he saw the baby lying in the road. It was kicking up its heels, cooing happily, when "a great billow of flame rolled over it, striking the ground beyond and leaving the baby in the center of a great arch of fire."

The man and the baby's mother stood rooted there, horrified. But when the flames slackened, the baby was still happily kicking. The Green Bay visitor leaped out of the ditch, grabbed the child and got safely back. "It is no wonder," the narrator of the tale added, "that the mother fainted when she secured the child."

226

●

Not long after the Peshtigo fire, a Green Bay physician prophesied that within ten years "all the unfortunate survivors of that terrible catastrophe will have paid the debt of nature, victims of the irreparable injury inflicted on their constitutions by smoke, air, water and fire."

This gloomy prediction was not fulfilled, although those survivors who died within the next few years were often believed to have been delayed casualties of the fire. It seems likely that in some cases this was true. Other survivors lived into their eighties or nineties—one or two reached a hundred —and for many years they held annual reunions at Peshtigo.

The gathering held on the eightieth anniversary of the fire was typical. By then there were known to be fifty-three persons still alive who had lived through the fire. Nineteen of the fifty-three arrived to swap tales that had been told many times before. Autumn hues colored the woods. Creeks and the river were running high after a season of plentiful rain. The nineteen gray-haired men and women were quick to point out this contrast with how it had been in 1871.

The patriarch of the group was Uncle Ed Slaughter, who

said with proud precision that his age was ninety-four years and eight months, making him fourteen years and eight months old the night of the fire. He talked about what had happened then: "Mother and my two sisters headed for the river. Father and one of my brothers and I stayed at the house and tried to save it. The inside of the house caught fire first. We finally gave up and started for the river.

"A flying board hit Father in the head and I started to cry. But he got up and we got behind a pine stump a block from the river. We spent the night there."

One of Slaughter's brothers was seriously burned but recovered. The brother's wife and young daughter burned to death.

Another of those at the eightieth reunion was Charles E. "Dad" Wright, who was ninety-one. He and his sister, Mrs. Nellie Race, then eighty-seven, had lived on the shore of the bay about six miles from Peshtigo the night of the fire.

"Mother was sick in bed and was carried, bed and all, into a boat," Wright recalled. "The fire destroyed all the houses around but somehow missed ours."

The men and women who had been children when the village burned climbed onto the stage in the Peshtigo High School gymnasium that afternoon of the anniversary and listened to speeches dedicating a plaque erected by the State Historical Society of Wisconsin to commemorate the fire. Then they were bundled into automobiles for the two-block ride to the Peshtigo Fire Cemetery. All but two of the survivors ignored the chill fall weather to take a close look at the plaque there. Near it, at the foot of a slope under a big oak tree, is a ten-by-sixteen-foot plot believed to be approximately where more than three hundred bodies of unidentified fire victims are buried. Later in the day, another marker was dedicated at the cemetery at Harmony, five miles from Peshtigo, where more than one hundred unidentified bodies of Sugar Bush residents were buried in another mass grave.

The marked graves of Peshtigo fire victims in the ceme-

228

teries have headstones engraved in English, German, or Norwegian. Under the names of twelve members of the McGregor family is the brief summary of what happened to them: "All lost in the calamity." Another gravestone marks the graves of the *frau and kinder* of a man named Lemke, who lost his wife and five daughters. There are many such examples.

Some years ago, there was talk of moving the Peshtigo cemetery which is near the site of Father Pernin's church. The town was growing, and the old burial ground was in the way of progress. But women of the town and some of the men rallied. They won a showdown battle with those who felt that sentiment should not stand in the way of change. Mrs. Fay Stuart Dooley, whose eighteen-year-old grandmother had started life again with the five-dollar bill that had survived in the well, led the successful fight to let the dead rest in peace.

To a present-day traveler in Wisconsin's north country, Peshtigo is but one of a series of small cities on U.S. Route 41 between Green Bay and the Wisconsin-Michigan border. The highway narrows from four lanes to two shortly before the stadium Green Bay built as a monument to its Packers. The road continues north, a few miles inland from the bay, past pleasant woods—birch, aspen, maples—and prosperous-looking dairy farms. There are big barns and comfortable white houses.

At a four-corners called Abrams, Route 41 separates from another main highway and angles toward the bay, turning north again in the vicinity of Pensaukee, which was a thriving sawmill community when all of northern Wisconsin was forest. It continues past Oconto, then northeast through slightly rolling countryside to Peshtigo, where the highway follows French Street to a bridge across the Peshtigo River. Six miles beyond Peshtigo, the highway crosses the Menominee River, which forms the boundary between the states and between the small cities of Marinette and Menominee.

Peshtigo—the name comes from a Chippewa word meaning "river of the wild goose"—is located 256 miles north of Chicago. It still bases its economy principally on lumber. A pulp mill and wood yard are located on the approximate site of the vanished woodenware factory. Across the river, about where Lister's Foundry was situated at the time of the fire, is a paper mill. Also included among present-day Peshtigo's industries are a boat factory and a manufacturer of laminated wooden roof supports. The population of about 2500 represents only a modest increase from 1871.

Many wooden buildings on the main street have the second-story false fronts which were considered an architectural necessity by the carpenters who built small towns sixty or seventy years ago—the same kind of false fronts which are familiar to fans of movies about places like Dodge City. An exception is the Cholette Hotel, a blocky brick building three stories high. It was constructed shortly after the fire.

To the east of the river, which is dammed just below the bridge, is a great pile of logs, the raw material the local mill uses to make specialized paper products. The logs are no longer cut from huge white pines and floated down the stream from an apparently inexhaustible forest. The logs the tourists see now as they head northeast from Peshtigo are puny by comparison. In the days when the shanty boys swarmed through the woods, such timber would have been used for stovewood.

A little south of Peshtigo, the highway passes through a farming area which old-timers still call the Sugar Bushes. So quickly are old ways forgotten that some Peshtigo residents assume this name came from a period lasting until comparatively recent times when sugar beets were grown in the region. The days when groves of sugar maples showed settlers that here was likely farmland in the midst of the great pine forest have been preserved only in a name which is itself rapidly passing out of use.

What was once called the Lower Sugar Bush begins about two miles from the village in an area now traversed by Route 41.

230

Aside from an occasional tavern and filling station, the region is still devoted to farming. One of the crossroads in what was the Lower Bush now has the picturesque name of Baby's Corners. To the north of the Lower Bush and a little northeast of Peshtigo is Harmony, located in what was the Middle Bush. North of this, above the Peshtigo River, is Porterfield, another four-corners settlement, in what was once the Upper Sugar Bush.

There are no main-traveled roads in what were the Middle and Upper Bushes. A stranger driving along the county trunk highways can relax at the wheel, seldom meeting another car. In some areas, he goes past swampy-looking woods, with ferns growing in profusion under deciduous trees. Cattails grow along the roadsides. In summer, the fields are splashed with color from buttercups and a weed called devil's paintbrush. The glaciers were here once, and they have left their legacy in the form of low, sandy hills thinly covered by vegetation. The melting ice also left numerous rocks, ranging in size from pebbles to boulders. The farmers have piled the stones in great mounds in the center of their fields, like idols of a primitive race.

In dairy country, prosperity is measured by the size of the barn and whether it is kept in paint and repair, so this is obviously good country for Holsteins. Some of the small outbuildings, used now for storage, are made of hand-squared logs. The farmers have not torn down the log cabins their grandfathers built, but the time is long since past when a cabin was good enough to house a man's cows, or even his family.

The Peshtigo River meanders into the Upper Bush from the west. It is about 150 feet wide here, doubling its size after it makes a sharp bend to the south toward Peshtigo. Below the dam in the village, the stream narrows again and winds in a series of horseshoe bends toward the southeast for six miles to discharge into the bay.

The time when the area around the river's mouth was one

of the busiest harbors on Lake Michigan is hardly remembered now. Fifteen hundred people lived there then. Steamers stopped on their way to Green Bay or Marinette. Timber was loaded to be carried by barge to Milwaukee and Chicago. Boats were built there, using a nearby stand of white oak to supply the raw material. Now there is no trace of all this activity but a few rotting pilings along the river. Except for an occasional fisherman in what is now called Peshtigo Harbor Wildlife Area, there are few signs of human life in a place which once bustled with activity and was an important part of William Ogden's great timber empire.

Unlike the harbor area, Peshtigo has held its own. Wood is still the basis for its economy, but it also competes with other north country communities for tourists. At the edge of town is a sign urging travelers to visit the Peshtigo Fire Museum, which contains a collection of miscellany, mostly unconnected with the fire. The museum is housed in what was once a church. Next to it is the cemetery on Oconto Avenue with the mass grave for the unidentified dead of 1871.

The few mementos of the big fire in the museum include a piece of ticking from a feather bed. Its owner somehow brought this fragile piece of property through the conflagration with only one small hole burned in it. The hole is neatly darned, for the ticking was used by its owner for years before it became a souvenir. In a glass case is a metal pie plate, proudly inscribed with the name of Emilie Brouette, who owned it at the time many of Peshtigo's residents were sure the world was ending. There are two charred ten-by-ten timbers of white pine which escaped relatively unscathed when the town was wiped off the earth. And that's about all that remains of the Peshtigo of 1871 in this museum named after the fire. The dearth of relics is mute testimony of how thoroughly the flames did their work.

The best evidences of what the fire did to Peshtigo are the tombstones. Some are in the little cemetery on Oconto Avenue. Some are in an old graveyard in Harmony Corners.

232

Still others are in a small, well-tended cemetery along a country road near Michael's tavern in what was once the Lower Sugar Bush.

One stone commemorates twelve persons buried under it. It was raised to mark the grave of Henry Newberry, 22; Selah F. Newberry, 20; Walter B. Newberry, 12; Louisa, wife of W. B. Newberry, 28; Nellie Newberry, 4; Walter Newberry, 2; an unnamed infant Newberry; Edward S. Newberry, 28; Louisa A. Newberry, Edward's 19-year-old wife; Charles O. Newberry, 32; Franklin H. Newberry, 2, and Jessie Newberry, 5.

"All died Oct. 8, 1871," the marker says. With so many names, there was no room for a fuller explanation. Those who raised the stone to the departed Newberrys must have felt none would ever be needed. They could not have imagined a time when the memory of that date would grow dim in northeastern Wisconsin.

The Peshtigo that travelers see as they drive through on Route 41 is laid out almost exactly as was the village that was destroyed in 1871. The streets bear the same names. The older houses are built in the same places as their predecessors. The bridge across the river is the direct descendant of the wooden structure that was there when the Peshtigo Company was putting its mark—a diamond with a P centered in it—onto most of the logs cut for miles around. The dam is made of concrete now instead of timber, but it is in the same place as the one that was opened to drain the river to hunt for the bodies of those drowned trying to escape the fire.

The ranch houses on the outskirts of the town are in what used to be open country. But the main part of the present-day Peshtigo, including its business district, is much the way it was after the new community was rebuilt on the ashes of the old.

The church which houses the museum once belonged to the Congregationalists, who built it on the east side of the river to replace the one lost in 1871. It was moved to its

233

present site when it was purchased by St. Mary's parish, before the Roman Catholics built a more modern structure several blocks away. In 1871, Father Pernin's church stood on this same corner of Oconto and Ellis avenues, but then the building faced on Ellis Avenue.

From the church-museum to the river is only two-and-a-half blocks, along what was then the main road to Oconto in one direction and Marinette in the other. Behind the church and adjoining the cemetery is Trout Creek, which flows into the river a little above the bridge.

As in the days when the Peshtigo Company flourished and lumberjacks strode down the plank sidewalks, the streets east of the river are named mostly for trees and for lumbermen—Oak, Linden, Spruce, Pine, Ogden, Stephenson. Those west of the river, where nearly all the retail establishments have always been located, commemorate such once-important men as Superintendent Ellis.

Most present residents of Peshtigo, when pressed by visitors for information about the big fire, refer them to a brief pamphlet prepared by the Chamber of Commerce for tourists. Beyond that, many of them imply, they're not much interested. Some seem to be weary of hearing about something that happened so long ago. They wish strangers would talk about something more pertinent, such as paper-making or fishing or how to keep more of the travelers from driving on north without spending money in the town. The talk at LaValley's, Pete's Uptown, and the other small taverns along French Street is not apt to be about history.

But some descendants of those who were in the fire talk of it as if the embers were still warm. One woman, whose grandmother used to tell her of seeing friends "roasted like marshmallows," said fiercely that a lot of nonsense has been talked and written about it. But she had heard of it from a woman who nearly died in the fire, so she knew it wasn't simply a lot of words in musty books.

On the street which runs along the east side of the river

234

lived old Ed Bruette, who said he had no first-hand knowledge because he was born a few years after the fire. But he had been told how his parents and two older brothers escaped by huddling in the flats all night and how his grandmother had been "smothered to death by the fire" near where the museum now stands.

"And just down this street, according to the stories I've heard, lived this fellow they were going to string up only they couldn't find a rope," he said. "But you've probably heard the story."

"Is it true?"

"So they say. I wasn't there. I'm only ninety-one, so I'm too young to remember."

It has been some time since any gathering of survivors has been held. By 1967, so far as was known, there were only two people left. Joseph Prue, who was a baby when he lived through the fire, had long since moved to California. Mrs. Amelia Desroches—born Amelia Dupuis—had been five that October. In her old age, she lived in the Pel-Bar Convalescent Home in Peshtigo, where she was sometimes pointed out to visitors.

When she was younger, Mrs. Desroches sometimes talked of the night she lived with her parents in Marinette and heard her mother tell her father: "Wake up. The end of the world is coming." It looked like the end of the world to a five-year-old child, too. The sky was red. As she ran with her parents toward the Menominee River, the wind blew sand against her face and legs so hard that each grain stung her skin.

The parents' first thought had been to cross the bridge to Menominee on the Michigan side, but a man advised them to get aboard a flat-bottomed barge with other refugees. As it floated down the river, sparks blown by the wind caught the boat on fire. But the flames were extinguished and the barge continued into the bay. Five-year-old Amelia looked back toward the land.

235

"Look," she told her mother, in wonder. "Look, it's snowing fire."

As the years went by, Mrs. Desroches talked less and less of what it had been like that night. The time came when she no longer was able to share the memories. The fire had faded into the hazy dreams of a distant time, even for her.

The memory of it now lives mainly in the minds of those who heard of it from their parents or grandparents. Some of the survivors' descendants were told surprisingly little about it. Some who lived through that night could never bring themselves to talk about what had happened. They wanted only to forget. But others handed on the story of the fire that destroyed the town.

"What it was like, my grandmother used to say, wasn't the way it was written down in a lot of the stuff that's been printed," a middle-aged woman said. "I wasn't there myself, of course. But I've talked with my grandmother. I've talked with others who went through it. I think I know something about it and I'll tell you what it was like in Peshtigo that night."

She fixed her visitor with a pair of stern blue eyes. Her hands were trembling.

"It was just plain hell."

INDEX

A

Abrams—229
Advocate, Green Bay—see
  Tilton
Ahnapee—185, 187
Albrecht, Charles—137-8
Albrecht, Louise—137
Army, U. S.—193
Arndt, Judge John P.—19
Arnold, R. Keith—201, 210
Ashland—16
Astor, John Jacob—27
Aust, Mrs. Friedrich—137

B

Backfiring—59-60
Bagley & Curry—151
Bagnall, John T.—178
Baldwin, Gov. Henry P.—
  163-4, 220
Bartels, Augusta—78, 94
Bartels, Charles—76, 95
Bartels, F. J.—4
Bartels, Henry—89-90
Bateman, Henry—89-90
Bay City—13, 15
Bay Settlement—29
Beach, Rev. Edwin R.—8, 37
Beebe, J. E.—220
Bernson, "Praying Peter"—
  55-6
Birch Creek—152-5, 168
Bird, H. P.—145-6
Births during fire—135-6
Blaisdell, James—207
Blowup fires—201, 209
Boston relief committee—191,
  199
Breweries—3, 32
Brice, Adele—31, 86
Brouette, Emilie—232
Brown, A. C.—151, 182

Brown County—23, 32-3, 187
Bruette, Ed—235
Brussels, Wis.—30, 32, 54, 58,
  185-8
Buck, Charles C.—201, 210
Bucklin, George—63
Bunday Creek—74, 137
Burkhart, Anton—48
Burns, Thomas—125
Bush, Thomas—68
Byram, George M.—211-2

C

Cameron, John—106-7, 113
Casco—49, 185
Case & Turner—158
Cato—160
Causes of fire—201, 203-13
Cavoit, Nick—9, 36, 195
Cedar River—101-2
Champion—29
Chase, Salmon P.—27
Chicago—5, 7, 15, 23, 36, 107,
  142, 164, 167, 180-1, 185,
  191, 195, 211, 230
Church, John—88
Church, Warren—88, 197
Churches—see religion
Circus, Older's—40-1
Clements, J. G.—45-6, 114-5
Cloquet fire—211
Cocoanut Grove fire—168
Cole & Co.—152
Coneya, Maxeme—71
Conlon, John—60
Conn, A. C.—39-40
Convection column—209-11,
  213
Cox, John—136
Crane, Dr. H. O.—193
Crown fires—212
Cryin, Joseph—71
Crying, Thomas—64, 68, 71

Cunnion, T. C.—21-2
Curry, Mike—148
Curtis, William—89

D

Death toll—41, 54, 57, 72, 78, 81, 86, 91, 94, 121, 137, 155, 157, 163, 167-8, 187, 211
Delano, Nettie—215-6
Delia, Big—14-5
De Marsh, Mrs. John—225
Demereau, Mrs. Nelson—65
Desroches, Mrs. Amelia— 235-6
Diederich, Christ—89
Dolan, Will—131
Donlon, James—68
Dooley, Mrs. Fay—208, 229
Door County—6, 26-7, 33, 40, 47, 53, 58, 86, 167-8, 184, 186-7, 191, 197, 206
Downey, Peter S.—146
Doyle, Pat—87
Drees, Henry—16
Drees, John B.—197
Drought—2-3, 5, 34, 74, 99, 204-5
Duket, Wesley—218-9
Dunlap, steamer—101, 144
Dunton—see Delano
Dupuis—see Desroches
Dycksville—186-7

E

Eagle, Marinette—4, 7-9, 45, 196-7, 205
Eamer, Mrs. James—218
Eames, Phineas—152-5
Ellis, W. A.—44, 131, 136, 139-40, 190, 234
Ellis, Mrs. W. A.—139-42

Elm Creek—159
England family—134-5
Escanaba—144

F

Fairchild, A. M.—150-1
Fairchild, Gov. Lucius—166, 180-1, 192
Fairchild, Mrs. Lucius—180-1
Filiatrault, J. W.—128
Firefighting methods—39-41, 43-4, 108-9, 122, 158, 214
Fire storms—203, 209-10, 213
First Belgian Settlement—see Robinsonville
Forester—159, 162
Forest Service, U. S.—203, 208, 211
Forests, description of—1-3, 5, 11-13, 19, 27, 37, 41, 44, 98, 106, 206
Forestville, Mich.—159-61
Forestville, Wis.—54, 185, 188
Fort Howard—144, 205
Fuller, Rev. H. T.—193

G

Gardner—58, 185
Gardner, F. B.—185-6
Gas, marsh—199, 208-9
General Slocum steamer fire— 168
Glenmore—187
Godfrey, George—187-8
Goodspeed, Rev. E. J.—159
Grandow, Mrs. Antone—222-3
Grand Rapids—15
Graniez—197
Gratiot County—158
Gray, Oscar—40
Green Bay, the—6, 26-7, 40-1, 52, 58, 156, 167, 184, 190,

192-3, 202, 204, 212
Green Bay, city of—5, 9, 11, 13-4, 16-7, 19, 26-9, 32, 34, 40-2, 47-8, 52, 106, 166-7, 183-4, 187, 190-1, 205, 226-7, 229
Green, Isaac—159
Ground fires—212
Guild, Leonard—149
Guillfoyle, Kate—136
Guse, Fred—220

H

Hale, Levi—196
Hall, Dr. Ben R.—182
Hanson, Lars—138-9
Harmony—73, 218, 228, 231-2
Harms, R. W.—115-6
Harris, J.—174
Hartford fire—165
Hauser, J. H.—202, 213
Hawley, Capt. Thomas—4, 144-5, 166-7
Hay, T. A.—108-9, 117-8, 195, 197
Hayward—16
Heath, Walter—168-9
Heidenworth, Carrie—118
Heydenberg, David—75
Hill, L. H.—79, 94, 173
Hime, Michael—53-5
Holbrook, Stewart—25, 168
Holland City—157-8, 163
Hospitals—166, 182-3, 193
Hotels—36, 124, 148, 150, 166, 182, 196
House, Charlie—222-3
Howard, George—157
Howard, M. D.   157 8
Howard, William A.—163
Hoyt, John—79-81, 94
Hubbard, R. B.—160

Huebner, Rev. Charles—37, 75-6
Hurley—16
Huron, city of—159-60
Huron, Lake—159-60, 162, 164

I

Immigrants—6, 26-33, 46, 48, 54, 57, 73, 124, 135, 185, 197-8
Indians—2, 12-3, 19, 27, 41, 90-1
Iroquois Theater fire—168

J

Jacksonport—178
Jacobs, Frank—225-6
Jacobson, August—138-9
Jarvis, Cyril—69, 71
Jaques, J. F.—7
Johnson, Charles—148
Johnston, James—120
Jones, David—19

K

Kelly, Terrance—77-8, 96-7
Kelsey, Dr. J. F.—4, 10, 118, 183, 193
Kent, John—160-2
Kewaunee, village of—27, 48-9, 185
Kewaunee County—6, 26-7, 33, 40, 47, 53, 86, 167-8, 184-7, 197, 206
Kirby Carpenter Co.—166
Kittner, Edward—74-6, 95-6
Kittner, Mrs. Edward—95-6
Kuchenberg, Adolph—5

L

Laird, Jacob—158-9
Lamb, Willard—48-9
Lamp, Charles—81-2
Land, price of—11
Lansing—158, 163
Lapham, Increase A.—206-7
Lasure, Floy—83-5
Lasure, Joseph—83-5
Laughrey, Charles—146
Lawson, G. A.—48-9
Leaguee, Louis—71-2
Leavenworth, Col. J. H.—168
Legends of fire—200-1, 213-4, 221-6
Lemke, John—89
Lezotte, Celestine—93-4
Lezotte, Frank—93-4
Lincoln—188
Lister, David—36, 230
Little Sturgeon Bay—58, 185, 187
Little Suamico—39
Logging—3, 5, 8-9, 11-4, 19, 21-3, 36, 193, 206-7, 230, 234
Ludington—15
Ludington Co.—151
Ludington, Wells & Van Schaick Co.—166
Lumberjacks—1, 3, 4, 8, 12-4, 16, 18-25, 91-2, 96-7, 106, 158, 169-71, 178-9, 194, 208, 230, 234
Lynchings—20-1, 224-5

M

Manistee—158
Manning, J. C.—183
Marinette—3, 5-8, 11, 15-6, 19, 21, 34-5, 37, 39-40, 85, 95, 98, 100-1, 113, 143-4, 150-1, 165-6, 169, 177, 182, 184, 190, 229, 235
Marshall, Nellie—104, 142
Martin, Xavier—29-31, 187, 197
Maxon, David—45, 125-6
May, Dr. Jacob—182
McAdams, Frank—62-4
McArdle, Richard E.—211
McCusker, Con—61, 68
McDonald, Donald—124, 132
McDonald, George—218
McGregor, Daniel—105, 123
McGregor, Duncan—123
McGregor, Jennie—105
McPherson, Mrs. Sally—78
Mendocino National Forest—211
Menekaune—8, 143-50, 174, 190
Menominee, city of—5, 46, 101, 143-4, 182, 190, 205, 229, 235
Menominee River—5, 143-4, 151, 212, 229, 235
Merkatoris, Henry—219
Merrill, Byron J.—69, 71
Merryman, A. C.—183
Michigan, fires in—152-164, 169
Michigan, Lake—6, 27, 36-7, 144
Milwaukee—15-6, 166, 187-8, 191, 193, 204-5
Mitchell, Alexander—188
Mitchell, Gen. Billy—188
Monahan, James—174
Moore, Capt. J. P.—195
Morris, Mary F.—181
Mulligan, John—127, 165-6
Museum, Peshtigo Fire—232, 234
Muskegon—14-5

N

Nasawaupee—54
Naze, Eugene—188
Neil, Maggie—see O'Neil
Nelding, Frederick—126-7
Nelligan, John E.—18-20, 22,
  92-3, 194, 223-4
Newberry family—233
New Franken—47-54, 60-1
Newspapers—4, 7-8, 17, 37,
  45, 167, 191, 186-7, 225
Newton, Adnah—78-9, 94
Newton, Samuel—78
Noyes, Luther B.—7-8, 45,
  143, 196-7, 205

O

Oakes, Nan—140-1
Oakes, W. C.—36
Oconto, city of—5, 9, 15, 18-
  20, 38-9, 41-2, 73, 92-4,
  176, 190-1, 202, 216, 229
Oconto County—19
Oconto River—5, 92
Ogden, William B.—7, 34-6,
  142, 195, 225, 232, 234
Oleson, John—94
O'Neil, Maggie—59-61, 63, 67
Oshkosh—16, 166

P

Paris, Mich.—162
Pasture-maker fires—156
Pensaukee—5, 19, 38-40, 229
Pernin, Father—37, 98-105,
  110-3, 116-7, 119, 130-1,
  139, 144, 149, 169-70, 175-
  7, 200, 202-3, 229, 234
Peshtigo Co.—7, 9, 36, 43-4,
  46, 75, 106, 116, 119, 134,
  139, 169, 174, 195, 214,
232-4
Peshtigo Fire Cemetery—228
Peshtigo Harbor—5-6, 16, 46,
  76, 107, 142, 195, 231-2
Peshtigo, population of—4,
  230, 232
Peshtigo River—4-5, 9, 35,
  73-4, 88, 96, 114, 116, 119,
  174, 177, 179, 194, 217,
  229, 231
Petrified man—179
Philbrook, S. V. D.—147,
  149-50
Phillips, A. B.—196
Phillips, Alf—173
Phillips, Austin—87
Phillips, Dr. B. T.—183
Physicians—7, 182-3, 193, 227
Pittsfield—40, 190
Place, Abraham—90-1
Place, Anton—113, 165-6
Place, Job—137
Port Huron—163
Porterfield—179, 231
Prostitution—1, 3, 12-6, 45
Prue, Joseph—135

R

Race, Martin—92
Race, Mrs. Nellie—228
Railroads—3, 5, 9-10, 13, 22,
  27, 34-5, 38, 40, 99, 107,
  170, 175, 181, 196
Reed, Lovell—85
Red River—55, 185-6
Relief efforts—163-6, 169-70,
  180-9, 191-3
Religion—3, 8, 16-7, 24, 30-1,
  37, 43, 46, 55-6, 75-6, 86,
  92, 98, 100-3, 111, 157,
  159, 172-3, 177, 193, 200,
  216-7, 233-4
Reunion of survivors—227-8

Rhinelander—16
Rice, Alexander H.—163
Richmondville—159
Roads—6, 19, 27, 31, 40-1, 109, 171
Robinson, Charles D.—85
Robinson, George—7
Robinsonville—29, 31, 86
Rock Falls—162
Rockstad, Helga—114
Roscommon—15
Rosiere—30, 54, 197
Roth, Filibert—206-7
Rubens, Charles—54-5
Rule, Joseph—20

S

Saginaw—13-5
Saginaw Bay—160, 163
St. Joseph, steamer—5
Saloons—3, 12, 14, 16, 20-1, 24, 36, 40, 42, 104, 108, 110-3, 196-7, 234
Sand Beach—159
Schauer, Casper—51
Scheller, Fred—41
Schwartz, Charles—131, 136, 221-2
Scofield's mill—186
Seney—15, 22
Settlers—5, 8, 19, 26-33, 37, 48, 86, 197-8, 207
Seymour, Charlotte—225
Shepherd, Fred—121-5, 131-2
Shepherd, William—121-5, 132-3, 141
Sherman, J. J.—145-9, 155
Slattery, Mayme—91
Slattery, Reuben—91-2
Slaughter, Amelia—119
Slaughter, Ed—227-8
Slaughter, Samuel—214

Smith, James D.—146
Spalding, Houghteling & Johnson—145, 148, 151
Spear, L. C.—94
State Historical Society of Wis. —228
Stephenson, Andrew—182
Stephenson, Isaac—11-2, 151, 165-6, 169, 180, 182, 205, 234
Stephenson, Robert—151, 166
Stephenson, Samuel—151, 166
Storey, Stephen—94
Strong, Gen. Moses—7
Stuart, Amanda—217-8, 229
Sturgeon Bay Canal—6
Sturgeon Bay, the—53-5, 184
Sturgeon Bay, village of—54, 56, 69-71
Suamico—39, 190
Sugar Bush—3, 5, 17, 35, 46, 73-4, 76-7, 83-95, 99, 168, 173, 200, 202, 210, 228, 230-1
Suicides—88-9, 197
Surface fires—212

T

Telegraph—36, 38-9, 40, 166-7, 180, 196, 200-1
Thompson, William—105
Tilton, Franklin 3, 7-9, 41, 74, 110, 136, 167, 205-6
Tisdale, G. J.—126
Tornado—171, 174, 190, 199, 201-3, 208, 212-3
Towsley, C. R.—46, 88-9
Trout Creek—9, 74, 126-7, 137-8, 221, 234
Trudell, Mrs. Theodore—46
Turnverein Society—193

U

Union, steamer—5, 144-5, 166
Union, Wis.—54

V

Van Raalte, Rev. A. C.—157

W

Walworth County—185
Washburn, Cadwallader—12
Washburn, Ira—105
Watson, George W.—47-54, 167
Wausau—16
Weather—203-4
Weinhart, Philip—35
Wells, Daniel—11

Whalen, Michael—63
White, Denny—20
White Rock—159-60
Wilke, Mrs. Elizabeth—219-20
Williamson, Fred—60, 62, 71
Williamson, James—60, 71
Williamson, John—60-2, 65, 69, 71
Williamson, Maggie—59-61, 63-5, 67, 69, 71
Williamson, Thomas—60-72
Williamson, Mrs.—62-6, 68, 70-1
Williamsonville—32, 54, 57-72, 168, 202
Woodruff & Co.—194
Wright, Charles E.—228

Y

Young, G. W.—185